The Vision of
Politics on the Eve
of the Reformation

The VISION of POLITICS on the EVE of the REFORMATION

More, Machiavelli, and Seyssel

J. H. HEXTER

Basic Books, Inc., *Publishers*
NEW YORK

TO WASHINGTON UNIVERSITY
IN ST. LOUIS

An institution I have
long admired and loved

Chapters II–V appeared, in somewhat different form, in the publications
listed below. Acknowledgment is hereby made to the publishers for
their permission to include the essays in this volume.

Chapter II: From *Utopia*, Volume IV of The Yale Edition of the Complete
Works of St. Thomas More, ed. Edward Surtz, S.J., and J. H. Hexter
(New Haven and London, 1965), Introduction, pp. xv–cxxiv, and
Appendix, pp. 573–576; and from *Action and Conviction in Early
Modern Europe*, ed. T. K. Rabb and J. E. Seigel (Princeton, 1969),
pp. 77–89.

Chapter III: From *Studies in the Renaissance*, IV (1957), 113–138.

Chapter IV: From *American Historical Review*, LXIX, No. 4 (July 1964),
945–968.

Chapter V: From *Art, Science and History in the Renaissance*, ed. Charles S.
Singleton (Baltimore, 1967), pp. 389–415.

PREFACE

ABOUT a quarter of a century ago I received a grant from the American Council of Learned Societies to prepare a translation of Claude de Seyssel's *La Monarchie de France*. Except for some minor revisions to ameliorate slightly the stylistic ineptitude of an author whose gifts for redundancy, flatness of phrasing, and the production of rhetorical clinkers were boundless, the translation was complete two years later. I then set to work on an introduction. That is not finished yet, twenty-odd years later. Lest the Council succumb to a natural temptation to charge me with misappropriation of funds, I am forthwith publishing the book that follows, *The Vision of Politics on the Eve of the Reformation*. In a time-hallowed waffling phrase which goes as far toward causal imputation as historians sometimes want to go, all the studies in this book "grew out of" investigations related to the still unfinished introduction to the translation of *La Monarchie de France*. Perhaps, in the reasonable belief that *The Vision of Politics* satisfies my debt to the Council, I can now get around to publishing the translation with a less elaborate introduction than I first planned.*

"*Il Principe* and *lo stato*" and "Normal Politics in the Age of Machiavelli" were initially published without considerable editorial revision. I am grateful to the Renaissance Society of America and to the Johns Hopkins University Press respectively for permission to republish the two essays. "The Loom of Language and the Fabric of Imperatives" was subject to considerable revision at the behest of the editor, Professor Stull Holt, before the *American Historical Review* accepted it. During his brief tenure of the editorship, Professor Holt set an unmatchable standard of patient editorial candor. I remember happily his avowal that he would like to publish the piece but that the readers to whom he sent it agreed that "it was not top-drawer Hexter." With some annoyance I replied that it seemed to me that "the proper standard was not top-drawer Hexter (whatever that was), but middle-

---

* Since I wrote the above preface, Professor Donald Kelley has undertaken to provide an introduction to *La Monarchie* and to prepare it for publication, a gain to scholarship and a relief to me.   J.H.H.

drawer *American Historical Review*." With unruffled patience he answered, "I do not know what top-drawer Hexter is either. I have not previously read a word you have written." He offered to go ahead and publish without revision but urged me to consider seriously the readers' reservations. He and they were right. When I got over my fit of author's pique, I drastically altered the early section of the article in line with the readers' suggestions. I thank the *American Historical Review* for permission to republish.

None of the studies mentioned above have undergone more than trivial modification in their reprinting here. I have made two considerable changes in "More's Utopia and Its Historical Milieux." That long essay first appeared as the historical introduction to *Utopia* in the Yale edition of the *Complete Works of St. Thomas More*. At that time it received the benign and beneficial editorial attention of Professor Richard Sylvester, the general editor of the entire edition. In appropriate exercise of editorial discretion, Professor Sylvester excised the section on "Utopia and Geneva," thus bringing an overlong introductory essay somewhat closer to its proper limits. The section was subsequently published in *Action and Conviction in Early Modern Europe: Essays in Memory of E. H. Harbison*. I thank the Princeton University Press for permission to replace it in its initial context. Finally, although my dating of the sequence of composition of *Utopia* is of consequence for my explication of More's book, the detailed grounds for that dating are not. I have therefore placed my argument in support of my dating in an appendix, where those interested in literary detective work will find it in full. My thanks to the Yale University Press for permission to publish the study.

In my preface to this volume I have followed what I recently noticed has been my lifelong custom of offering no justification, apologia or excuse for its publication. I suppose I have always been intuitively aware that a good book needs no justification, that a bad book has none, and that readers are given to following their own leading and do not need to have an author whispering sweet nothings in their ears about the delights or disasters that await them.

It is not, I believe, customary to dedicate a book to an institution. The place of Washington University in my heart and life has been such, however, that nice customs can curtsey to it. I had been a professional academic for nearly two decades when, in 1957, I joined the faculty of Washington University in St. Louis. It was there for the first time that I saw at work the relentless concern for and pursuit of quality in higher education which alone and fully redeems an enterprise that is often and in many places ill-conducted. It was Washington's firm policy of encouraging scholarship and of finding means to give scholars on the faculty an opportunity to pursue their vocation that enabled me to write while I was there, among other studies, two included in this book, *"Utopia* and Its Historical Milieux" and "The Loom of Language and the Fabric of Imperatives." Washington University was neither a very rich school nor a very big one. It was just a great one. Its excellences shone out in that fine and magnanimous man, Ethan Sheply, who was chancellor when I came to St. Louis, and in a multitude of my colleagues whom I remember still with the warmest affection. The people of St. Louis have a noble treasure in their midst. From time to time they seem less acutely aware of this fact than they might be.

I also owe thanks to Yale University. For a longer time than Washington, it has undertaken the care, feeding, and encouragement of scholars, wisely without exempting them from responsibility for classroom teaching. This book and I have benefited both from Yale's generosity and its firm rule on teaching. I am also indebted for assistance to four philanthropic foundations. I first began an intensive study of Machiavelli with the support of the Ford Foundation, in 1953–54. Work on *"Utopia* and Its Historical Milieux" began during a leave in Scotland in 1959–60, afforded me by a Fulbright Senior Fellowship. During the summer of 1960 I received a helpful grant from the Rockefeller Foundation. Finally, it all began with an act of faith by the John Simon Guggenheim Memorial Foundation, which in 1947 renewed the grant of a fellowship to me with little concrete evidence to support the belief that something of scholarly worth would come of it.

J. H. H.

Yale University
New Haven, Connecticut
July 1972

A NOTE ON
CITATIONS

THE essays included in this book were written over a space of nearly two decades. This has resulted in the adoption of divergent systems of citation among them. The divergences in citation are also related to differences in structure, focus, and method among the essays, and, in one case (Chapter III), to a curious set of accidents. For the convenience of readers, an explanation of the methods of citation from *Utopia* and *Il Principe* follows:

Chapter II. Citations from More's *Utopia* are enclosed in parentheses in the body of the text. The edition cited from is Thomas More, *Utopia,* ed. Edward Surtz, S. J., and J. H. Hexter (The Yale Edition of the Complete Works of St. Thomas More, Volume 4, New Haven, 1965). Citation is by page and line. For example (240/7–242/5) means "page 240, line 7 to page 242, line 5." (240/7–8) means "page 240, lines 7 to 8." When the author *quotes directly* from the English translation of *Utopia*, which appears on right-hand pages of the Yale edition, *the page numbers are odd*, for example (231/5–12). When he simply *refers to* a passage in that edition, citation is to *the even-numbered pages* of the Latin text, for example (230/4–10).

Chapter III. As indicated on p. 154 n. 8, the footnote citations to *Il Principe* are to Niccolò Machiavelli, *Tutte le opere,* ed. Mazzoni and Casella (Florence, 1929) referring first to chapter, second to page and column; for example, Chapter 12, page 25, column b is given as 12;26b. In the summer of 1971 a grant from the Social Science Research Council made possible the preparation of a page-and-line index of *Il Principe.* The edition used for this purpose was Niccolò Machiavelli, *Opere,* 8 vols. (Feltrinelli, Milan, 1960–65), Volume *1, Il Principe e Discorsi sopra la prima deca di Tito Livio,* ed. S. Bertelli.

Before the index was ready, copy for this book was on its way to the printer. This unfortunate sequence of events rendered it inconvenient and overcostly to amend in proof all the citations to *Il Principe* in Chapter III. For the convenience of properly skeptical readers, however, there is provided 1) in Appendix D an index of occurrences of *stato, stati* by chapter, page, and column in the Mazzoni and Casella edition of *Il Principe*; 2) in Appendix E a similar index by chapter, page, and line to occurrences of *stato, stati* in *Il Principe* in the first volume of the Bertelli-Feltrinelli edition; 3) in Appendix F a conflated table of initial pages of chapters of *Il Principe* in Mazzoni and Casella and Bertelli-Feltrinelli.

Chapters IV and V. Utopia is cited in the footnotes using the same method of notation as in Chapter II, except for citations to the Tudor translation into English by Ralph Robinson, for which the edition edited by J. H. Lupton (Oxford, 1895) is used. Citation to *Il Principe* is by chapter, to the *Discorsi* by book and chapter. For the convenience of readers a list by chapter, page, and line of all occurrences of *virtù* and *virtuoso* in *Il Principe*, using the Feltrinelli edition, appears in Appendix G.

Throughout the book, "Eras. *Ep.*" refers to Desiderius Erasmus, *Opus Epistolarum Des. Erasmi Roterodami*, ed. P. S. and H. M. Allen, 11 vols. (Oxford, 1906–1947); and *Corresp.* refers to *The Correspondence of Sir Thomas More*, ed. E. F. Rogers (Princeton, 1947).

CONTENTS

CHAPTER IV

The Predatory and the Utopian Vision: Machiavelli and More.
The Loom of Language and the Fabric of Imperatives: The Case
of *Il Principe* and *Utopia*   179

CHAPTER V

The Predatory, the Utopian, and the Constitutional Vision:
Machiavelli, More, and Claude de Seyssel. *La Monarchie de
France* and Normal Politics on the Eve of the Reformation

The Vision of Politics on the Eve of the Reformation

CHAPTER I

A Discourse on Method*

I N September 1516, on the eastern fringe of the Germano-Romanic world, in one of the backwater universities of Europe, a professor of theology and member of the Observant Congregation of the Augustinian friars began the lectures that would wind up his three-semester course on St. Paul's Epistle to the Romans. The segment of the Epistles under consideration, Romans 9 to 16, had imbedded in it the verses of Chapter 13:1–8:

> Let every soul be subject unto the higher powers. For there is no power but of God: the powers that be are ordained of God.
> Whosoever therefore resisteth the power, resisteth the ordinance of God: and they that resist shall receive to themselves damnation.
> For rulers are not a terror to good works, but to the evil. Wilt thou then not be afraid of the power? do that which is good, and thou shalt have praise of the same:
> For he is the minister of God to thee for good. But if thou do that which is evil, be afraid; for he beareth not the sword in vain: for he is the minister of God, a revenger to *execute* wrath upon him that doeth evil.
> Wherefore *ye* must needs be subject, not only for wrath, but also for conscience sake.
> For this cause pay ye tribute also: for they are God's ministers, attending continually upon this very thing.
> Render therefore to all their dues: tribute to whom tribute *is due*; custom to whom custom; fear to whom fear; honour to whom honour.
> Owe no man anything, but to love one another: for he that loveth another hath fulfilled the law.

Centuries before 1516 and more emphatically during the century to come, those verses were to be at the center of an intense debate on the political obligation of Christians.

* See "A Note on Citations."

Since the Investiture controversy in the twelfth century, embroilments of Popes with Christian emperors and of Popes with Christian kings, each king claiming to be *imperator in regno suo,* had revolved around this text. In each struggle the contestants, whoever they were, assigned divergent and self-serving meanings to the admonition that the Apostle to the Gentiles directed to the Christian congregation of pagan Rome in the first century of our era.

Four decades after Professor Martin Luther of the University of Wittenberg delivered his Lectures on Romans, the issues he raised then and later swirled out of the political botch of Germany, where nothing was ever quite clear, into England, France, and the Netherlands, where a good many things were clear enough. There the key passage from Romans became a controversial text in one of the most vigorous and penetrating controversies of all time over the nature, the source, the extent, and the limits of political authority, the obligations and rights of subjects, and the power and responsibilities of rulers.

Such deep arguments did not enter the mind of Martin Luther as he wrote about the Epistle to the Romans. Not that he failed to comment on Romans 13. Indeed he glossed the chapter as a whole for his lectures and wrote several pages of commentary on verses 1 through 8.[1] The gloss is a flat, brief, and traditional assertion of the duty of Christians to obey their rulers, even "evil and unbelieving" ones, because "the order of government and their power to rule are nevertheless good and from God."[2]

Intrinsically this is a little disappointing. It blandly avoids all complexities concerning which higher power to obey, and when, and under what circumstances. Within a year Martin Luther was to challenge the right of the Pope, the spiritual head of the Christian community, to issue indulgences. Within four years he was to reject entirely the Pope's general authority, both in temporal and spiritual causes, to refuse to obey him, and to burn the volumes of the canon law. Within five years he was to stand before the Holy Roman Emperor, the chief temporal prince of Christendom, and the assembled rulers of the German nation at Worms. There, charged with disobedience and asked to revoke his pamphlets, he asserted the sovereignty of his conscience against all the "higher powers," temporal or spiritual.

Unless I am convicted by the testimony of Scripture or by evident reason . . . my conscience is captive to the Word of God. Therefore I can-

[1] Martin Luther, *Lectures on Romans,* tr. and ed. Wilhelm Pauck, Library of Christian Classics, vol. 15 (Philadelphia, 1961). The gloss is on p. 358, n. 1, the comment, pp. 358–66.
[2] Ibid., p. 358, n. 1.

not and will not recant, since it is difficult, unprofitable and dangerous indeed to do anything against one's conscience. God help me. Amen.[3]

In the wake of those tremendous, proud, and humble challenges, the complex issues of obedience were gradually churned up until, decades later, Europe was sucked into an agonizing religious civil war. In his gloss of 1516 there is no sign that Luther even glimpsed the theoretical possibility of such issues.

No more is there such a sign in his scholium, over 3,000 words long, on Romans 13:1–8. To the contrary. In 1516 Luther is full of his discovery of the sufficiency of Christ's unique sacrifice to redeem from sin and death all who believe his promises, the true freedom of the Christian man. His recent religious experience and theological discovery boil over into his commentary on Romans 13:1–8, where one would have thought that other matters were more germane.[4] In the commentary he has almost nothing to say about the obedience owed to temporal rulers, except that it is owed. He does not deny the jurisdictional rights of the clerical hierarchy ("I do not say these rights are evil."), even though he is somewhat queasy about how they work in practice. For the rest he gives his commentary over to a homily in the manner of Erasmus on the failures of the clergy to earn by righteous living the privileges and powers that they possess and that they claim as rights by virtue of their offices.

The Erasmian echo from the Saxon frontier reminds us that in 1516 we are not yet in the age of the Reformation, that indeed Luther was not in the age of the Reformation either but was still an orthodox university professor, still unaware of the shattering implications of his religious convictions. The echo should also remind us that the vision of politics that Luther's revolt ultimately impressed on the world was not sketched in the ninety-five theses he posted in 1517 at Wittenberg, that Luther himself never in his life saw that vision clearly, and that it only gradually forced itself on Western Christendom, slowly passing from the dimness with which most men perceive things in the beginning to the harsh clarity with which they perceive them in the end.

In the end, a little before or after 1555, statesmen and churchmen alike had to adjust their political vision to a new reality. In most lands in Europe the ruler had to deal with the presence in his country of organized groups of men opposed to the religious settlement there as it stood, whatever it was, men ready to adopt any necessary and practical means to force the prince to alter it. Even when a man wrote

[3] Hans J. Hillerbrand, *The Reformation in Its Own Words* (London: SCM Press, Ltd., 1964), p. 91.
[4] Luther, *Lectures*, pp. 358–66, esp. pp. 359, 365.

about politics with no explicit reference to this situation, his very silence was in a way audible—an expected note not played.[5] The pressures of the New Politics of the second half of the sixteenth century ran an irregular course from Edinburgh through London, Antwerp, and Paris, and south to Languedoc, a giant political fault with many side-faults. In this unstable structure, charged with rigidities and tensions, a shift of forces anywhere reverberated like a great earthquake throughout the system, to Amsterdam, the principalities of Germany, Madrid, and Rome. Europe was violently bound together by the very force that most violently tore it apart. Its tragic situation reached a climax in the complex constellation of events that fed into and spun off from "the enterprise of England," the Armada campaign.[6]

On the eve of the Reformation the crisis of Western Christendom in the latter half of the sixteenth century was neither visible nor imaginable. In the ten years or so before the Diet of Worms no confessional conflict pressed simultaneously on all centers of political power in Western Christendom, nor did any other single pervasive force condition the vision of politics of all men who concentrated their thought on such matters. There was, however, an event nearly as characteristic of the prologue to the Reformation as the Armada was of its catastrophic climax—the Concordat of Bologna.

In 1515 the new young king of France, Francis I, following the precedent sanctified by his revered predecessors, Charles VIII and Louis XII, began once again to pour the human and material resources of his kingdom down the rat hole of Italy. His rapid success, like that of his predecessors, further stirred the muddy waters of Italian politics and called for a certain number of modifications and readjustments of the ongoing confusion to take account of the French presence in Milan, as long as it lasted. The situation particularly required action on the part of the princely Italian house of Medici. Three years earlier that house had been restored to control in Florence under the now inauspicious auspices of Ferdinand of Aragon, to whom the French monarchs owed and gave nothing but unremitting malevolence for past humiliations. It was up to the head of the house of Medici, Giovanni, to make the deals which altered circumstances demanded. Indirectly ruler of Florence, Giovanni, as Pope Leo X, was also directly ruler of that odd anomaly among principalities which so perplexed Niccolò Machiavelli, the Papal States. Besides its feeble temporal power over the States of the Church, the papal office carried with it

---

[5] E.g., Sir Thomas Smith, *De Republica Anglorum*, ed. L. Alston (Cambridge, England, 1906).

[6] The classical study of the European "fault structure" in its time of maximum convulsion is, of course, Garrett Mattingly, *The Armada* (Boston, 1959).

certain actual or claimed fiscal and jurisdictional perquisites throughout Western Christendom. Useful counters those, in bargaining with
monarchs, and Leo might have made a better deal with Francis if he
had not had to concern himself with the Medici principate in Tuscany.
As it was, first things first, Leo negotiated French recognition of the
princely interests of his family, and then met with Francis in Bologna
to finish off the residual ecclesiastical business. It did not take long.
In effect, the shepherd of the whole Christian flock and the Most
Christian King quickly came to terms on the convenient way not to
feed but to fleece the part of the flock resident in France. The division of the loot was proportional to the political power of the bar-
gainers: the Most Christian King got the lion's share—effective power
to appoint all the bishops in France and all but a few of the abbots
and priors; the Vicar of Christ got the fox's share—a considerable
number of less considerable appointments. Later, in a side deal, he
picked up the annates, the first year's revenue, of newly-appointed
French bishops, which for more than half a century those bishops had
refused to pay. Then Francis went home, where he had to ram the
agreement down the throats of the *parlements* and the Sorbonne, both
of which put up a considerable resistance.

This unedifying episode compressed within itself several of the more
conspicuous traits of the world of European politics on the eve of the
Reformation—the actualities, which, if they paid heed to actualities,
men with a vision of politics had before their eyes. In the north and
west of Europe, there were the great monarchies—England, Spain, the
Netherlands-Burgundian principality and, greatest of all, France—
which had the resources and the political organization to play the game
of European great-power politics; and there was the Holy Roman
Emperor who lacked the resources and organization, but who tried
to play the game anyhow. And there was Italy—a cluster of weak
principalities and republics, of cities grown into territorial states—the
natural victim of foreign monarchs to whom its internal divisions provided chances for honor, glory, war, loot, and landgrabbing. In the
midst of Italy was the Papacy with claims to spiritual leadership of
the whole of Western Christendom, with further claim to authority
over the whole clergy of the West in some matters, and appellate jurisdiction over all Christians in a few. The Popes ruled, or often failed
to rule, a feeble, central-Italian principality, stretching northeast across
the peninsula from the Tyrrhenian Sea to the Adriatic. For fifty years
the throne of St. Peter had been occupied four-fifths of the time by
men heavily preoccupied with the advancement of their brothers,
nephews, and sons to princely power in the States of the Church or
elsewhere in Italy. The Vicars of Christ were diverted from doing the

work of their Heavenly Rector (supposing they had any inclination to do it) by a somewhat excessive involvement in the temporal welfare of assorted Riarios, della Roveres, Borgias, and Medicis.

Since 1494 the onset of the more acute malaises of the *corpus Christianum* had responded to the means and whims of the kings of France. Four times, between 1494 and 1515, those monarchs poured their armies across the Alps into Italy and grabbed whatever there was for easy taking. Then the greed and incompetence with which the French exploited their conquests and the formation of anti-French coalitions ended in the expulsion of the conquerors until another French king (or the same one) started the process again. When Francis met Leo X at Bologna in 1515, the cycle had already entered its fourth time around. The monarchies of Northern and Western Europe were the ones that had the resources to win—or to lose big—in the power games on the eve of the Reformation. The principalities and republics of Italy, including the Papal principality, were not up to it. The Italian princes tried to keep a hand in, but their principalities were the stakes in a game beyond their control. The display of raw force of which France and Spain and occasionally even England and Netherlands-Burgundy were capable can, however, be misleading. The difficulties that Francis had in getting his deal with Leo at Bologna turned into the law of the land he ruled displayed the weakness behind the spectacular façade of pre-Reformation monarchy in Western Europe. In all the great monarchies there were resistant groups entrenched behind customs, charters of privilege and franchises, laws and traditions. Towns, nobilities, provinces, bodies of magistrates, universities, religious orders, guilds, assemblies of estates—none were invulnerable to a ruler determined to encroach on their liberties, but all in different degrees had means to make his way hard and slow. The monarchs got what they wanted mainly by taking care not often to want much that clearly ran counter to the rooted, traditional expectations and interests of resistant and entrenched groups among their subjects. The current notion that monarchs (at least some of them) were "absolute" had to allow room for the other notion that subjects (at least most of them) were free men.

Such, then, were the conspicuous actors in the politics of the years before the Reformation—great princes in the hereditary monarchies of the north and west, a few republics and little princelings in Italy, including the little elected princeling who ruled the States of the Church, a hodge-podge of lay and ecclesiastic principalities in Germany, ready along with the Swiss to provide mercenaries to any power ready to pay the price. The cast was not much different from what it was to be between the 1550's and the 1590's, but all the relations among them were looser. Men who looked at politics did not have their gaze caught by a Europe in the rigid tensions of religious civil war. The wars of Italy were not really a crisis except to the rulers of Italy. Indeed, in a land where for a long while back princely power had tended to become unstuck rather easily, it was not all that much of a crisis even to the Italian rulers. Only in the chaotic States of the Church were subversions of regime occasionally accompanied by massacres, perhaps less an indication of acute political intensity than of the local mores. Indeed, although the misery of Italy fired the desperate political imagination of Niccolò Machiavelli, already by 1516 Baldassare Castiglione had accommodated himself to Italian political servitude and tranquilly incorporated the peculiar virtues of French and Spanish gentlemen into his conception of that cosmopolitan creature, the perfect courtier.

The juxtaposition of Machiavelli and Castiglione raises awkward questions, especially about the title of this volume of essays, *The Vision of Politics on the Eve of the Reformation*. Machiavelli surely had a vision of politics, but Castiglione . . . ? *The Book of the Courtier* does not read much like a treatise on politics. And was Machiavelli's vision, if indeed he had only one, *the* vision of politics on the eve of the Reformation?

Castiglione's book was not, certainly, a treatise on politics, yet better than any writing of the sixteenth century it reflected the habitual outlook of the residents of the corridors of power in every European principality. The scene of *Il Cortegiano*, the tiny Duchy of Urbino, offers a miniaturized sample of what was to be in Florence, Paris, Brussels, Madrid, and London before the century was out. As to Machiavelli, obviously his whole vision of politics was shared by no man of his own time. Nor were the visions of Thomas More and Claude de Seyssel, the other writers whom the following essays are about, common currency in the second decade of the sixteenth century. Indeed, one of the conclusions of this essay is that More's *Utopia*, Machiavelli's *Il Principe*, and Seyssel's *La Monarchie de France* are the archetypes, if not the antecedents, of three divergent modes of perceiving political life characteristic of the Western world in modern times.

Yet *Utopia*, *Il Principe*, and *La Monarchie* have three traits in common that help to characterize the vision of politics on the eve of the Reformation. The first trait is negative. Nowhere in any of the three little treatises is there any reference to Romans 13:1–8. This is not coincidence or accident. What Passerin d'Entrèves rightly describes as the central problem of political thought, the problem of political obligation, is not central for More, Machiavelli, and Seyssel in the 1510's. Of the King of France, Seyssel asserts both that he is absolute and that his authority is bridled by religion, justice, and police. He adds that if any French monarch willfully exercises his power against rather than within these constraints, he is in danger of being disobeyed. But that French subjects *ought* to obey or to disobey a willful and arbitrary French monarch Seyssel does not assert. The *problems* of political obligation do not interest him; he is far more interested in the problems of political efficacy and expediency. As to More, compared to Utopia every realm in Europe is a tyranny, veiled by law, of the ruler and the rich over the ruled and the poor. Yet nowhere in *Utopia* does More suggest that Christians are not bound to obey the parasites that command them and feed off them. No more for him than for Seyssel is political obligation a live *problem*. And of course in *Il Principe* it is no problem at all; it is not even a concept. Princes rule by force, fraud, and craft; they acquire and keep dominion over men by *fortuna* (which is luck) and *virtù* (which is not Christian virtue); and in politics no one owes to another anything but what he can be forced or conned into paying.

So Machiavelli had no place in *Il Principe* for political obligation; and although More and Seyssel had a place for political obligation, they did not see it as a problem. It was not a problem in their political world. Outside Italy it was a tranquil world from 1500 to 1520, dominated by princes—Ferdinand and Isabella, Henry VII and Henry VIII, Philip the Handsome, and Louis XII and Francis I—who succeeded remarkably well in maintaining peace within their realms. Not everyone was satisfied all the time, but most of the men and groups of men with enough clout to make trouble did not feel strongly moved to make it or to make a great deal of it. In the early 1500's Europe was little inclined to the resumption of great debates over the sources of political authority and the ultimate division of the obligations of Christians between their spiritual and their temporal rulers.

The affair of the two councils showed this clearly enough. Louis XII, finally aware that Pope Julius II had gulled him for several years and was about to put together an alliance to throw the French out of Milan, got together a council of the Church (very ill attended) and called on the Pope to appear before it. Julius summoned his own council. The bones of the conciliar movement, dead nearly a century since Constance and Basel, stirred a little but not much. Louis's schismatic council, chased from Pisa to Milan, evaporated when the Holy League drove the French out of Italy. A few uninteresting statements of the Gallican view of ecclesiastic authority circulated in France. Julius' Lateran Council restated the claims of Papal supremacy. Still no minds of great quality entered the lists of controversy on either side. Why should they? What the whole uproar was about was already settled when Julius's great scheme for getting the foreigners out of Italy got the French out of Milan at the cost of getting the Swiss in and tightening the grip of Spain elsewhere in the peninsula. From the beginning Louis had hid (all too visibly) behind the Council of Pisa, so that such polemic as there was dwelt on the constitution of the Church and the status and authority of Church Councils *vis à vis* the Papacy. In the Lateran Council Julius had started an attack on the liberties of the Gallican Church, but that headlong, headstrong Pope died before the Council could act, so a situation that might have pitted the Pope and his Council not only against Louis, but against Ferdinand of Spain and the Emperor, was averted.

Perhaps then the peculiar barrenness of Luther's gloss on Romans 13 and the irrelevance of his commentary on verses 1–8 to serious issues of political obligation were not just the consequence of the political naiveté of a Saxon monk. If the issues of political obligation were not a live problem for him, neither were they so for Machiavelli, or More, or Seyssel, who were not Saxons, nor monks, nor at all politically naive. Those issues were not alive in the European world from 1500 to 1520 with respect to the relation of the Pope to temporal princes. Were they alive with respect to the relation of temporal rulers to their subjects?

Not if one thinks of political obligation in terms of its classical formulation (paraphrasing Rousseau): "Men are born free, yet everywhere they are bound to obey their rulers. What can make this bond legitimate?" As we have seen, this formulation does not fit *La Monarchie,* or *Il Principe,* or *Utopia.* Seyssel assumes the legitimacy of the French monarchy; Machiavelli disregards the notions of legitimacy and obligation altogether; and one might infer from *Utopia* that no one was bound to obey rulers as wicked as the ruling classes of the Christian states of Europe—but to do so would leave the author of *Utopia* behind, since More makes no such inference. Yet all three authors are fascinated by princes. The Utopian commonwealth is a meritocratic republic, not a monarchy; but when he turned from the Discourse on Utopia to the Dialogue of Counsel,[7] the princes of Europe, and especially his native prince, became and remained the focus of More's attention. As for *La Monarchie* and *Il Principe,* they were mutants of a very common genre of political writings—the "Mirrors of Princes," the books of advice to monarchs on how to rule. They are mutants because both Seyssel and Machiavelli held the genre in considerable and warranted contempt. Consequently, their prince books were like none that had ever been written before. Nevertheless, all three works do abundantly give advice to princes, More's literary pretense to the contrary notwithstanding.[8] This is the second way in which

---

[7] See below, pp. 30–37.

[8] More sets in motion the Dialogue of Counsel in Utopia by having Hythlodaeus, the protagonist of the Dialogue, repudiate the obligation of rendering advice to rulers (54/19–57).

the visions of politics of More, Machiavelli and Seyssel blend with the common vision of politics on the eve of the Reformation.

It is my impression that there was an extraordinarily dense outpouring of books of advice to princes in the years before the Reformation. To systematically check this impression might be an onerous but perhaps worthwhile task.[9] One thing, however, is certain: Machiavelli finished writing *Il Principe* about the beginning of 1514; Seyssel presented *La Monarchie* to Francis I in 1515; Erasmus published the *Institutio principis Christiani* in 1516; Budé completed *De l'institution du prince* in 1519. Surely in no period of five or six years, before or after, did as many men of such extraordinary distinction in their own day and later write books of advice to princes. Granting the singularly vapid character of almost all such books (including those of Erasmus and Budé), granting their singular lack of distinctive and individuating substance, the dense distribution of works in the genre indicates that the authors of prince books were not quite so detached from political life as the vacuousness of the final product suggests. About the politics of their day they may have known only one thing, but they knew it very well. They knew that, as one of them remarked, "From the prince as from a fountain comes all that is good or ill to their subjects." A curious concatenation of *virtù* and *fortuna* had provided Western Europe with an array of vigorous monarchs—Ferdinand and Isabella, Henry VII and Henry VIII, the Archduke Charles who became Charles V, Francis I, even Louis XII—at a moment in history when, to rulers with a will to act, wide opportunities for decisive action in both foreign and domestic affairs opened up. At the same time the external limit on that will was solely the power of the other monarchs, and the limits within each realm were ill defined. The intention of the authors of books of advice to princes makes sense in such a context, however limited the efficacy of their labors. In the phraseology of the early sixteenth century, the books figured forth to actual monarchs the ideal of the perfect prince. In terms of more recent vintage, they sought to restrain the ids and the egos of monarchs by appealing to their ego-ideals and superegos. One of them at least knew exactly what he was doing and why he was doing it that way. Explaining

---

[9] It would, however, present serious difficulties. The invention of printing may have both increased the number of books written and the number that have survived. Therefore, the issue of a disproportionate gross number of prince books between 1480 and 1520 compared to any equal earlier time span might not be particularly significant. A more useful comparison might be made between the *ratio* of the prince books to other genres of books on politics. The problem here would be one of classification: just what is a "book on politics"? After all, it demands a considerable relaxation of one's critical faculties to classify most prince books as books on politics. Still a comparison of the ratios of books of advice to princes to other forms of political writing over different time spans might indicate something about shifts in the preoccupations of writers on politics.

somewhat apologetically his reason for writing his hack-work panegyric
to Philip the Handsome, he observed:

> There is no such efficacious mode of making a prince better, as that of
> setting before him, under the guise of praise, the example of a good
> sovereign, provided you so attribute virtues and deny vices, as to persuade
> him to the former and deter him from the latter. . . . Persons who think
> Panegyrics are nothing but flattery appear not to know with what design
> this kind of writing was invented by men of great sagacity, whose object
> it was, that by having the image of virtue put before them, bad princes
> might be made better, the good encouraged, the ignorant instructed, the
> mistaken set right, the wavering quickened, and even the abandoned
> brought to some sense of shame. . . . The defence I have made would, I
> think, be admitted to be a fair one by wise judges, even if some Phalaris
> or Sardanapalus or Heliogabalus had been praised in this Panegyric.[10]

If Erasmus' view of the way to keep rulers within some limits sounds
like a literary man's daydream, no more firm than a fleeting cloud easily
dispersed by the first vigorous gust of royal willfulness, nevertheless
it was a view shared by men closer to the gear-trains of royal power
than was the detached Dutch humanist. After fifteen years in the
service of Henry VIII, Erasmus' friend Thomas More resigned from
the service of that monarch. Shortly thereafter he had a conversation
with one who was then high in the King's favor:

> Master Cromwell, you are now entered into the service of a most noble,
> wise and liberal prince. If you will follow my poor advice, you shall, in
> your counsel-giving unto his grace, ever tell him what he ought to do, but
> never what he is able to do. So shall you show yourself a true faithful
> servant and a right worthy Counsellor. For if a lion knew his own strength,
> hard were it for any man to rule him.[11]

In substance More is saying to Thomas Cromwell something like what
Erasmus said in justification for writing a prince book: Hold up to
Henry VIII the model of a perfect prince. It adds poignancy or a
sharp edge to the advice when we recall that the man who rendered
it and the man to whom it was rendered were both brought to the
block at the behest of the king with respect to whom it was rendered.

The pattern explicit in Erasmus' remarks in his panegyric and
implicit in More's advice to Cromwell was the pattern of all prince
books, all that is but two—*Il Principe* and *La Monarchie de France*.
In his little book, Machiavelli was not concerned with imposing and

---

[10] *Opus Epistolarum Des. Erasmi Roterdami*, ed. P. S. Allen, et al., 12 vols.
(Oxford, 1906–58) 1, 397, 400–401.

[11] William Roper, *The Lyfe of Sir Thomas Moore, Knighte*, ed. E. V. Hitchcock,
Early English Text Society, Original Series, 197 (London, 1935), 56–57.

maintaining restraints on the will of the prince but with exploring
means available to princes for removing or evading such restraints.
Seyssel was very much concerned with maintaining them, but he did
not think that the endlessly reiterated homilies of the prince books
were an efficacious means of doing so. Rather, he put his faith in what
we might call the viable existing institutional restraints on the King
of France and in persuading the king that his power would be greater
and more lasting if he acted within the limits of those restraints than
if he tried willfully to shatter them. So in *La Monarchie* Seyssel attempted for the first time in history a specific examination of the
structure of French government and society and of their interplay in
the French monarchical commonwealth.

In their vision of politics, *La Monarchie de France, Il Principe*, and
Utopia shared a third trait. That trait is easier to sense clearly than
it is to describe succinctly. It is impossible to apply a simple label to
the trait in question, because all the more or less appropriate labels
—realism, empiricism, historicism, institutionalism—have already been
too widely appropriated. They have been casually stuck onto too many
boxes, diverse and divergent in content. As the number and diversity
of the boxes increased, the utility of the words themselves decreased,
until now a writer can use them with almost complete certainty that
they will convey to all readers something more or less or different than
what he had in mind. So, in the interest of precision, it is necessary
for me to spell out in some detail here what I have in mind. The trait
shared by More, Machiavelli, and Seyssel, which differentiates them
from the ordinary writers of books of advice to princes, is their common awareness that in politics, general principles usually operate
through specific institutional structures, when they operate at all. For
all three writers this implies that mere exhortation to a ruler to act
this way or that is futile unless there exist institutional structures guid-
ing his action in the desired direction and impeding him from taking
alternative directions. In Machiavelli this characteristic is more easily
identifiable in the *Discorsi* than in *Il Principe*, but it is evident enough
in the smaller work. Given that in order to be a prince at all a man
must acquire (or inherit) a *stato*, hold onto it, keep it in his grasp,
not lose it nor have it taken from him, what he must do to accomplish
his purpose will depend on a variety of circumstances. It will depend
on whether he inherited his whole *stato*, whether he inherited part and
lately acquired part, or whether he is a new prince who got a *stato*
into his grasp only recently. The situation will also vary, depending
on whether he made his acquisition by his own valor and prowess
(*virtù*) or by mere chance (*fortuna*) and on whether he used his own
military force in taking his *stato* or depended on armies in the obedience of other men. The institutional structure of the *stato* will also

prescribe the means for maintaining a hold on it, divergent practices being required for a corrupt *stato*, a *stato libero*, and a *stato civile*.

Machiavelli's prince has only one purpose, to acquire a *stato*, if he has none, and to keep it, however he came by it. In contrast, Seyssel assumes that the French king should seek primarily for the honor, glory, greatness, wealth, and power of the French monarchical commonwealth and that he enhances his own glory only through the augmentation (which does not mean merely the geographical expansion) of the society he rules. Although the ultimate goals it sets for the king are bounded by the traditional morality and the conventional wisdom, *La Monarchie* is by no means merely hortatory. Before Seyssel prescribes what the king should do for the preservation and augmentation of the French monarchy, he describes how that monarchy is *"regulée,"* that is, he writes about the rules imbedded in law and custom under which the kingdom operates. This description does not confine itself to the organs of government, about which Seyssel's remarks are in fact rather sketchy. He also provides an account of what we would call the social structure. Only when he has done that does Seyssel turn to advising the king on the "preservation and augmentation of the monarchy of France by policy."[12]

The advice differs from the standard exhortations of the prince books that the ruler exhibit in perfection all the natural and Christian virtues. It concerns itself rather with ways of keeping in repair the bridles on the monarchy—religion, justice, and *police*—so that they will better restrain the arbitrary actions of the ruler, and with ways of dealing with the social orders so that they will not oppress each other or gang up on the King. It is through the institutions of the realm, political and social, and by his relation to them, rather than by exemplifying an abstract set of virtues, that the King of France preserves and augments the monarchy of France and thereby preserves and magnifies himself.

As for More in *Utopia*, he traces the ills of the realms of Christendom to identifiable institutional defects and proposes institutional remedies for some of them. More than that, from one point of view his Utopian commonwealth is organized for the suppression of the three deadly sins of avarice, indolence, and pride. More devotes his considerable imagination to conjuring up laws and social arrangements which prevent not only crime but sin from paying. In modern economic jargon the institutions of *Utopia* are primarily directed to achieving

---

[12] Claude de Seyssel, *La Monarchie de France*, ed. J. Poujol (Paris, 1961), p. 129. Seyssel's term is *police*, a word he uses frequently. Not only the connotations but even the denotations of *police* in *La Monarchie* are sometimes difficult to make out. In the instance at hand, however, it seems unambiguously to mean actions within the king's power.

justice and harmony by maintaining institutional disincentives to the sins that carry the highest social cost.

Il Principe, La Monarchie, and *Utopia,* then, share a common trait in their acute awareness of the consequences of institutions, in their sense that whatever ends are aimed at, they can be achieved only through the actually available socio-political structure. Therefore they address themselves immediately to the problems of political behavior and only mediately to ultimate purposes and goals.

Was this sifting of ideals and ends through the fine mesh of available (or, in More's case, plausible) means, this unwillingness to slip one's moorings in experience and float substanceless on a cloudbed of ideals, a trait unique to More, Machiavelli, and Seyssel? Did it begin with them? In their time was it confined to them? Or were they rather particularly conspicuous exemplars of a more widely diffused shift in patterns and habits of thought on the eve of the Reformation? To answer these questions adequately would require a far deeper and broader grounding in the literature (in the most inclusive sense of the word) of the decades before 1520 than I possess or ever will possess. Someday the questions raised may attract the interest and attention of a scholar adequately equipped to answer them. In the meantime, I can only offer uncertain signs of what may or may not be a more extensive historical process.

For example, a half-century before the Reformation, having decided that the best form of a political order was a *dominium politicum et regale,* a lordship both political and regal, Sir John Fortescue set out to show how certain actual English institutions worked to make England such a *dominium.* He also made suggestions as to how some of those institutions, especially the king's council, could be reformed to prevent them from upsetting what was much later called "the balance of the constitution." He further attempted to show that the freedom of Englishmen resulted from the legal lordship of the English kings, as the servitude of Frenchmen was a consequence of the *dominium regale merum,* the purely regal lordship, of the kings of France. So spoke Fortescue in *The Governance of England.* In his *De laudibus legum Anglie* he tried to explain why the jury system and accusatory process, which he admired, was viable in England and would not work in France. He argued (perhaps more optimistically than the evidence warranted) that in England there was an abundance of free men sufficiently secure in their economic position and legal status to arrive at verdicts on the facts and not merely in response to the pressures of the powerful. In France no such independent middling sort of men existed. Thus Fortescue links the attainment of general political desiderata—a limited royal power and an equitable system of criminal justice—to the availability of solid social and institutional structures through and by means of which those desiderata could be realized.

In the 1480's and 1490's, Philippe de Commines, a Burgundian-Netherlander in the service of the French crown, wrote his *Memoires*. They were actually a history of his own times at the level of high politics. In the *Memoires*, God is an active omnipresence and usually a rather angry one. For Commines, disasters especially are evidence of the wrathful intervention of Divine Providence. He sees the Hand of the Lord in almost every resolution of a crisis, particularly in the misfortunes of the losers. But there is another side to it. God acts in history not immediately but intermediately, through the deeds of earthly men, undertaken by them for earthly ends. Events are linked to the characters, purposes, and means available to the participants in them. They happen as a consequence of the conjuncture of different men with different aims in specific situations. The aims are not always sensible —in the case of Charles the Bold of Burgundy and Charles VIII of France they rarely are. But they are always intelligible. Given the rashness of both Charleses, the civil councilors they favored, and the bad advice they got and took, it is easy to understand the disasters they stumbled into. In fact, Commines' *Memoires* proceed in two layers. There is the superimposed, discontinuous layer of Providential interventions. There is also the continuous layer of interconnected human motives, frailties, intentions, and actions, and the events consequent on collisions among them. The focus in Commines as in the others we have examined is not on the lofty universe of ultimate principles or on the chaotic world of just one damn thing after another, but in the intermediate area where one can find intelligible patterns of human conduct.

From Commines, inquiry can move in two directions. Surely not in quest of another Commines. If there were others like him in the decades before the Reformation, historians would have found them by now. A sifting of the chronicles and histories written during the appropriate period, however, might determine whether sporadically, at least, some writers at some time were exhibiting an outlook, a vision of politics, congruent with his, and with Fortescue's, Machiavelli's, More's, and Seyssel's. The second direction would take us out of the range of what we ordinarily think of as political thinking, or even as a vision of politics, into a wider sphere that might be described as the vision of life. This opens all sorts of doors to inquiry, perhaps too many; and we stand in danger of losing track of what we are looking for, or extending our initial conception so far that it becomes shapeless. With due caution, however, such an inquiry might, for example, take us into Erasmus' *Adagia*, into Castiglione's *Book of the Courtier*, into the

Florentine writings on family life, and into the debates of the Florentine *pratiche* and the French Estates General of 1484, in quest of habits of thought that linked together the ideal and the actual, the imperative and the necessary, through a consideration of the institutional structures and the patterns of habit, custom, and belief within which men live. But this is not the place for such an inquiry. We have already cast an eye too casual and vagrant over the European scene on the eve of the Reformation. It is time now to narrow our scrutiny to the historical milieu of Thomas More and its relation to his *Utopia*.

*C*HAPTER II The Utopian Vision: Thomas More. *Utopia* and Its Historical Milieux[*]

1. The Author and the Book

IN 1515 Thomas More was a man in his late thirties. To make a living he practised law in London. As Undersheriff of the city he also sat once a week as a judge in the Sheriff's Court. By avocation and preference he was a scholar and literary man. For years he had read deeply in the literature of ancient Greece and Rome, in the Bible, and in the works of the Church Fathers. For years, too, he had been a member of a cluster of *literati*, the most eminent of their day in England. Several of them lived in London after 1500 and others came to the capital frequently. Collectively they made that city the equal of any in Europe as a center of the New Learning, which placed knowledge of Greek alongside and even ahead of Latin as prerequisite to a claim to erudition. Four of these scholars, William Grocyn, William Latimer, Thomas Linacre, and William Lily had gone to fountainheads of Greek scholarship in Italy to acquire Greek or strengthen their command of it. They had direct contact there with the erudite circle of Hellenic scholars with whom Lorenzo de' Medici surrounded himself. John Colet, Dean of St. Paul's and founder of a great school there, did not learn Greek, but he corresponded with the most eminent of the Florentine Platonists, Marsilio Ficino. When he was in England, Desiderius Erasmus, who towered over all the men of letters and scholars of his day, added luster to this distinguished group. Such was the intellectual company Thomas More kept.

Nearing forty, More earned much and had read much, but he had written little. In the summer of 1515 his sovereign Henry VIII sent Thomas More to Bruges as a member of a mission to treat with the emissaries of the ruler of the Netherlands, Archduke Charles, on matters concerning trade between England and the Low Countries. While engaged on this service More began to write a book. He wrote it in Latin. Months later, after his return to London, he brought the work to completion. He sent it to his friend Erasmus, who saw to its publication by Thierry Martens, a Louvain printer. The book, which came off the press near the end of the year 1516, bore the title:

DE OPTIMO REIPUBLICAE
STATU DEQUE
nova insula Utopia libellus vere aureus
nec minus salutaris quam festivus

The world which four hundred and fifty years later still reads this "Truly Golden Handbook, No Less Beneficial than Entertaining, concerning the Best State of a Commonwealth. . ." has long since reduced its title to the name of "the new island" which it tells about—*Utopia*.

Formally *Utopia* is divided into two books, and the second book topically into several sections. It is convenient, however, to analyze the structure of the little treatise somewhat more precisely.

In the beginning of Book I of *Utopia* More introduces himself and describes the circumstances that in the early summer of 1515 brought him first to Bruges and then to Antwerp. In the latter city, he says, he met Erasmus' friend Peter Giles. Only so far (46/6–48/15) in the book does the author cling close to actuality. With the appearance in it of a mythical Raphael Hythlodaeus (48/17–32) *Utopia* takes off into fantasy. Raphael is a cultured world traveler, whom Giles introduces to More. Having met, the three go to More's lodging, where Raphael, so More says, gives a long account of his adventures and of the many lands and peoples he has visited. More then adds that he will now relate only what Hythlodaeus "told us of the manners and customs" of one of those peoples, the Utopians (54/5–8). Here the first distinct section of *Utopia*, the Introduction (46/6–54/8), ends.

Before More gets around to reporting Raphael's account of Utopia, he tells about an interchange that Peter Giles precipitated by asking Raphael why he did not attach himself as adviser to some king (54/13–19). The latter rejects the idea, and the three argue, pro and con, about the desirability of serving as a royal councilor, Giles and

More mildly pro, Hythlodaeus vehemently con. In the course of this dialogue about counsel Hythlodaeus is diverted from his argument to tell about his acquaintance with More's old mentor Cardinal Morton (58/13). He describes a conversation at the Cardinal's table in which Morton, a stupid lawyer, a hanger-on, a friar, and Raphael himself took part. It ranged over the social ills England suffered, their causes, and the way to ameliorate them. Having finished his tale Hythlodaeus brings the conversation back to the matter of counsel again (84/20–30).

The argument about counsel goes on vigorously until Raphael asks More what he thinks would happen if he advised a king to model his land on Utopia, a country where property is held in common (100/10–12), a "commonwealth . . . more wisely governed and more happily flourishing than ours" (109/19–20). More then urges Raphael to describe fully the land whose institutions he has so warmly praised (108/19–23). Raphael agrees to do so after they have dined, and Book I of *Utopia* ends just before Raphael starts his account of the Utopian commonwealth. In addition to the Introduction, then, Book I consists of a Dialogue of Counsel (54/13–102/20) with an interjected Dialogue on the Condition of England (58/15–84/20), and an Exordium on Utopia, linking Book I and Book II (102/20–108/31).

From the beginning (110/7) nearly to the end of Book II (236/31) Hythlodaeus discourses on Utopia. In this discourse he complies with More's earlier request that he "not be brief, but set forth in order the terrain, the rivers, the cities, the inhabitants, the traditions, the customs, the laws, and, in fact, everything you think we should like to know" (109/22–25). When with a description of the religious practises of the Utopians he has finished his account of the Utopian commonwealth (236/31), Raphael ends his discourse with an eloquent peroration on the virtues and excellences of the way of life of Utopia. Then More winds up his little book with some brief concluding reflections, ascribed to himself, on Hythlodaeus' account of Utopia. Book II, then, comprises Hythlodaeus' Discourse on Utopia (110/7–236/31), his Peroration (236/31–244/13), and the Conclusion (244/13–246/2). Such, briefly, is the structure of *Utopia*. The task of the rest of this essay is to set *Utopia* in its historical milieu. To do so we need to examine the book itself carefully; but we also need to make clear what we have in mind when we speak of a book's historical milieu.

2. Some General and Particular Considerations on Milieux

The phrase "the historical milieu of *Utopia*," so forthright in appearance, actually enfolds a few ambiguities which will impede our investigation if we do not remove them at the outset. The historical milieu of a book has two aspects, overlapping but not fully congruent. It includes what was going on in the world at some roughly limited time before and during the book's conception, and it also includes the furniture of the author's mind at the time he wrote the book. At the center of a book's historical milieu, where its two aspects overlap, there are those happenings in its author's time which, making an impact on him as he wrote, clearly affected the book. Of such happenings there were many in the case of *Utopia*—for example, the English treatment of criminals (60), enclosure of open fields for sheep grazing (64–70), the hiring of Swiss mercenaries (206–208). Outside this area of unmistakable relevance, and shading into an area of dubious relevance, lie two twilight zones:

1. There were the important things going on while More was accumulating the experience that enabled him to produce *Utopia*, things *indirectly* related to that experience, of which nevertheless More was unaware and which therefore could not have shaped *Utopia* in any way. Luther was suffering a fearful ordeal of doubt and despair and emerging from it with a new kind of conviction about God's love to man, and Machiavelli was writing *The Prince* and much of what became the *Discourses on Livy* while More was accumulating the experience which *Utopia* assimilated and organized. More was concerned, although in a very different way, with some of the matters that concerned both these men. But in 1515 he did not know there was such a man as Martin Luther, and he may never have known that there was such a man as Niccolò Machiavelli. In 1515 Luther and Machiavelli were part of More's times but not of his life.

2. When we consider the furnishings of More's mind, we must recognize among them much that came from the distant past. In the age More lived in and the intellectual circle he belonged to, such furnishings were regarded as the best of all. So while his mind did not comprehend some things that were directly present in his own day, it did comprehend much that belonged to an ancient time. And while the fragments of the present which did not touch him and the fragments of the past which did were in a sense both parts of the historical milieu of *Utopia*, they were parts in very different ways: the latter may have had a considerable effect on what More wrote in *Utopia*, but the former could have had none. As obvious as this point is, it needs firm emphasis. Because of More's vigorous opposition to the Lutheran movement only a few years after 1516, the propensity to relate *Utopia* in one way or another to that movement has been very strong. So it is important to remember that in the years 1515–16 there could have been nothing further from Thomas More's mind (or indeed from Martin Luther's) than any intimation that the unity of the Church was about to be irrepa-

rably rent by a conflict over the fundamentals of Christian theology. All the difficult dilemmas, painful heart-searchings, and hard decisions which the words and deeds of Luther, the Popes, and Henry VIII were to impose on More lay beyond his horizon in 1516, quite invisible to and unimagined by him. To read into the record of More in 1516 what we can clearly discern in his mind after the Lutheran revolt and "the King's great matter" is an obvious anachronism. It prematurely forces that mind into the rigid posture which under terrible stress it subsequently assumed, a posture more pleasing to those engaged in the quest for proofs, wholly supererogatory, of More's orthodoxy, than to those merely curious to understand the writer and the writing of *Utopia*.

Since More was quite unaware of such important figures in his milieu as Luther and Machiavelli, we may well hesitate to ascribe to him a vision of his times identical with that of twentieth-century historians addicted to the study of the early sixteenth century, who are likely to be reasonably well informed about Luther and Machiavelli. It is precisely where More seems to share the vision of recent historians as he looks sharply at what those historians have looked at sharply that we need be most careful. When they have looked at the agrarian change in More's England, many present-day historians have seen it in connection with the conflict of classes defined by their relations to the means of production.[1] More was deeply disturbed by enclosure and castigated it with a vigor and fervor forever memorable (64–68), but he saw enclosure as the abuse of the poor by the rich. In the same way during the current century historians tended to see in the wars of the early 1500's the conflicts of nascent nations struggling into existence under the aegis of their rulers.[2] But More saw only the insatiable greed for glory and possessions of warrior-tyrants (86–94). We need make no judgment of relative merit between the perceptiveness of More and that of historians today (or yesterday). We need only take care not to ascribe to More perceptions identical with those of modern historians, or indeed any precocious perceptions at all except those for which his words provide us with clear and exact evidence.

We are not without clues as to More's concerns and preoccupations in 1515–16. His correspondence serves to explain why certain particular matters preoccupied him when he wrote *Utopia*; it also indicates that for pressing personal reasons some of the matters he dealt with in *Utopia* were of special concern to him as he wrote. Evidence drawn

---

[1] Christopher Hill, *Puritanism and Revolution* (London, 1958), pp. 32–49. R. H. Tawney, *Agrarian Problems in the Sixteenth Century* (London, 1912), especially pp. 177–310.
[2] A. F. Pollard, *Factors in Modern History* (New York, 1907), pp. 1–25, 52–78. Cf. Garrett Mattingly, *Renaissance Diplomacy* (London, 1955), pp. 162–63.

from the earlier part of More's life clearly must be used with greater caution. The spiritual disarray of the young bachelor, pressed toward a career for which he doubted his vocation and toward marriage and family responsibilities, may have occasioned the *cri de coeur* More sent to Colet in 1504;[3] but it cannot be taken to reflect the state of mind of the twice-married family man nearing forty in 1516. Even further removed from reliability for determining the hierarchy of More's interests and concerns in 1515–16 is his literary output at any time after 1521, when his attention was sharply directed to the Protestant Revolution. Although that Revolution may not have altered his formal creed, it undoubtedly led him to a drastic reordering of his structure of religious priorities.

Least useful in helping us relate *Utopia* through its author's mind to its milieu are the remarkable group of biographies of More written after his death by men who admired him.[4] Even the earliest of these biographies was set down twenty years after More's execution and forty after the writing of *Utopia*; this one alone is the work at first hand of a man, William Roper, who knew More personally; and even Roper probably did not know his future father-in-law well in 1515–16.[5] The most elaborate of these biographies, that of Nicholas Harpsfield, is, as R. W. Chambers observes, "as much a manifesto as, later, was Foxe's *Book of Martyrs* on the other side."[6] While other lives of More written during the sixteenth century may not be so polemical, they all focus on More's later life and especially his martyrdom. They see the candidate for canonization through the saintly aura that surrounded More on the scaffold, their martyr-hero through the distorting medium of the Catholic Counter-Revolution. Therefore they play down the humanist More, the dearest friend of Erasmus, that dubious character whose works were or were shortly to be put on the Index of Prohibited Books.[7] This alone makes their biographies almost useless for our purposes, since 1515–16 marks the point of maximum convergence of the trajectories of More and Erasmus, the time when the area of opinions and sentiment shared between them was greatest.[8] Except for a few excerpts from More's correspondence in Stapleton's *Tres*

---

[3] *The Correspondence of Sir Thomas More*, ed. E. F. Rogers (Princeton, 1947), p. 6. Cited hereafter as *Corresp.*

[4] These are discussed by R. W. Chambers, *Thomas More* (London, 1935), pp. 24–42.

[5] For the conjectured dates of Roper's entry into More's household (1518) and his writing of More's life (1555–57), see Roper, *More*, pp. xxxii, xlv.

[6] Chambers, *Thomas More*, p. 31.

[7] Preserved Smith, *Erasmus* (New York, 1923), pp. 421–22.

[8] See below, pp. 57–65.

Thomae, these biographies provide no guidance to the immediate milieu of *Utopia* in the mind of Thomas More in 1515–16.

For this loss there is a small compensation. In a loose sense the part of any book which its author writes first becomes the milieu of what he writes later. In the *Utopia*, however, this is the case in a peculiar and exceptional way. The peculiarity results from the odd circumstances of the composition of *Utopia*. From those circumstances, as we shall see, it follows that, before he wrote the Dialogue of Counsel, the Exordium, and the Peroration, More had the opportunity to reflect for a while on the Discourse on Utopia. Indeed in order to decide how he wanted to integrate the Dialogue with the Discourse, he had to reflect considerably on the latter. The sum of the matter is that those points of view, opinions, modes of thinking and feeling that occur in both the Discourse and the Dialogue cannot be dismissed as passing fancies or ill-considered trifles. If they do not embody More's ultimate convictions and concerns, they do embody his deepest convictions and concerns as of 1515–16.

Such considerations may suggest a possible answer to two related though not identical questions about More's *Utopia*: Is the More of *Utopia* the real More? Did More *really* believe what he wrote in *Utopia*? In dealing with them it is helpful to consider a work of a contemporary of More which has persistently elicited very similar questions. Did Machiavelli *really* mean what he wrote in *The Prince*? Is the Machiavelli of *The Prince* the *real* Machiavelli? Is not the real Machiavelli the author of the *Discourses on Livy*? Now if by the real Machiavelli one means that aspect of the man which expressed itself in his most durable habits of thought and patterns of action, then beyond doubt the *Discourses* better than *The Prince* reflects the real Machiavelli. But this identification of the real Machiavelli is a dangerous game; it has led to the dubious inference that only those elements in *The Prince* duplicated in or reconcilable with the *Discourses* represent the real Machiavelli, and that what is left over is to be disregarded or explained away. Yet so to treat *The Prince* is to miss perhaps the most important point about it. What gives *The Prince* its remarkable power and its perennial liveliness is that in it Machiavelli's imagination takes wing and his vision soars above his ordinary perceptions to a new height.

And so it is with Thomas More in *Utopia*. If the Machiavelli of the *Discourses* rather than of *The Prince* is the real Machiavelli, the More of the letter to Dorp and the *Dialogue Concerning Heresies* rather than of *Utopia* is the real More. The unique heights they attain above their own times put *The Prince* and *Utopia* beyond the ordinary reach of the contemporaries of Machiavelli and More, beyond the reach of *all*

their contemporaries—and that includes More and Machiavelli too.
For it is not necessary to believe that almost two decades later, or
even two years later, More saw all things precisely as he saw them in
the moments of acute perception which took possession of him when
he wrote *Utopia*. Sustained imaginative vision is indeed like being
possessed; it is not necessarily progressive or cumulative or even readily
preserved intact. It is a dizzy height which a very few men scale once
or twice in a lifetime and fewer still attain more often. When such
vision is turned on the ways in which men live together, it may bring
some facets of human affairs into focus with a fierce brilliance, but in
so doing it is almost bound to throw whole spans of men's experience,
the visionary's as well as others', into the shadow. The greatness of a
book which does this lies not in its harmony but in its intensity. This
is why afterwards the writer of such a book may seem not to advance
from it but to recede from it. In regaining his balance he loses some
of his impetus. This happened to Machiavelli after he wrote *The Prince*;
it happened to More after he wrote *Utopia*. In both cases the convictions the books express are not so much repudiated as drawn back into
the setting from which something like poetic inspiration had momentarily freed them. The convictions may not be consciously rejected, but
they are integrated with their writers' previous habit of thought and
thereby transmuted and toned down.

With this conception of the place of *Utopia* in the spiritual continuum that was the mind of Thomas More, with internal evidence
provided by the book itself, and with external evidence about More's
situation and concerns in 1515 and 1516, we can reconstruct the circumstances surrounding the writing of *Utopia* that help to render
intelligible some of its traits and peculiarities.

3. The Immediate Circumstances

In the five years before his mission to the Netherlands in the year
1515 Thomas More was an inordinately busy man.[1] He was the father
of four young children and the foster father of another. His eldest child
was only six when More was left a widower in 1511. Within a month
of the death of his first wife he married again to have someone to help
care for his house and his brood—"help" care, because the raising of

---

[1] The data for the following reconstruction of More's situation just before the
Netherlands mission are drawn mainly from Roper, previously cited, and from the
following works: Erasmus' letter to Hutten, in Eras., *Ep., 4, 21.* Nicholas Harpsfield, *The Life and Death of Sr Thomas Moore, Knight*, ed. E. V. Hitchcock, Early
English Text Society, Original Series, *186* (London, 1932), More's correspondence,
along with the information in Chambers' biography and the notes to Harpsfield in
the edition cited here.

his children was a matter to which More himself devoted close attention. To provide for this large family, and for the household of servants
and tutors they required, and to indulge his generous inclinations
toward friends and anyone in need, he required a large income. He
got it from his work as a lawyer, in which he did extremely well but
at a heavy price in time. Nevertheless he managed to eke out a little
leisure for other pursuits. Thus sometime about 1513 he probably
began his *Life of Richard III*.[2] And a half day each week as Undersheriff of London he sat as judge in the Sheriff's Court, not for the
fees, which were trivial and which in any case he usually remitted, but
out of duty to and love for his native city. He also must have given
generously of his small hoard of spare hours to Lincoln's Inn, whence
he had been called to the bar. He was a Bencher of the Inn and a
double Reader, an unusual distinction, especially unusual in More's
case, since he was called upon to make his second reading in 1515,
only three years after his first.

For years, then, the man who set off for the Netherlands in May 1515
had been under almost unremitting pressure from the excessive demands made upon him. And despite the gay face he showed the world
in which he had prospered by the world's measure, More had moments
of misgiving about the course that his life had taken so far and the way
it might run in the future. For with all his large gifts of humane wit,
humor, and fantasy, he had used those gifts only in conversation, in
the exercise of writing Latin epigrams and some English poems, and
in translating four dialogues of Lucian from Greek into Latin. This
slim product of More's wit was also a large part of the whole product
of his learning. Yet along with his faith, his family, and his friends,
learning of the kind most fashionable in his day was one of the
things nearest his heart. And he was not growing any younger. By
1515 he was nudging forty, and his proficiency in classical literature
probably went back as much as two decades. His closest friend was
the leading man of letters in Europe, Erasmus, who had already written much, and won himself a great name. Erasmus was about to crown
his studies with new editions of the letters of St. Jerome and of the
New Testament. But besides his sheaf of epigrams and translations,
all More had to show for his erudition was a *Life of Richard III*, done
after the manner of Roman historians, and a translation into English
of the brief biography of Pico della Mirandola by his nephew, Giovanni Francesco Pico.[3]

As with learning, so too perhaps with contemplation—not in the

[2] See *The History of King Richard III*, ed. R. S. Sylvester, The Yale Edition of
the Complete Works of St. Thomas More, Vol. 2 (New Haven, 1963), pp. lxiii f.
[3] Thomas More, *The Workes of Sir Thomas More, Knyght . . . in the Englysh
tonge* (London, 1557), sigs. a₁–c₁v.

purely religious sense, but in the sense of standing back from his experience, thinking it over, considering its implications in a fairly orderly way instead of by bits and snatches, and relating it to his larger conception of the nature, destiny, and duty of man. His brisk and busy life had left him all too little time for such contemplation. And, of course, in the ten years before 1515 the content of More's experience had enormously expanded to include the law of England and its practice and uses, the ways of those who came before the Sheriff's Court, the problems and joys of marriage, of earning a living, and of raising a family. In 1504, in the spiritual vacuum and partial panic that sometimes precede the assumption of full responsibility for one's own affairs and those of a family soon to be, the young man More, like the Victorians, had doubts of some unspecified sort, and having once escaped "almost from the very gates of hell," feared "falling back again into gruesome darkness."[4] The doubts of the More of 1515 were of a different kind, the doubts of a man approaching middle age, successful and prosperous in the eyes of the world, who had begun to wonder if, in his successful career, he was making the best use of the talents God gave him in stewardship.

Some men are born to leisure, some seek leisure, and some have leisure thrust upon them. In 1515 Thomas More had leisure thrust upon him, an odd sort of leisure and very suddenly thrust on him.[5] In mid-May, Henry VIII appointed him along with four others—Cuthbert Tunstal, Richard Sampson, Sir Thomas Spinelly, and John Clifford—to negotiate with Prince Charles, ruler of the Netherlands, an agreement settling the terms of commercial intercourse between England and the Netherlands.[6] For several weeks after the mission reached Bruges it dealt vigorously, actively, and quite ineffectively with the Prince's representatives. By mid-July the conflict between the demands of the two sets of negotiators was such that it could be resolved only by the intervention of authorities higher than they. The negotiations were recessed to allow the Prince's representatives to go to court and consult with him and his advisers. It was soon evident that they

[4] *Corresp.*, p. 6.

[5] The reconstruction of the events here narrated is based on a minute examination of the available record of relevant events and their chronological relationship. The only sources, outside *Utopia* itself, available for such a reconstruction are scattered through *Corresp.*, pp. 16–84, Eras., *Ep.*, 2, 67–196, and *Letters and Papers, Foreign and Domestic, of the Reign of Henry VIII*, ed. J. S. Brewer, James Gairdner, and R. H. Brodie (London, 1862–1932), *1515–16*. Cited hereafter as *LP 1515–16*. The data and arguments in support of this reconstruction have been placed in Appendix A. A useful account of More's mission is provided by Edward Surtz, "Sir Thomas More and His Utopian Embassy of 1515," *The Catholic Historical Review*, 39 (1953), 272–98.

[6] *Corresp.*, pp. 16–20.

would be a long time gone, and the English emissaries drifted away from Bruges to do other work.

That left More with very little to do; he had no other work. He was, indeed, at leisure, but his leisure was not the sort that can be projected into a distant future and therefore be made the basis of some broadly conceived scholarly effort. There was no telling how short it would be, how long it would last. On the other hand, while it lasted it was nearly pure leisure—complete, indeed forced, freedom from all the ordinary obligations of a busy lawyer and a zealous father. More had the chance for the first time in years to think things over, to contemplate for days on end. But it was in an odd atmosphere that the chance came. The dutiful More had no duties. Cares he still had, cares about separation from his loved ones, about the money his mission was costing him out of his own pocket, about the loss of the lawyer's fees which supported his family; but about such cares he could do almost nothing as long as he was away from home.

It was the kind of situation that snaps the durable ties which imprison a man's fancy, which chain his imagination to the actual with the strong bonds of habit, which falsely make him conceive that the way things in fact are is the way they must be, the only possible reality. Thus More's mind was freed to move in unaccustomed ways; but to produce the Discourse on Utopia something more than the negative relaxation of the bonds of habitual thinking was needed—some positive thrust to help the imagination soar.

That, too, circumstance provided. One use that More made of his unexpected freedom was to visit old friends of Erasmus, men whom he no doubt knew already by name and fame from Erasmus' conversations. He went to see Jerome Busleyden, a rich pluralist churchman, a friend of More's chief-of-mission, Tunstal, as well as of Erasmus, and the owner of a fine house in Mechlin.[7] Late in July or early in August he also went to Antwerp. He had a little business to do there (46/29–48/1), but he also went to acquaint himself with Erasmus' friend, Peter Giles. Erasmus very much wanted these two men of whom he was so fond to meet one another. Even before More had left England, Erasmus had written thence to Giles to ask him to extend hospitality to his friend.[8] No doubt Erasmus also spoke of Giles to More both in England and when he went through Bruges in June on his way to Basel.[9] And since his way lay through Antwerp, he had a further chance to

[7] See The Latin Epigrams of Thomas More, ed. and trans. Leicester Bradner and Charles Arthur Lynch (Chicago, 1953), pp. 221–23, for More's poems on Busleyden's house. Cf. Busleyden's letter to Erasmus (Ep., 2, 375) of November 9, 1516.
[8] Eras., Ep., 2, 68.
[9] Ibid., 2, 90, 151, 194.

remind Giles of More's presence in the Low Countries. More tells about most of this in the Introduction to Book I of *Utopia*.

To meet new people and to have ample time to converse with them have certain advantages. Under ordinary circumstances talk with old friends is the most pleasant and least enlightening kind of dialogue. One knows them too well; they know one too well. The kind of broad exploratory talk that tends to reveal the contours of men's minds is unnecessary; the contours of their minds are already familiar, a well-known scene which one accepts and loves. With new friends exploratory talk is more likely. Through it one identifies the kind of man one is dealing with—his style, his tone, his character. Such talk More had, no doubt, with Busleyden, but more importantly with Peter Giles. They talked about many things in the pleasant summer of 1515 as the English commissioners waited for Charles' emissaries to clarify their instructions—perhaps about the late discoveries in the New World, and the sorry condition of the old one. Mainly, however, they talked about how best to order a commonwealth. This was an old staple item of speculation among intellectuals, having got off to a good start in the literary world with Plato and Aristotle. Within about a year of the conversations of More and Giles two other very intelligent men gave their attention to the same problem: Claude de Seyssel, as, returning to attend the coronation of his new king, Francis I, he meditated on the advice he should give that rash boy, advice which found its way into the *Monarchie de France*,[10] and Niccolò Machiavelli, as he tried to impose some order on his lifelong intent observation of political affairs by assimilating it to his lifelong annotation of his beloved Livy.[11] Between More and Giles, however, the old conversational trot took a new path. What if one could really start building a society from scratch? What kind of commonwealth could one then erect, men by nature being what they are? In 1515 More and Giles could imagine just such a thing happening. There was after all the New World, with which More was acquainted not only from the account of Vespucci's voyages but from the active interest of his brother-in-law John Rastell in voyaging to the northern American continent, up to then untouched by the Spanish.[12] In that New World there were primitive folk living rudely, but ready to be molded into a new order of society. What had Vespucci said of these folk? A number of things indeed. For example

[10] Claude de Seyssel's *La Monarchie de France* was presented to Francis in 1515.
[11] See Niccolò Machiavelli, *The Discourses of Niccolò Machiavelli*, ed. and trans. Leslie J. Walker (London, 1950); Hans Baron, "Machiavelli: The Republican Citizen and the Author of 'The Prince,'" *English Historical Review*, 76 (1961), 217–53.
[12] Although Rastell's venture to the newfound lands took place in 1517, it was probably the fruition of an earlier interest. See A. W. Reed, *Early Tudor Drama* (London, 1926), pp. 6, 11–12, and Chambers, *Thomas More*, pp. 141–43.

that in outlook they were epicureans. And also that they held everything in common.[13]

That they held everything in common! Here More's imagination took
the decisive leap into a region for centuries not seriously explored. For
in Plato's *Republic*, too, all things were held in common. So the new
society, the best-ordered commonwealth, might be like the *Republic*
at least in this, that there would be no private property, no money, no
markets in the ordinary sense.[14] The *Republic*, however, did not merely
capture More's fancy in his talks with Giles any more than Vespucci's
Voyages did; together Plato and Vespucci freed More's fancy. There
was not, after all, in Vespucci's slim narrative much more than a spark
for the imagination; and we shall later note how little More was bound
either in detail or in essence by Plato's imaginary commonwealth. We
shall see how More organized large tracts of the experience of Western
men other than the Greeks and since the Greeks, and how he assembled
them in a new way. And so in Antwerp in the summer More let his
imagination run free as he discoursed on the best-ordered commonwealth—on Utopia.

The Discourse on Utopia is discursive. It is not tightly organized,
even though in part it may casually reflect a sequence of topics as they
appeared in ancient political treatises with which More was acquainted.[15] Instead of trying to offer a rational account of the order
of topics in the Discourse, we may do well to think of his new friend
Giles prodding More in the exercise of his imagination with questions
—How did the Utopians dress? How was work allotted? Were not even
meals private? Not even wives and children? What did the Utopians
do about surplus population?—and so on.

As with his new-found friend Giles, More roamed somewhat capri-
ciously through the fields of fancy, he would occasionally pause to
consider some particular detail of the terrain made especially vivid
for him by immediate circumstances or very recent experience. During
his stay in Bruges his normal aversion to finery and show was exacer-
bated by the obligation his position imposed on him to dress in a style
then deemed suitable to the ambassador of a great prince. By clothing
his Utopians in a uniform gray habit, he expressed his distaste for such
lavish pomposity (132–134), and he tells how the Utopian mother explains to her child that the Anemolian ambassador, decked out in silly

[13] For Vespucci, whose book More knew and described as being "in everyone's
hand," see Martin Waldseemüller, *The Cosmographiae Introductio*, ed. C. G. Herbermann, United States Catholic Historical Society Monograph 4 (1907), sig. c and
pp. 97–98.
[14] For these and other correspondences between the *Utopia* and Plato's work,
see the discussion below, pp. 43–4, 53–4, 88–9, 120–23.
[15] As suggested by P. Albert Duhamel, "Medievalism of More's *Utopia*," *Studies
in Philology*, 52 (1955), 99–126.

splendor, is the ambassador's fool (154/31). He had brooded on his dislike of the practice of law, of the chicanery of lawyers, and of the formality of court procedure. So in Utopia there are no lawyers (194), and the judges help the litigants to put their cases properly, as More may have done in the Sheriff's Court. And with large domestic expenses piling on top of the costs of his mission for his king and his country, with an income which ceased when he left England, and with a family which, as he once observed, he could not persuade to go without food during his absence, More was more than abstractly drawn to a condition of things where a man could serve his country wherever he was needed without sacrificing the welfare of those nearest him in love and kinship. And thus it would be or was in the land of More's summer fantasy. Somewhere along the line it occurred to More that some or all of this ought to be written down, perhaps to provide guide lines for subsequent conversation, perhaps because increasingly it became evident that he had got onto something lively and interesting.

All good things end, however. Negotiation may have begun again in Bruges,[16] but for whatever reason, More left Antwerp. Since he still had time and nothing much to do, he began to set down the substance of his conversations with Peter, elaborating on this or that matter that took his fancy, giving the whole a fictitious narrator, Raphael Hythlodaeus, and making himself and Giles the present but silent auditors to whom the narrator spoke. Later, before More went back to England, he had another chance to visit his new-found friend in Antwerp.[17] At that time he showed Peter the nearly complete rough draft of what became the Introduction and the Discourse on Utopia. Clearly it would not take long to finish it, and this is the real reason why More, in his letter to Giles, "is almost ashamed . . . to send you this little book about the commonwealth of Utopia after almost a year when I am sure you looked for it within a month and a half (39)."

While he was still in the Netherlands More's attention had been sharply diverted from *Utopia* to one of the largest concerns of his age and his own most immediate intellectual concern—the direct defense of a new kind of learning and of a reoriented outlook on the proper ordering of Christian imperatives. Of these views the pre-eminent exponent was More's comrade Erasmus, and for better or worse the views themselves have come to be called Christian humanism. When his work brought down on Erasmus the vigorous attack of a former friend, Martin Dorp of Louvain, More wrote in answer a fierce polemic defending Erasmus on every point at issue. It was not More's last letter in support of the New Learning against the Old, but it was his longest,

---

[16] There is no indication of a resumption of negotiations in Bruges between July 21 and October 22, 1515, in *LP 1515–16*, Nos. 732–1057.

[17] See Appendix B.

something like two-thirds the length of *Utopia*; and he was still busy with it when at long last his recall summoned him home toward the end of October 1515.

Very soon after he got back he found himself wrestling with a problem and decision of inordinate complexity. Henry VIII and Wolsey offered him a place in the royal service along with a pension, "which, whether one looked to the profit or the honor, was not to be despised."[18] To serve or not to serve was the question; and to it More had no easy answer. At about the time Wolsey began to press More to enter Henry's service, Erasmus became a councilor to his native ruler, Charles, Prince of Castile and, among other things, Count of Holland.[19] But Erasmus' councilorship was what in academic circles today would be called a prestige appointment, with a concomitant absence of responsibilities. Erasmus received the post, as he put it, with "my liberty reserved by the vote of the Council."[20] The terms were indeed such as any man might have found gratifying—no duties and a regular stipend.[21]

However little to be despised was the honor or profit of the place Wolsey offered More, he was not offering him a sinecure, but a career, a new career in place of the old one. To take a post at court meant no partial or temporary commitment; it was usually for keeps. Men who entered onto that path seldom turned off it; they kept on it until they dropped. It was not too late for More sharply to alter the course of his life, but it would be very late indeed, once he had altered it, to shift back again. Before making up his mind in a matter so decisive for his future, he needed to think hard and long, and he did think hard and long.

His choice did not, like Erasmus', lie between leisure for scholarship and literature on the one hand, and immersion in affairs on the other. Erasmus had made his choice, and a very courageous choice it was. He chose a life of persistent, humiliating mendicancy and patronage-hunting in preference to the riches and security that would have come to him with a permanent and active place in a prince's court, a place he could have had for the asking with any of the three greatest princes of Europe—Henry, or Francis, or Charles.[22] For him it was a choice

---

[18] Eras., *Ep.*, 2, 196.

[19] Ibid., 2, 161.

[20] Ibid., 2, 204.

[21] 'Regular' in the sixteenth-century sense of being a recognized obligation, not that it was always paid regularly. See Eras., *Ep.*, 3, 50.

[22] In a long and interesting study by Jean Hoyoux, "Les moyens d'existence d'Erasme," *Bibliothèque d'Humanisme et Renaissance*, 5 (Paris, 1944), 7–59 much is made of the sizeable fortune that Erasmus made as an author and literary lion. Even by Hoyoux's estimate, however, good times did not come to Erasmus before 1511, when he was already forty-two years old, and the really thick evidence of a rapidly rising income scarcely antedates the publication of the *Novum instrumentum*.

between freedom and slavery—freedom to come and go where he chose, to write pretty nearly what he chose and not what someone else chose to have him write, to have, so far as his financial means allowed, the full direction of his own life. To be forced to acquire the means by a refined sort of beggary was not pleasant, but that much Erasmus was willing to pay the piper for the privilege of dancing the way he wanted.

The Erasmian choice—study or affairs, *otium* or *negotium*—did not exist for More; he had given too many hostages to fortune—a wife, a foster daughter, an adopted daughter, and three daughters and a son of his own. The children were to be educated in a quite costly way by tutors in More's house, the daughters to be married with the appropriate portions. Added to all this was the generosity of a very kindly man to friends and acquaintances in need. More did not have to live well to live expensively. And, given the age of the children, the oldest just entering their teens, the coming decade was going to be the most difficult of all to finance. More had no reason to doubt that he could do it. At thirty-eight he was already an eminent lawyer, who readily enough earned £400 a year, a very good income in the days before the Price Revolution.[23] The cost of such an income was time, a great deal of time, hours and days in the law courts, hours and days with clients. And now, on his return from the economically dreary interlude of his embassy, More found that his net financial loss had run to perhaps as much as a half-year's income. To make up that gap would take some hard running. There would be little time for the work he loved best—the study of ancient literature. Under such pressure the law, which he had taken as a career to please his father rather than himself, looked more wearisome and barren than ever. In June 1516, he said it was "remote from every kind of learning." Six months later, and more bitterly, he described it as a prison.[24]

But Henry and Wolsey opened another prospect, one by which, given his remarkable talents, More could as well provide for his family as he could by the law. Perhaps this very prospect made the chains that bound him to his demanding practice more galling, and led him uncharacteristically to grumble time and again about his lot. For whatever Erasmus might think—and what Erasmus said much later when More capitulated to Wolsey was that he "was lost to letters"[25]—a councilor of the King was probably better off for leisure than a successful practicing lawyer. Erasmus, after all, had no experience of what provision for the care and feeding of a big family required of a lawyer. On the other side good friends of both More and Erasmus, men who shared their tastes, interests, and concerns, notably More's recent chief-of-

[23] Roper, *More*, pp. 8–9.
[24] Eras., *Ep.*, 2, 259 and 414.
[25] Ibid., 3, 295 (c. April 23, 1518).

mission, Tunstal, now Master of the Rolls, and Richard Pace, had entered the service of the King, and serious patrons of letters like Mountjoy and Archbishop Warham were already at Court. If time for literary work had been the only consideration, the decision to become a courtier would have been easier—but it was by no means the only consideration.

Serving a king meant more than putting in time; it meant giving advice on policy; and it meant actively consenting to or silently condoning the course the King in the end decided to take, or in actuality, in England in 1516, the course Wolsey decided to take. To his general knowledge of what went on in the councils of kings, the knowledge of a man who knew his way around and who had long had friends close to the center of power, More had added a little experience during his recent mission. He had watched Wolsey, through his agent Sampson, greedily grasping at the revenues of the bishopric of Tournai and, to gain his end, proposing every device that a natural bully, enamored of chicanery, could conceive, up to and including the suggestion that Sampson excommunicate the uncooperative Archbishop of Rheims.[26] It was a performance likely to upset the digestion of a man with a stronger stomach for such doings than More possessed. And it was Wolsey who would be More's superior in the King's service. Then, too, while More was in the Netherlands, Francis I, newly ascended to the French throne, hurled his forces across the Alps, defeated the hitherto invincible Swiss, and seized Milan. For a while it looked as though the whole of Western Europe would very shortly be enveloped in flames. Soon after he came back to England More had to ponder such things as these, for it was just such things that were woven into the pattern of the life Wolsey wanted him to follow. Suppose he had been in Francis' council when the question of the Milan campaign came up. What would he have advised? And what would have come of his advice? What difference would it have made?

As he pondered his decision, we may surmise, More remembered his literary creation, Raphael Hythlodaeus, somewhat amorphous still as he appeared in the Introduction and Discourse, not really fully characterized in the little book about Utopia that was almost finished. Nevertheless Hythlodaeus was a creation in some respects very like More himself, sharing his aspirations, sharing his literary tastes, sharing his moral convictions, sharing his feelings about so many very important things—about justice, and luxury, and pomp, and war, and peace, and study, and work. And as More thought of Hythlodaeus, a very clever idea occurred to him. He took out his manuscript about Utopia, and just at the point where the introduction to the Discourse ended

[26] *LP 1515–16*, No. 769.

he inserted a few lines, lines that enabled him to divert his character, Hythlodaeus, from his impending (and already written) discourse and turn him to arguing with Giles and More about the rights and wrongs of a man such as he becoming the adviser of a prince. More thus set Hythlodaeus up as the protagonist of a dialogue about counsel, a dialogue in which the perplexities coursing through his own mind were worked over in an exchange of views among Hythlodaeus, Giles, and More. By mid-February at the latest he had got as far along with his writing as the imaginary interview in the French King's council,[27] with its mordant treatment of the dilemma of a man of peace acting as councilor to a warlike king surrounded by a host of sycophants. And as More wrote now, his creation Hythlodaeus took on new sharpness and definition.

How much further he got before he was again diverted we cannot say. At some point, however, he became acutely aware of another dimension of the problem about counsel. It was not only on great affairs among princes that the adviser to a ruler would be called to speak. An adviser to an English king would have to give advice on the condition of England, the state of his own nation. And on the condition of England More had strong opinions. He was a man very alert to what was going on around him, and that alertness was intensified by one of the jobs that he had taken on. In the Sheriff's Court he did not dispose of great cases, the kind of cases that made lawyers rich, like the one he handled for the Merchants of the Staple.[28] There he saw poor men, and he learned something of what the poor suffered from laws they had not made and scarcely understood. And he learned not to like what the laws did to the humble, small in power and feeble in understanding. In matters like these a man who had the ear of those nearest the throne might perhaps do something worth doing. Why was the condition of the poor, who were most of the people of England, what it was? And if—just if—he should take the road to Court along which Henry and Wolsey were beckoning him, what would he feel obliged to say in the councils of England's King about what England's laws and England's great were doing to England's people? Certainly anyone who could reach Thomas Wolsey might hope to do something

[27] No later than mid-February, because of the indication (88/7) that More thought Ferdinand, King of Aragon, was alive when the passage was written. Ferdinand died on January 23, 1516, and news reached England about February 14th *LP 1515–16*, no. 1541, 1546).

[28] For extracts from the London records dealing with More's relation to the City, see Harpsfield, *More*, pp. 312–14. Cf. J. H. Hexter, *More's "Utopia": The Biography of an Idea*, History of Ideas Series 5 (Princeton, 1952), pp. 99–102, and references there. I am greatly indebted to Mr. Philip E. Jones, Deputy Keeper of the Records at the Guild Hall Record Office, London, for much information regarding the office of Deputy (or Under) Sheriff in the sixteenth century.

about these matters, for, with the resignation of Warham, Wolsey had become chancellor, and thus not only final judge in chancery cases but also the chief figure in the King's Council sitting as a court in the Star Chamber, a body of almost infinitely flexible powers.[29]

And again—his little book was still in his mind—More thought of the device, a fictitious dialogue, which he had used, perhaps at the moment was using, to talk to himself, as it were, about the problem most immediately before him for decision—the problem of counsel. By now the part of the Dialogue of Counsel More had already written had shaped and sharpened the outlines of Hythlodaeus' character; in the course of the Dialogue he had stamped on his creation all that was hard and clear and austere about his own character—and nothing of what was mild and soft and gentle. More decided to use Hythlodaeus once more, this time to set out his views on the condition of England. So again he opened a seam in his book—this time in the Dialogue of Counsel—to insert an addition, the dialogue on the condition of England. For good literary and personal reasons he did not make his new dialogue continuous with the old. In the close argument about counsel, he did not hesitate to set himself up as *advocatus diaboli*. It was after all a matter on which he was of two minds. The role he assigned himself in the Dialogue did represent a judgment, albeit a minority judgment, of the Bench of his intellect. With respect to the injustices rampant in English society it was another matter. He did not wish to represent himself as opposed to the positions that Hythlodaeus would be taking on the condition of England, when in fact he most warmly favored them. On this issue his whole mind and spirit spoke with a single voice. He had to put someone in his place as Hythlodaeus' antagonist. He achieved this end by having Hythlodaeus interject into the Dialogue an account of his visit to England years before and of the conversation in which he took part while there at the table of Cardinal Morton, a close and trusted adviser of Henry VII. It is of interest to note the kind of antagonist More gave to Hythlodaeus in this encapsulated dialogue. In the Dialogue of Counsel Hythlodaeus has shrewd and worthy opponents—Giles and More. In the conversation at Morton's table (70) Hythlodaeus' opponent is a lawyer and a dolt, a tedious and nasty dolt, too. More may have had doubts hard to resolve about the wisdom of a man like himself becoming a councilor to a king. He did not have any doubts whatever about the social condition of England, about the kind of reformation it needed right away without tarrying for any, and about his opinion of the kind of man who would oppose that reformation.

Writing by fits and starts in the very little leisure that his onerous

---

[29] See A. F. Pollard, *Wolsey* (London, 1929), pp. 57–58, 72–73.

duties allowed him, More tried to finish what had become Book I of
Utopia. When he was almost but not quite done early in August, he
had as a house guest his old friend Erasmus.[30] Naturally he showed his
brainchild to his friend, naturally Erasmus praised it. Together More
and Erasmus made plans for publication. Erasmus would take care of
the necessary arrangements when he got to the Netherlands, where he
intended to stay for a good while. On September 3 More sent the manuscript on to him[31] and in December *Utopia* made its debut in the literary world.

The Utopian mission of Thomas More affected in more ways than
one the character of the Dialogue he wrote when he got back home,
returning to the treadmill of humdrum after his curious experience in
the Netherlands of being suddenly projected out of and above the
daily routine. In England he felt the more sharply the tension between
his aspirations and his actions. Even more important, he saw his own
doings and the way of his world with a new perspective, from the
peculiar point of view with which he had provided himself in the
process of creating the Discourse on Utopia. It was the effects produced by this new perspective that we had in mind when we suggested
that the parts of *Utopia* which More wrote in the Netherlands were
a significant element in the historical milieu of the parts he wrote in
London, the Dialogue, Exordium and Peroration, and Conclusion. The
final result, *Utopia* as Erasmus received it, is thus an instance of that
"withdrawal and return" of which Arnold Toynbee has written.

To think of *Utopia* in this way enables us to offer a solution to a
literary riddle about the work. Most of its substance is in the Discourse;
but on the literary side, other parts—the Dialogue, the Exordium, the
Peroration—achieve a more powerful impact. The Discourse is loose-
jointed, a little rambling; it has its moments of intensity, but it does
not build up to them; rather they crop up quite unexpectedly, almost
whimsically sometimes, at points where we would not expect them.
For example, although Utopian communism—political equality of the
citizens, common duty to labor, abolition of private ownership, markets,
and money—is the solid constitutional foundation of Utopia, in the
Discourse it never appears in one piece, but breaks through bit by bit,
as the narrative wanders discursively along from one topic to the next.
But in the other sections of the book, the Dialogue and Exordium, the
Peroration and Conclusion, Utopian communism is firmly integrated
into the literary structure. Moreover, although these sections are discontinuous in the final form of *Utopia*, even though one of them con-

---

[30] Almost done because less than three weeks after Erasmus left his house More
sent the manuscript of the book to him. Not quite done because, had it been,
Erasmus could have taken the book with him. See Eras., *Ep.*, 2, 317.

[31] Ibid., 2, 339.

tains an interior Dialogue, there is no diffuseness, no looseness in them. The structure is tight, the line of argument tidy, the focus always clear, never hazy. In those parts of *Utopia* More achieves a relentless intensity and continuity of feeling.

At first it may seem odd that what More wrote when he had no business on his hands *per otium* should be inferior as a literary effort to what he wrote *ex tempore* and *per occasionem*, snatching hours from sleep amid the press of an overextended commitment of his time. Yet if our reconstruction of the circumstances under which *Utopia* was written is correct, there is nothing surprising about this. Indeed it is what we would expect. As Giles and More whiled away some days of the latter's enforced leisure with their speculations on the best ordering of society, they moved from topic to topic in no very systematic fashion, trying out ideas on how the well-ordered commonwealth would deal with this or that particular matter—housing, clothing, marriage, meals, agriculture, industry, leisure, and so on. They maintained a considerable internal consistency, but they did not carry on their conversation systematically. They expanded the notion of a true community of living, drawing out its consequences, developing related ideas where the topic suggested such development. And they carefully introduced this arrangement into the structure of all major Utopian institutions. Elsewhere they worked in other convictions that they shared—hatred of war and detestation of blood sports, for example. And sometimes, as in the case of the pseudo-Epicureanism of Utopian philosophy, they embroidered a pattern and ran it more or less consistently through their speculation in a spirit of intellectual play.

Such a procedure conduced to a wide-ranging expression of view but also to a certain amount of rambling. The Discourse has a tone of disengagement which vanishes from the portions of *Utopia* written later, because, as he dealt with the matter of the Discourse in the Netherlands, More was as disengaged as he ever would be. This disengagement ended when More, home once again, got back to work, and simultaneously began to wrestle with the problems posed by the demand for his services on the part of Wolsey and the King. Suddenly what had been semi-detached speculation in the Netherlands was transmuted into the most germane and poignant criticism of everything More saw about him; and as he considered what he saw and what he was being asked to do, the structure of values in the Discourse, hitherto somewhat loose in his mind, became firm. Elements of the Discourse to which in his time of detached speculation he had devoted some of his considerable skill in mental acrobatics cease to interest him at all —the philosophy of the Utopians and their religious beliefs and practices, for example. Now unmistakably to the fore were the Utopian positions on crime and punishment, on war and peace, on equality, on

luxury and idleness, on money and property, that is, on those matters
in which, by evidence thrust daily before More's eyes, the way things
were ordered in Christian states most manifestly fell short of Utopia,
the matters, too, on which he would have to render advice if—just if—
he succumbed to the persuasions of Wolsey.

So much we can understand of the relations between *Utopia* and its
historical milieu by investigating the structure and composition of the
book in the light of More's immediate circumstances during the time
he was writing it and by telling the most likely story we can to account
for the facts as we reconstruct them. But this does not take us very
deeply into the relations we are investigating. We shall need to go
deeper. To the specific question, "What went into the writing of a
great book?" the answer is likely to come even shorter of adequacy
than the always incomplete answer to the generic question, "What
explains a particular event?" Capsule sentences for answering such
questions are bound to be unsatisfactory. Tentatively, by way of pointing both to where we have been and to where we are going, we may
say of *Utopia* that it was what happened when in a period of leisure
a humanist undersheriff of London on the fringes of high politics re-
thought the implications of Plato's *Republic* under the influence of
Holy Scripture, and before he was done, had to face the personal and
ethical problems posed by an invitation to enter the service of his ruler.
The words "humanist," "under the influence of Holy Scripture," and
"ethical problems" carry us beyond the point our exposition has so far
reached. To deal with them we shall have to take further into account
both the content of *Utopia* and the larger historical configurations
which are connected with that content.

4. The Perdurable Milieu: *Utopia* and the Family

Much that has been written about the relation of *Utopia* to its historical milieu has been concerned with the extent to which and the
senses in which the book may be said to be medieval or Renaissance
or modern. Such a framework of discussion cautiously and discreetly
used may be helpful; but it does tend to conceal one of the most pervasive themes of *Utopia*, a theme that commentators on *Utopia* have
dealt with scantily or disregarded altogether. The neglected theme is
that of patriarchal familism. The character and place of the family in
the Utopian commonwealth are at once pre-medieval and post-Renais-
sance. It is one of those perdurable phenomena which rudely defy our
traditional systems of historical periodization.

Once we begin to look for it in *Utopia*, the family unit turns out to
be ubiquitous. At any given time about half the Utopians are farmers

and half city folk.[1] To use current terminology, the agricultural units are not collectives or state farms. They are family farms, although the farm family is somewhat extended, consisting of forty adult members (114/5). And the industrial activity of the towns seems to be organized in family units, too, with son ordinarily succeeding father in the family trade, and the women working in the house on the wool for the simple gray cloth in which all Utopians dress (126/10). Moreover, the family is the political unit, since every thirty families are said to choose one magistrate (122/9). Even in war the Utopian soldier marches out and fights accompanied by his wife, children, and other relatives (208/30–210/4). And—a trivial but characteristic detail—just to go on a little sightseeing trip in his small city-state a Utopian must have both the leave of his wife and the permission of his father (146/10–11).

Here we notice two fundamental traits of Utopian family organization: it is strictly monogamous and solidly patriarchal. The law permits divorce, but even this is a family matter since it requires agreement of both parties and the consent not only of the magistrates but of the magistrates' wives (190/4–5). The punishment for adultery is penal servitude, and, for repeaters, death (190/7–8, 14–15). The authority of parents over children, of husbands over wives, and of the eldest, the patriarch, as long as he is of sound mind, over all is affirmed again and again in *Utopia* and tightly woven into the fabric of Utopian institutions. On marriage the women go to live with their husbands, to whom they commend themselves by deference (134/26, 192/23). The sons, whether of the second or third generation, stay at home and are subject to the patriarch "unless he has become a dotard," in which case "the next oldest is put in his place" (135/31–34). The family provides a powerful cohesive force for the whole commonwealth both as a coercive institution and as a training place for citizens. It is one of the means by which Utopians counteract the possible disruptive effects of their egalitarianism. Thus when Hythlodaeus gives More and Giles the first hint of the extraordinary character of the Utopian social order, they suspect that in so democratic a society all respect for authority would be in jeopardy (106/10–12). In the Discourse, however, he describes a society in which there is no lack of such respect. The everyday life of the Utopian is steeped in ceremonial acts of obedience and reverence to his parents. "Wives wait on their husbands, children on their parents, and generally the younger on their elders" (137/31–33). This form of domestic order the Utopians maintain in their public life on

---

[1] At least so it seems (114). But there are some Utopians who prefer the rural life, and they do not have to participate in the biennial rotation of Utopians between town and country (114/15–16). The extent and the consequences of the "stickiness" in the mobility of the rural population are some of the stray ends which More does not get around to tying up.

the two most frequent occasions of common gathering—the common meals and the common religious worship. And on the monthly day of penance "wives fall down at the feet of their husbands, children at the feet of their parents," (233/25–26) where they confess their faults and seek pardon to cleanse their spirit before the religious sacrifices. The penal structure is parallel to the penitential. "Husbands correct their wives and parents their children" (191/26–27).

The importance of the patriarchal family as an institution in *Utopia* throws light on the historical milieu of the book and on the book itself. For several reasons we tend to underemphasize the fundamental importance of the patriarchal family in the pre-industrial society of the West. Probably the oversight is the effect of our own social milieu. As a consequence of major changes during the past two centuries in the organization of work, education, recreation, and police, the patriarchal family has ceased to perform many of the functions which it had performed for centuries, indeed for millennia. For us to recapture a sense of its former social pervasiveness and omnicompetence requires a straining of our imaginations. We tend further to underestimate the place of the patriarchal family in the pre-industrial West, because in proportion to its importance it was not very often written about in that systematic way which is likely to attract close attention from historians. Unlike papal supremacy or the influence of the stars, the family was too firm and its operations too certain, its workings too much a part of the universally accepted fabric of life to elicit widespread systematic discussion. It was never news.

Two able English historians, Lawrence Stone and Peter Laslett, have recently reminded us that "firm belief in the subjection of children to parental control . . . was natural in a society in which family discipline was the main guarantee of public order."[2] Such was society in Renaissance England, in ancient Israel, or for that matter in Confucian China. Thomas More so abundantly provided his imaginary commonwealth with welfare institutions—hospitals, public dining halls, schools, beyond anything known anywhere in his time—that we are likely to think of its structure as more modern than it actually is. But as we have seen, Utopian society is rooted in patriarchal familism.

The place of the patriarchal family in the habits of mind and patterns of action of More and his contemporaries helps to explain a peculiarity in the way they thought. Today we distinguish between the social and the economic. We conceive of an interplay between two spheres of human activity and an area of overlap; but however we envisage the

---

[2] Lawrence Stone, "Marriage among the English Nobility in the Sixteenth and Seventeenth Centuries," *Comparative Studies in History and Society*, 3 (1961), 182–83; Peter Laslett, *The World We Have Lost* (London, 1965), *passim*, esp. pp. 11–21.

extent of common ground between economy and society we feel bound
in the main to deal with the two separately. This is precisely what men
in More's time and More himself did not do and felt no inclination to
do. They did recognize several distinct broad regions of human activity
—politics, war, education, religion, even foreign trade. Most of these
are represented in separate chapters of the Discourse on Utopia. In the
Discourse, however, there is not one chapter devoted to the economy
and another to the society; and data which nowadays would be par-
celed out under these headings are scattered and jumbled seemingly
at random in several chapters. Usually the ways of classifying human
doings contemporary with the doings in question are reasonably well
justified; to use the jargon of our day, they meet a felt need; they do
reflect an actual fact about those doings. In our society the political,
the military, the educational, the religious, the economic, are separate
activities in a very literal sense; by and large they are carried on in
places separate from where the participants live—the church, the
school, the battlefield, the factory or the office; and so on. Language
is a fairly flexible thing; when the Felt Need whispers low, "You must!"
Language usually replies, "I will." Language's long-standing failure to
provide precise means of distinguishing the economic from the social
suggests that people in More's day, and long before and after, were
not powerfully impelled to make the distinction. For most people, living
and earning a living, unlike war, schooling, worship, and politics, went
on in the same place—the family. In the country almost everybody
lived with his family and in his family's house or hovel, and lived from
his family holding. And of course most people were country people.
The unit of agriculture was also the unit of industry, commerce, and
banking. The greatest enterprises, the businesses of the Medici, the
Welsers, the Fuggers, like the smallest, were family firms.[3] Household
production and family trading were as common as other modes of
organizing work were rare. The social and economic merged and sub-
merged in the familial. This merger is reflected in the thought and
expression of *Utopia*. As its title *De optimo reipublicae statu deque
nova insula Utopia* indicates, More's masterpiece is not about an
economy or a society; it is about a commonwealth.

So dominant in the pattern of the world More lived in was the patriarchal family that, once we note its importance in *Utopia*, our first
inclination is to dismiss it as a mere reflex of More's immediate his-

---

[3] See Raymond De Roover, *The Medici Bank* (New York, 1948), pp. 5–13, esp.
pp. 6–7. One rare exception to this rule seems to have been a state enterprise, the
Arsenal of Venice. There were few, if any, other considerable economic units of
this sort. Cf. Frederick Lane, *Venetian Ships and Shipbuilders of the Renaissance*
(Baltimore, 1934), pp. 129–75 and R. Ehrenberg, *Das Zeitalter der Fugger*, 2 vols.
(Jena, 1912), 1.

torical milieu.[4] Yet at the time he was writing *Utopia* More most surely
did not take the monogamous patriarchal family as a mere datum. As
he wrote he had the imaginary *polis* of Plato's *Republic* before his
mind's eye, and domestic relations among the rulers of that *polis* were
not organized on the basis of the patriarchal family. Perhaps the most
startling feature of Plato's argument was its insistence on the community of wives and children among those warrior rulers. More incorporated so many traits of Plato's *polis* in *Utopia* that his rejection of the
most striking of these traits could hardly have been the result of anything but conscious choice. And while he extended to all Utopians the
community of property and goods which Plato confined to the warrior-
guardian élite, he rejected for all of them the community of wives and
children of the guardians.

Made acutely conscious of the patriarchal family by Plato's specific
rejection of it for his rulers, More moved off in the opposite direction;
instead of minimizing the function of the family he magnified it. For,
important as the patriarchal family was in early sixteenth-century
Europe, it was far more important in Utopia. There it was the *only*
organized grouping between ordinary men and their rulers. In this,
Utopia differed greatly from the Western world that More knew. In
that world from the twelfth century on, a host of communities, cor-
porations, societies, and orders came into being—organizations of
clergy, lawyers, knights, townsmen, villagers, dwellers in a particular
county or duchy, teachers, students, merchants, masons, weavers,
butchers, bakers, candlestickmakers, and so on and on. These groups
were more than free extralegal fellowships; more, even, than groupings
recognized by law. They were legally privileged bodies each with its
own jurisdiction. So characteristic of the Middle Ages was the prolifera-
tion of such bodies that some historians call medieval society corporative. Utopians allow none of this. They apparently outlaw fellowships
under the name of *conciliabula* (146/15–21); in any case we hear nothing of such associations in the Discourse on Utopia. There are the
rulers, secular and priestly, and the families of the ruled; and that is
all. The notion, propagated by R. W. Chambers, author of the best-

---

[4] The curious silence of More's friends on this subject reinforces this inclination.
Those highly perceptive men, whose letters were published in the various editions,
have something sensible to say about many of the main themes of *Utopia*, but
about the domestic arrangements of the Utopian Commonwealth they say nothing.
This inclination is further strengthened by the first argument offered in the Dialogue of Counsel to persuade Hythlodaeus to enter the service of a prince. The
argument, put quite candidly, is that by so doing he will be able to enrich his
whole family. And so much a commonplace of the day is this conception of the
proper use of what we call public service that it does not in the least stir to indignation the inveterate moralizer to whom it is addressed. Hythlodaeus merely
observes that since he already has given his goods to his family he does not feel
obliged to submit to the yoke of princely service for their welfare (54/21–27).

known twentieth-century biography of More, that Utopia is a medieval corporate society,[5] rests on a curious misreading of More's book or an equally curious misconception of medieval corporatism. The magnitude of the patriarchal family in Utopia is greatly enhanced simply by the lack of corporatism, by the absence of all other organs of formal and durable human association below the supreme one.

5. *Utopia* and the Medieval

Since one of the universal elements of Western society in the Middle Ages—corporative life above the level of the family—is wholly lacking in Utopia, in this important respect *Utopia* is distinctly unmedieval. This serves to remind us of the need to discriminate carefully when we say that *Utopia* was the work of a medieval—or Renaissance or modern—mind.[1] In some respects, no doubt, *Utopia* reflected the medieval predilections and the medieval milieu of Thomas More. If the medieval elements in *Utopia* are not emphasized here, it is because for twenty-five years they have been emphasized and perhaps over-emphasized by R. W. Chambers and those who have followed his line of argument. His *Thomas More*, published almost thirty years ago, marked an epoch in the understanding of the man and his work. At the focus of his attention is the crowning and final event of More's life, his martyrdom for his ultimate faithfulness to the unity of Christendom in the face of death at the hands of its destroyer and his King. Orienting their saint-hero's words and deeds toward that tragic climax, Chambers and his followers have seen in Thomas More one of the last great medieval Christians. More's affinities, "his closest links are with the men of the Middle Ages." He "belongs to the last transitional era of the Middle Ages" and "stands nearer to St. Francis . . . than he does to the later Tudors of Elizabeth's reign." His death was the price of his resistance to a modernity which he dreaded and detested. He stood for self-mortification—for the hair shirt—against self-indulgence, for the pomp of medieval church ritual against those who would destroy it, for the monasteries against their plunderers. He stood for the corporate life of the Middle Ages against individualism, for the communal life of the Middle Ages against modern commercial exploitation, for medieval faith against modern skepticism. No turncoat, no renegade from an inchoate modernity, he died for what he lived for. What he lived for was medieval, not modern.

[5] Chambers, *Thomas More*, pp. 88, 131–32, 257–58.

[1] What follows is a reworking of my essay "Thomas More: On the Margins of Modernity," *Journal of British Studies*, 1 (1961), 20–37.

Not only lived for but wrote for, all his life long. For the second major theme of the currently accepted understanding of Thomas More is his consistency—consistency in "his works, his acts, and his sufferings." It follows from these two premises—More's medievalism and his consistency—that in studying his works, in studying *Utopia*, for example, the thing to look for is his affinity with the Middle Ages.

Now it is very likely that More approved of sacerdotal pomp, of monasticism in principle, if not in most of its practice, of symbolic ritual, of the beauty of solemn churches, of Christian unity and papal primacy, of the regular and proper administration of the sacraments, of quiet discussion in coping with the more recondite problems of creed. It is also true that these practices, although not uniquely medieval, were approved in the Middle Ages and by the medieval Catholic Church. And finally, it is true that More ascribes these practices to the Utopians (232–36). In this way More, the medieval Catholic, manifests himself in *Utopia*. Furthermore, the things done in Utopia which are squarely contrary to medieval Catholic doctrine almost certainly did not have More's approval. Thus in Utopia men hopelessly ill and suffering bodily torments might freely choose release from this life (186/5–13); and under the severest provocation the wronged partner in a marriage might receive a divorce with the right to remarry (188/26–28). No medieval Catholic could rightfully do these things; and it is a fair inference that as an orthodox Catholic More would not have approved of them.[2] Within these limits *Utopia* is the work of a medieval Catholic.

One general and one particular way of placing *Utopia* in a medieval historical milieu deserve a little further cautionary comment. The general way is to discover some shadow (or even some substance) of a similarity between a notion current in the Middle Ages and a standpoint expounded in *Utopia*, and on the basis of the resemblance to impute paternity to the medieval notion, since it patently came first. The inference is formally unwarranted (though I came before my brother, I am not his father), and substantially erroneous in the case of *Utopia*. It is especially true of More's age, and even more so of his circle of friends and of himself, that a similarity between a position taken in the Middle Ages and one emerging from his milieu does not necessarily imply any direct dependence of the latter on the former *unless the position is uniquely and distinctively medieval*. For it was precisely the achievement of Renaissance humanism, a movement of the intellect and spirit in which More took an active part, that it

[2] The term "approved" as used here conceals a possible ambiguity in More's view. He certainly conceived himself to be subject to the command and jurisdiction of the Church in these matters. Whether in 1515 he deemed that the law of the Church represented perfect wisdom and ultimate truth on the issue of divorce and euthanasia is a somewhat different question, and one to which, as far as I know, the best possible answer would still be tinged with very considerable uncertainty.

restored to Western men a direct access to some of the hitherto unknown or misread literature of classical and Christian antiquity, and made accessible to them a new understanding of the culture of these ancient sources of medieval civilization. So there is a considerable group of notions more or less shared by humanists like More and some men of the Middle Ages, concerning which, barring evidence to the contrary, it is safer to think of common ancestry than of lineal descent. So much by way of general caveat.

The particular way of placing *Utopia* in a medieval milieu about which some caution is called for goes somewhat as follows: In Utopia there is no pursuit of gain. Pursuit of gain is a capitalist trait. Capitalism is modern. The Middle Ages were pre-capitalist and hostile to the pursuit of gain. Therefore *Utopia* is medieval.[3]

To describe More's antipathy to the pursuit of gain as medieval is to do less or more but certainly other than justice both to him and to the Middle Ages. We shall postpone until later an attempt to orient to their historical milieu the views on gain and other such matters which More expressed in *Utopia*. With respect to medieval opinion on the pursuit of gain, the belief that in the Middle Ages the Church opposed all economic effort aimed at profit, though it still haunts innumerable textbooks, is about due for burial. Historians who traverse the slightly tortuous but generally comfortable and heavily traveled road which leads from the eleventh-century usurer to the fifteenth-century merchant prince[4] are not likely to think of the Middle Ages as pre-capitalist or of the medieval Church as particularly and consistently hostile to competitive enterprise, free markets, and the accumulation of wealth.[5] Of course the medieval church officially disapproved of avarice; but medieval theologians and canonists alike acknowledge the rightfulness of various kinds of commercial profit not gained through interest on loans. And in any case the illusion that avarice is a vice peculiar to middle-class capitalists is most easily maintained by those who know little of the history of the French peasantry, or of the English gentry, or of the Roman curia in the later Middle Ages. It is, in fact, on a par with the notion that the various ethical creeds of modern men all have been either indifferent to avarice or warmly approving of it. Recurrent denunciations of grasping merchants by some medieval moralists seem on the whole to have served

---

[3] This view is set forth tangentially in H. W. Donner, *Introduction to Utopia* (London, 1945), pp. 57–59, and explictly and throughout in a very odd book, W. E. Campbell, *More's Utopia and His Social Teaching* (London, 1930). See also Chambers, *Thomas More*, pp. 131–32, 386–87.

[4] Cf. Benjamin Nelson, "Usurer and Merchant Prince," *Journal of Economic History*, 7 (1947), Supplement, pp. 104–22.

[5] See Raymond De Roover, "The Concept of the Just Price: Theory and Economic Policy," *Journal of Economic History*, 18 (1958), 418–34.

functions similar to present-day invectives against chain-store distribu-
tors; they consoled the greedy incompetent without preventing the
world's work from being done with a modicum of greedy competence.
The gradual and occasionally embarrassed accommodation of the
medieval church to the doings of a mercantile world culminated in
More's day with the elevation to the papal throne of Giovanni de'
Medici—son, grandson, and great-grandson of the greatest bankers
of the fifteenth century; but it had got under way a long while back.

Again in connection with the medievalism of *Utopia*, consider the
problem of war and peace. Budé, the shrewdest and most perceptive
commentator on the book at the time of its publication, noted that one
of the "three divine principles" of the Utopian commonwealth was
"resolute and tenacious love of peace and quiet" (11/11–12). More's
deep hatred of the organized violence and the disastrous and pitiful
legacy of warfare stands out in passage after passage of *Utopia*. There
is his picture of the disabled and discharged veterans, crippled and
forgotten, too badly maimed to ply their old trades, too old to learn
new ones (60/27–62/2). There is the Utopian way of dealing with the
barbaric Zapoletans, who are mercenary soldiers, strikingly like the
Swiss mercenaries in More's Europe, brutal, sottish, ready to sell themselves to the highest bidder, and therefore always available to any
power determined on war and able to pay them. The Utopians, who
detest war but are sometimes forced into it, always buy up Zapoletans
by bidding highest for them in the open market. Then they thrust them
into the places of the most danger, not caring "in the least how many
Zapoletans they lose, thinking that they would be the greatest benefactors to the human race if they could relieve the world of all the
dregs of this abominable and impious people" (209/12–15).

Justly the best-known expression of More's detestation of war in
Utopia is Hythlodaeus' brilliant description of what would happen if
in the council of a European prince he gave his honest advice on the
waging of war (86/13–92/15). All the other councilors would make
warlike proposals to enable the King to grab territory on all sides by
fraud or force. Hythlodaeus would then feel impelled to tell the King
about the Achorians. Having seized a kingdom which their ruler
claimed in virtue of an old marriage tie, the Achorians were faced
continually by rebellion or invasion; and war took its eventual toll:
the cost of an army always on foot, the plundering of their land, the
spilling of their blood, the corruption of their morals by lust for violence and rapine, contempt for law, and the collapse of public order.
Then, as a councilor, Hythlodaeus would inform the King that the
Achorians solved their problem by telling their ruler to choose which
kingdom he would govern and to give up the other (90/7–12). What,

Hythlodaeus asks, would be the response of a European king to the advice that he give up expansionist warmongering and concern himself with the right ruling of his own land? "Not very favorable," replies More ruefully (90/14–22). In Utopia, on the other hand, since it is fit only for beasts but practiced by no beast so constantly as by men, war is looked on with loathing (198/30–31).

How does More's indubitable antipathy to war and his passion for peace relate him and his book to the Middle Ages? We have been told that his concern for peace is medieval, an aspect of his devotion to an irenic Christian unity. Yet surely such a view confuses counsel. It ill represents the remarkably contorted and ambivalent posture that medieval men assumed with respect to war and peace; and it does inadequate justice to the quality and connections of More's own views as expressed in Utopia. It is impossible here to offer more than a few cursory remarks about the problem of war and peace in the Middle Ages.[6] In brief, the problem had, in theory at least, enmeshed Western men in ethical dilemmas, paradoxes, and contradictions which were bound to strain the considerable proficiency of moralists in the arts of self-deception, obfuscation, and weaseling. On the one hand the West gave formal allegiance to the teachings of the Prince of Peace. Therefore, unlike a number of other societies, Western Christendom could never overtly accept war as if it were in general good, but only if it were made to appear a lesser evil. On the other hand, from time immemorial warriors had dominated the West; and for the ways of living which those warriors esteemed some place had to be found in the pattern of medieval Western values—a pattern over which the Church had assumed universal custody, direction, and control. For about a century and a half—roughly from the early days of the Crusades to the death of St. Louis—off and on, it may have seemed that the warrior ethos might be brought into some sort of rational adjustment to the Christian ethic. Hope of such an adjustment faded during the thirteenth century when the spiritual head of Christendom, the Pope, perverted the only practical instrument for its attainment, Holy War, by using the proclamation of a Crusade as a weapon against opponents in purely temporal quarrels. From that time some preachers lamented war and some theologians dealt with the circumstances which might justify it;[7] but what they said or wrote seems to have made little

[6] For a fuller treatment, see John Hale, "War and Public Opinion in the Fifteenth and Sixteenth Centuries," Past and Present, 22 (1962), 18–20.

[7] In addition to Hale (ibid.), see Edward Surtz, The Praise of Wisdom (Chicago, 1957), chapter 17, especially pp. 270–71; the article Guerre in the Dictionnaire de théologie catholique; and G. R. Owst, Literature and Pulpit in Medieval England (Cambridge, 1933), pp. 174, 330–31, 334.

impression on the rulers of Christendom, ecclesiastical or lay.[8] In any case a rough, practical *modus vivendi* had long since been found. It is imbedded in the venerable medieval classification of society into those who pray, those who fight, and those who work (for those who fight and pray). The three-way division became a sort of folk wisdom of the rulers, ecclesiastical and lay, cozily condoning the exploitation of the laborer by the clergy and the military. After all it merely generalized medieval practice, which could be illustrated from thousands of particular instances. The successors of the Apostles and the sons of Mars found modalities of mutual accommodation not unduly inconvenient to the latter.

Just a few years before More wrote *Utopia*, at the Lateran Council Egidio of Viterbo called war the most serious, perilous, and deplorable evil of the times, an evil that had almost succeeded in extinguishing the ecumenical authority and God-given liberty of the Church.[9] But to a Europe which had recently enjoyed the ministrations of two such unlikely vicars of Christ as the Borgia Alexander VI and the ruthless warrior Julius II, and in a Council called to patch up some of the damage which Julius had done the Universal Church by making it a pawn in the shoddy power squeezes and war games of Italy, the sermon must have echoed somewhat hollowly. Although before his martyrdom he rallied to the papacy because he deemed it the sole guarantor of Christian unity, it is not surprising that in *Utopia*, two years after the death of the martial Julius, More did not clearly associate papacy, peace, and Christian unity. Indeed the papacy makes only one appearance in *Utopia* and then it is as the butt of the bitterest anti-military gibe in the book. The Utopians do not make treaties of alliance because in their part of the world such treaties are mere scraps of paper; so different, remarks Hythlodaeus, from Europe where alliances are "holy and inviolable . . . partly through reverence to the Sovereign Pontiffs," who "undertake nothing which they do not most conscientiously perform" and "command all other rulers to abide by their promises in every way and compel the recalcitrant by pastoral censure and severe reproof" (197/28–33). A likely story!

6. *Utopia* and Europe's Warriors

General reproofs of gratuitous indulgence in armed violence were more or less the standard equipment of medieval homiletics. *Utopia*,

[8] The clergy, caught in the dilemma of the effusion of Christian blood on one hand and the hereditary claims of their own ruler on the other, had to talk alternately out of opposite sides of their mouths. See G. R. Owst, *Preaching in Medieval England* (Cambridge, 1926), pp. 204–205.

[9] Surtz, *Wisdom*, p. 271.

however, goes far beyond such exhortation. What distinguishes the treatment of war in *Utopia* from medieval treatments of the problem is the way in which More has inextricably woven together an invective against war and a powerful satirical assault on Europe's warrior class. One need not engage in the chicken-egg inquiry: did More attack the chivalry because they made war or did he attack war because it supported the chivalry? *Utopia* provides no answer to this question. It only makes it evident that, as he wrote *Utopia*, the warrior class and war itself were so intimately linked in More's mind that he felt no impulse to nice discrimination in his invective against them, but fervently and impartially vented his detestation of both. The attack on the chivalry in *Utopia* is remarkably comprehensive. It includes the whole order from bottom to top. For almost two centuries England had drawn much of its ready military reserve from the household retainers of the magnates and of the lesser landlords who were their followers.[1] If such men are actually to be a strong and reliable garrison force, More points out, there must always be wars to give them experience. This habituates them to violence. "How dangerous it is to rear such wild beasts" is shown by "the examples of Rome, Carthage, and Syria," whose own "land and even their cities have been more than once destroyed" by the soldiers supposedly held in readiness for wars against their enemies (65/9–14). As for the armed English soldier-retainers of his own day, grown rusty at their craft during the long peace of the first Tudor, More dismisses them as a "rabble of good-for-nothing swashbucklers" (131/6–7), "a huge crowd of idle attendants who have never learned a trade for a livelihood" (63/10–11). They are not even fit for the task they are supposed to do; they are no stronger or tougher than the town workers or the plowmen. In short, they are worthless.

Like men, like master. The idle, worthless retainers are the dependents of idle, worthless lords—the gentry and the nobility, who live like drones on the labors of others, who fleece and rack their tenants to maintain themselves in slothful luxury (62/3–9). Vain in dress, vain about the servility of their underlings, vain about their ancestors, they are mad with counterfeit pleasure (166/23–170/5). It is the born warriors of Europe, the gentlemen and the nobility, who, by giving them soft womanish work to do, in fact debilitate and corrupt the stout fellows, once vigorous and strong, whom they keep in service, so that the habitual practices of the chivalry weaken rather than strengthen the very fighting force which provides them with an excuse for living

---

[1] On the subject of retaining, see W. H. Dunham, Jr., "Lord Hastings' Indentured Retainers," *Transactions of the Connecticut Academy of Arts and Sciences*, 39 (New Haven, 1955), and E. F. Jacob, *The Fifteenth Century* (Oxford, 1961), pp. 338–45.

(64/21–25). And at the top of the chivalric heap, on the peak of the predatory pyramid, stand the princes, the kings of Christendom. For in early sixteenth-century Europe, with civil order restored after the turbulence of the previous hundred and fifty years, the ultimate responsibility for organized violence rested quite unmistakably in the hands of monarchs. The choice was theirs, and they made it: they preferred "to occupy themselves in the pursuits of war . . . rather than in the honorable activities of peace" (57/26–28). Although More attacks in detail the policy of conquest of the kings of France (and rightly, since they were the chronic aggressors in his day), he does not spare his own ruler—for "England never has a war unless its king wants one."[2] Indeed one overriding indictment comprehends all rulers in its scope: it is their insanity which stirs ordinary folk to war (204/25–26).

The onslaught on the chivalry in *Utopia* assails the whole aristocratic way of life, even its tastes and pastimes. The nobles' vain love of fine dress contrasts with the simple sobriety of Utopian costume (166/23–33), their pride in decorating themselves with gems and gold contrasts with Utopian practice, according to which gems are toys for children, quickly outgrown, and gold chains, gold rings, and even gold crowns are the badges of servitude (150/33–152/26). The amusements by which from time out of mind soldiers have dispelled the tedium of military life—gambling, boozing, and whoring—of course come in for their share of reprobation. Corrupting to the common people, they are naturally forbidden in Utopia (128/16–17, 146/15–21). About blood sports, the favorite pastime of the warrior aristocracy, More writes with even deeper repugnance. The other vices are a vile enough respite from the soldier's ghastly trade, but hunting and hawking serve to indurate the warrior in cruelty, and even in peacetime they whet his blood lust. In Utopia the butchery of animals, whether in the field or in the shambles, is work for slaves;[3] freemen do not engage in it lest it dull in them the quality of mercy (138/14–18, 170/21–28). Yet to enjoy such brutalizing sports the English aristocrats drive their poor tenants off the land in order to make game preserves (66/9–11).

So intimately bound in with the whole normative structure of *Utopia* is aversion to the chivalry that it almost automatically effects a kind of transformation of the values which, in More's time, men ordinarily attached to certain words.[4] In the sixteenth century, *generosus*

[2] The foregoing is a deliberate paraphrase, since direct quotation, "*habetis nisi quum*" (64/27), might seem to point more directly at the English king than, in the context, Hythlodaeus is actually doing.

[3] Servitude in Utopia is not hereditary. It is a punishment for Utopian citizens and a privilege for inhabitants of other lands who choose it in preference to what is called freedom in their native countries.

[4] The points in the following paragraph are made in greater detail in Chapter IV below, pp. 194–9.

and *nobilis* were not only nouns of status determination, "gentleman" and "nobleman," but adjectives connoting moral excellence, "gentle" and "noble." In *Utopia* very often they appear as terms of opprobrium and contempt. Thus More remarks on the readiness of *generosi animi*, out of jobs as retainers, to turn to robbery (68/21–24). "Honorable" conduct is in fact dishonorable (92/6–8); a lofty and noble spirit is in fact base (62/21–23). *Splendor* is childish vanity (154/8 f.); *majestas* something as bad or worse (88/4–6). *Gloria* is not glory but vainglory (138/6–7), when it is not *gloriola*, the petty pride of petty men. So frequent is More's devaluation of words ordinarily laudatory in his own day that to restore one of them to its honorific function he sometimes feels impelled to take special rhetorical measures. Thus the somewhat odd conduct of the Utopian priests, who pray for peace on the battlefield before the fighting starts and try to dampen the fury of their compatriots against the routed enemy, does not show merely their *majestas*, but their *vera majestas*, their real majesty (230/15). More's shifting of the traditional value of words is most drastic at the very end of *Utopia*. There he says that Utopian communism would deprive a commonwealth of "nobility, magnificence, splendor, and majesty, which are, in the estimation of the general public, the true glories and ornaments of the commonwealth" (245/24–26). The reference to "the estimation of the general public" only reinforces the satirical thrust of this list of "true glories." For earlier in the book More has already switched the signs on three out of four of these traditionally honorific terms—nobility, splendor, majesty. Of commonwealths they are not the true but the false glories.

If one lumps all this together—the express contempt for the whole European warrior class, the distaste for their pastimes and way of life, the transvaluation of the current vocabulary of praise (or self-praise) of the military—it adds up to a rejection of most of what is characteristic of medieval chivalry.[5] In *Utopia* More does not follow the pattern of medieval moralists who castigate the abuses of the actual military aristocracy by contrasting them with the chivalric ideal.[6] The chivalric ideal insofar as it has any specific traits of its own has no place at all in *Utopia*. And here again we note an eccentricity in More's use of Plato's *Republic*. For with a bit of adaptation that work could very neatly be made to fit the requirements of Europe's military aristocracy. Indeed, with or without the benefit of Plato, the adaptation of new

[5] Not, of course, a rejection of the Christian virtues which all Christians, even Christian warriors, are supposed to practice.

[6] For the literature on this subject, see Ruth Mohl, *The Three Estates in Medieval and Renaissance Literature* (New York, 1933), pp. 73–77, 267–340, 346–47; Alain Chartier, *Le Quadrilogue invectif*, ed. E. Droz (Paris, 1950), pp. 10–25; G. R. Owst, *Literature and Pulpit*, pp. 237–331, and *Preaching in Medieval England*, pp. 182, 264.

forms of education to the requirements of Europe's military aristocracy had gotten under way in the courts of the soldier-princes of north
Italy—Carrara, Gonzaga, and Este—a century before More wrote
Utopia. This process can be traced at least as far back as the treatise
on education which Vergerio wrote for Francesco Carrara's son about
1402, and it carries on through the court-school of Vittorino da Feltre
at Mantua; with Castiglione's *Il Cortegiano* the Italian tradition links
with what may have been an independent northern tradition originating in the court of the dukes of Burgundy.[7] In England itself in
the decades after More's death, and elsewhere north of the Alps, increasing numbers of aristocrats put themselves to school and acquired
at least a smattering of that intellectual culture prerequisite for Plato's
guardians,[8] while they retained their pre-eminence in Europe's military
life by becoming the officer class in the armies of the Renaissance
monarchies. More did not conform his imaginary commonwealth to
that adaptation of the *Republic* which was becoming the pattern of
history in his own day. As Utopia is patriarchal and familial while the
Plato's Republic is not, so the Republic is a military aristocracy while
Utopia is not.

7. *Utopia* and the "Middle Class"

In one of its aspects, then, *Utopia* is a blanket condemnation of a
very large section of Europe's "power élite," its ruling class. That
power élite was military; at least the ethic which distinguished it from
the ruled was of warrior origin, and it was the main reservoir for the
recruitment of officers for Europe's armies. Moreover, while by vocation many of its members fought against each other in Europe's wars,
they were aware of a companionship among themselves that transcended local limits. Recent fashions in historical thought almost require one to assume that if a writer vigorously attacks a currently
powerful class, he does so as a member of or in behalf of another class
which at the time threatens or challenges the position of the former.
It has long been believed on very scant and most ambiguous evidence

---

[7] On these matters see W. H. Woodward's *Vittorino da Feltre and Other Humanist Educators* (Cambridge, 1897), and *Studies in Education During the Age of
the Renaissance, 1400–1600* (Cambridge, 1906); Eugenio Garin, *L'educazione in
Europa (1400–1600)* (Bari, 1957); J. H. Hexter, "The Education of the Aristocracy
in the Renaissance," in *Reappraisals in History* (London, 1961), pp. 45–70.

[8] On schooling for the upper classes, see J. H. Hexter, ibid.; Fritz Caspari,
Humanism and the Social Order in Tudor England (Chicago, 1954), pp. 132–56;
and Mark Curtis, *Oxford and Cambridge in Transition, 1558–1642* (Oxford, 1959),
pp. 54–82.

that a group called the middle class or the bourgeoisie threatened the position of the aristocracy, the cosmopolitan military élite, in sixteenth-century Europe. One scholar has therefore argued that the repudiation in *Utopia* of the ethic of the military aristocracy points to More's attachment to the rising middle class, his role as an enlightened bourgeois.[1]

Of course it is gratuitous to assume that, because More detested the way the military aristocrats ruled, and because he spent some of his harshest satire on them, he necessarily did so as a representative of the bourgeoisie or of any other class or social group. To determine whether in fact in *Utopia* More spoke for the middle class has been rendered a little awkward by the self-appointed custodians of the term, since they have shown considerable irresolution about deciding who in the sixteenth century is middle-class and who is not. The main ambiguity has resulted from indecision as to whether to include the English gentry in the middle class or to exclude it. Since the gentry were collectively the richest social group in England—that is, they probably had the largest disposable cash income—this indecision has proved a great inconvenience to historians dealing with a variety of problems in sixteenth-century history. It need not, however, seriously inconvenience a student of *Utopia*. For quite clearly whichever way one packages the bourgeoisie—with the gentry or without—More has literally no use for it. The English gentry come off badly on all counts in *Utopia*. On the side of expenditure they are the wastrels who squander their substance on hordes of idle retainers, corrupting the commonwealth while they corrupt themselves (62/3–64/25). On the side of income they are ruthless rackrenters and enclosers who turn poor tenants off their lands to beg, to starve, or in desperation to steal and then hang (64/31–66/30).

If we disembarrass the bourgeoisie of the despicable gentry, in More's eyes it manages to remain quite detestable still. The town rich and the lawyers, the only other considerable components traditionally assigned to the middle class, are about equally vile. There are no lawyers and very few merchants in the Utopian commonwealth. The observant Budé noticed the broad streak of anti-legalism which runs through the whole of *Utopia* (6 ff.). In the Dialogue of Counsel, Hythlodaeus makes a lawyer into a figure of malicious fun (60 ff.); but that lawyer's defense of what More considered a brutal and unjust legal system is not merely a joke. Whatever More came to think of the laws of England in his later life, he had no warm feeling for them in 1515–16. In Utopia, the land of Nowhere, there are nowhere any lawyers. In that land the law is left simple; it affords no chance for the crafty handling of cases or the tricky arguing of technical points.

---

[1] Russell Ames, *Citizen Thomas More and His Utopia* (Princeton, 1949).

And the judge himself helps the simple to defeat the designs of sharpers. So the Utopians "absolutely banish from their country all lawyers" (195/15–16).

Shorn of lawyers and landed gentry, the sixteenth-century middle class is pretty much reduced to the bourgeoisie in the old-fashioned sense of the word, the rich or well-to-do townsmen who lived by trade. But it is hard indeed to discover in *Utopia* any marked sympathy for the doings of the town rich. While the rich landlord is no doubt most frequently the target of More's satire, often enough he spreads his wrath to cover the rich in general. *Aurifer* and *foenerator*, goldsmith and money changer as well as *nobilis*, are objects of his indignation (238/21–25). The rich are greedy, unscrupulous, and useless (104/13–14). Not only the idle aristocrats, but merchants whose activity is of little use to the commonwealth, have no place in Utopia (240/6–9). All the things they live by lie under the ban there: money, private property, accumulation of wealth, a pricing mechanism to establish the exchange values of goods. They would have as slim pickings in More's "best order of a commonwealth" as poets had in Plato's.

So *Utopia* expresses a detestation of both war and the social groups committed to warfare as a way of life. It shows an unqualified antipathy for Europe's cosmopolitan military élite. But in *Utopia* we find no counterbalancing admiration for the middle class, defined in any terms which do not spread it through the whole social spectrum. Indeed the only reason for arguing More's attachment to the middle class is his patent disenchantment with the military aristocracy. That reason is not in fact a reason at all; it is only a *non sequitur* sometimes accepted as a sound inference because of its coincidence with an old pattern of historical explanation, whose popularity is far more impressive than are its intellectual credentials. That it is in fact quite feasible to detest the rural rich without showing the slightest affection for the town rich is exactly what is evident on the face of *Utopia*, as it had been long before in the prophets of Israel.

In the very process of arguing that More rejected the middle class as the appropriate successors to the power which the aristocracy of Christendom had so egregiously abused, we may be distorting his way of thinking. For to reject a class as a possible heir to power one must conceive of it as a possible heir, and to do that one must conceive of it *tout court*. It is very doubtful that More did either of these things. While he characterizes or, if you will, caricatures, the military aristocracy very effectively and thoroughly, the lineaments of the bourgeoisie as actualized either in their activities or their ethic (if any) appear nowhere in *Utopia*. It is to be doubted whether the terms "middle class" or "bourgeoisie" or any equivalent of them would have evoked in More's mind the image of a social group which might come to power in Christian Europe. Indeed it is possible that those terms would have evoked for him no substantial or coherent image whatever, and certain that they would not have evoked any of the several images they evoke today.[2]

Granted that More did not conceive of the bourgeoisie as appropriate successors to the power of Europe's military aristocracy, did he regard any group of men in Europe as fit to hold the reins of power which the aristocracy misused so disastrously? To know the answer to this question would tell us much of More's relation to his historical milieu, but it is a question we will not be ready to consider until we examine another aspect of that relation. The element of More's milieu that will concern us now is not an institutional structure or a social class or order but a man—Desiderius Erasmus.

8. More and Erasmus

The problem of the relation between More and Erasmus has been clouded rather than clarified by controversy. From shortly after his martyrdom down to the present, a number of those who have written about More have tended to minimize the significance of his relations with Erasmus for reasons having not much to do with concern for historical accuracy and precision. Thus the first biographer of More after his death, William Roper, mentions Erasmus only once.[1] Although Harpsfield often mentions him, he does not pause to describe the long friendship between his hero and the greatest literary man of his age.[2] The biographer known only as Ro. Ba. includes, in a list of More's friends, Edward Lee, "who wrote learnedly against Erasmus."[3] He does not indicate that More wrote vehemently in defense of Erasmus against Lee,[4] and from the same list of about two dozen of More's closest friends Ro. Ba. wholly omits Erasmus' name! In recent times some writers have laid heavy emphasis on More's warning against identifying Erasmus' opinions with his own.[5] Others have compiled extraordinarily jejune lists of points on which the opinions of the two men did

[2] Cf. R. H. Tawney, "Rise of the Gentry: A Postscript," *Economic History Review*, Series 2, 7 (1954–56), 91–97.

[1] Roper, *More*, p. 3.

[2] Harpsfield, *passim*. The underplaying of the friendship of the two men seems especially conspicuous in view of Harpsfield's knowledge of Erasmus' letter to Hutten.

[3] Ro. Ba., *The Life of Syr Thomas More*, ed. E. V. Hitchcock and P. E. Hallett, Early English Text Society, Original Series, 222 (London, 1950), 100.

[4] *Corresp.*, pp. 137–54.

[5] For the passage from More, see *Workes*, sigs. dd₇–dd₇v. Cf. *The Apologye of Syr Thomas More, Knyght*, ed. A. I. Taft, Early English Text Society, Original Series, 180 (London, 1930), vii–viii; and Donner, *Introduction*, pp. 66–67.

not always coincide.[6] The motives of More's early biographers are
evident enough. They felt it inappropriate that More, the man who
died for the Catholic faith, should be closely associated with Erasmus,
the man whose orthodoxy was so suspect that all his writings, even
those without doctrinal taint, were at one time placed on the Index
of Prohibited Books on the ground that he was a professed heretic of
the first class.[7]

Since no one could imagine that throughout their long and varied
careers two such originals as Erasmus and More would have all opinions and attitudes in common, evidence that on this or that point their
views were not identical may be valid but is of little intrinsic interest.
First one needs to know the priority that each set on his various
opinions, views, and sentiments at different times during his life. Then
one must try to assess the extent to which, at a particular time, their
judgments were congruent on those matters to which each assigned
a high priority. When the congruence is very considerable it is of small
concern that their judgment diverged on points which both men at the
time considered things indifferent or not very important, or did not
then consider at all. And this is so even when they later came to consider such matters seriously and to differ about them. This way of
examining the views of Erasmus and More helps avoid futile arguments about the consistency of one or the other. Only very obtuse
men could have felt exactly the same about things before Luther as
after. Things, to put it tersely, were not the same to feel about. What
we are concerned to know here, then, is what things More and Erasmus
held to be of most importance in 1515–16, whether they were the same
things, and whether by and large the two agreed on what ought to be
done about them and what could be done about them.

The author of *Utopia* was the kind of man now usually described
as a humanist, but in More's time often called simply *literatus*, which
is perhaps best translated as "man of letters." The indispensable marks
of a man of letters in More's day were wide familiarity with the literature of Roman antiquity; increasingly, some acquaintance with the
literature of Greek antiquity in its original tongue; and, finally, command of a Latin style modeled with more or less precision on classical
Roman prose. That the author of *Utopia* was a man of letters, a humanist in the most elementary sense, is evident from the way he writes
Latin, from his easy, offhand way of dealing with Latin literature, and
from his knowledge of and concern with the language and literature

---

[6] Rainer Pineas, "Erasmus and More: Some Contrasting Theological Opinions,"
Renaissance News, 13 (1960), 298–300.

[7] Marcel Bataillon, *Erasme et l'Espagne* (Paris, 1937), p. 60. For the general
ecclesiastical reaction against Erasmus during the Counter-Reformation, ibid., pp.
759–67.

of Greece. Of all the men of letters of More's day, More's friend Erasmus was beyond doubt the most eminent. In the literary world he held a position such as no man since, except possibly Voltaire, has ever attained. At the very least, then, More and Erasmus shared a concern with the same sort of literary life.

But this is not all. Occasionally, it is true, *humanitas* or its vernacular equivalent meant no more than aptitude or grace in literary expression, as when Amerigo Vespucci described his letter to Soderini narrating his voyages to the New World as *"con barbaro stilo scripto, & fuora d'ogni ordine di humanita."*[8] But though for some humanists a graceful style and a knowledge of classical literature were mainly means of personal enjoyment, or of making a reputation, or of securing jobs and promotions, many humanists justified their literary preferences on grounds less self-seeking and less superficial than these. Beyond their technical equipment, literary and philological, perhaps the trait most widespread among humanists was concern with education.[9] Among the humanists were to be found the most active and vigorous educational reformers of the age of the Renaissance. Although on peripheral matters they might differ, they shared a common central educational aim—a radical revision of the ordinary academic curriculum. In that curriculum the place of honor had for centuries belonged to logic. Not only was it essential for the arts degrees in the universities; it also underpropped the main graduate studies—medicine, law, theology. For both the methods and the achievements of an education focused on logic many humanists felt and expressed supreme contempt. They advocated its extirpation and its replacement by a new curriculum organized not around logic but around grammar and rhetoric—the arts of writing and speaking well. Other staples of the new curriculum were classical literature, history (largely ancient), and moral philosophy.

More himself was deeply committed to this kind of education. It was the kind he had received or had provided for himself, and it was the kind he intended to provide for his children, not only for his son but for his daughters.[10] He was even prepared to inflict it on so unlikely and difficult a pupil as his second wife, Dame Alice.[11] And the Utopian commonwealth, of course, was soaked in education, education for every citizen (158/8–9). Even the least apt received the rudiments. Those more gifted had opportunity to continue the formal educational process indefinitely since the hours before daybreak were set aside for the

---

[8] For Vespucci, *The First Four Voyages of Amerigo Vespucci*, see Waldseemüller, sig. a₁v.

[9] See the works by Woodward cited, p. 54, n. 7. See also Garin, p. 67, n. 3, P. O. Kristeller, *Renaissance Thought* (New York, 1961).

[10] *Corresp.*, pp. 96–98, 120–23, 134, 249–51, 255–57.

[11] Chambers, *Thomas More*, pp. 110, 179–80.

schooling of those who sought it, and its attraction even at such early hours may have been enhanced by the alternative, which was bodily labor during those same hours (128/3–12).

Erasmus was of course the educational reformer *par excellence* of his day. In the effectiveness of his propaganda for his views on education his only rivals in later times were Jean Jacques Rousseau and John Dewey. He wrote indefatigably on what would today be called the philosophy of education, but, unlike Rousseau and Dewey, he was equally energetic about the details of pedagogics—specification of curricula and provision of textbooks, into both of which he threw himself with his customary energy.[12] He did not take the educational reformers' easy way, that of simply scourging the available textbooks. He wrote his own to supplant them, and he did supplant them.[13] At about the time More wrote *Utopia*, Erasmus' impact on the educational institutions of Europe was having its maximum effect. He had just begun to correspond with Guillaume Budé, through whose mediation Francis I's collegiate foundation was to become the trilingual Collège de France; and Francis invited him to Paris to lend his prestige to the new enterprise.[14] His rich friend Jerome Busleyden, dying in 1516, left a great sum to endow a College of Three Tongues (Latin, Greek, Hebrew) at Louvain.[15] Erasmus himself was invited to teach at both Paris and Louvain.[16] But it was in England, especially during his long residence there between 1509 and 1514, that the kind of study closest to his heart made the most rapid strides. John Colet, who in 1510 established his school at St. Paul's, was affected by Erasmus' writings on the education of the young. At Oxford, in his new foundation, Corpus Christi College, Bishop Foxe was ready to introduce the sort of instruction that Erasmus advocated.[17] At Cambridge two new foundations—Christ's College and St. John's—under the influence of his friend John Fisher began to propagate the new learning;[18] and

[12] Woodward, *Education*, pp. 104–26, especially pp. 108–10, 115, 121.

[13] For the very extensive use at Oxford in 1520 of the work of Erasmus, including his translation of the grammar of Theodore of Gaza, see "Day-Book of John Dorne," ed. F. Madan in *Collecteana*, ed. C.R.L. Fletcher, 1, 71–177, especially the index at pp. 155–57, 159, *Oxford Historical Society*, 5 (1885).

[14] Eras., *Ep.*, 2, 252, dated by Allen c. June 19, 1516, is the first surviving letter in the correspondence of the two men, but their acquaintance may have been considerably older. For the invitation to Erasmus, see *Ep.* 2, 445–46, and *Histoire de France*, ed. E. Lavisse, 9 vols., V, i, H. Lemonnier, *Les Gueres d'Italie—La France sous Charles VIII, Louis XII et François Ier* (Paris, 1911), pp. 291–94.

[15] Eras., *Ep.*, 3, 230; 4, 548.

[16] Ibid., 2, 503.

[17] J. H. Lupton, *A Life of John Colet* (London, 1887), p. 171. The introduction of Greek into the curriculum at St. Paul's was almost entirely a result of the influence of Erasmus.

[18] C. E. Mallet, *History of the University of Oxford*, 3 vols. (London, 1924–27), 2, 22–23.

Erasmus himself, living at Queens', taught Greek there for three years.[19] Again, then, More and Erasmus attached great consequence to education, and between them there was as little difference about what the substance of education ought to be as about its proper tools and mechanisms.

But why educate men in a particular way? What sort or sorts of men is education supposed to develop? By and large, whether it was the kind that craft-masters gave their apprentices or the kind that men received in the universities, organized education in the Middle Ages aimed primarily at the training of experts—craftsmen, merchants, physicians, lawyers both civil and canon, clerics, administrators ecclesiastical and lay, teachers, professional philosophers, and theologians.[20] According to More and Erasmus what was the function of the kind of education that they advocated? And were they in agreement about the ends as well as about the means of education?

One function actually performed by the humanist sort of education was the production of those experts necessary to perpetuate it—rhetoricians and philologists to teach the humanities in schools and universities. In Italy especially, where the political life of the city-states was a good deal more in the open than in the North, rhetoricians became professional propagandists by speaking and writing for their city.[21] Their training led to their inclusion in foreign missions, to their selection for the new vocation of resident ambassador,[22] and occasionally to their promotion to high office at home.[23] Nevertheless, for most humanists since the early days of the revival of learning in Florence, the aim of educational reform was not merely an improved curriculum, or improved speakers and writers, but improved men. The gravamen of the charges against the kind of education ordinarily provided in the European universities of the fifteenth century was that men were no better as men for having had it, that it produced only adepts in logic-chopping and chicanery, and louts at living. Not all humanists, as we have said, were dedicated educational reformers, and among those who

[19] See James B. Mullinger, *The University of Cambridge*, 2 vols. (Cambridge, 1873–1911), *1*, 423–552, especially 453–65; and Eras., *Ep.*, *1*, 465, 590–92.

[20] The part of medieval education of which this seems to be least true, despite the contempt of the humanists for it, was the education of the warrior élite. It did indeed aim to produce technical military competence, but it also aimed to produce a kind of man. It is perhaps for this reason that there is an unmistakable ideal type of medieval knight, but there is no single ideal type of medieval cleric. Cf. Rudolf Limmer, *Bildungszustände und Bildungsideen des 13 Jahrhunderts* (Munich, 1928).

[21] P. O. Kristeller, *Studies in Renaissance Thought and Letters* (Rome, 1956), pp. 563–64.

[22] G. Mattingly, *Renaissance Diplomacy* (London, 1955), pp. 103–118, especially 116–17.

[23] Such was the case with Coluccio Salutati, Leonardo Bruni, and Poggio Bracciolini, heads of the Florentine chancery during the period from 1375 to 1449.

were, not all envisaged educational reform as a means of moral reform; but many did. Italian humanists like Vittorino da Feltre and Guarino of Verona found in the literature of classical antiquity and in the educational models provided by classical writers, especially Plutarch, Cicero, and Quintilian, the inspiration for their own educational designs.[24] They held their students to rigorous standards of training in mind and body, and they held before those students the highest standards of conduct to be found in the moralists, poets, and historians of Greece and Rome. Men so trained, they believed, would be better equipped than men trained in the traditional curricula of the universities or men steeped in the tradition of chivalry, both to live well themselves and to rule well, to perform their duties and to govern their fellows in Christian commonwealths. By and large the vision of the Italian humanist was confined to Italy, and within Italy it was mainly civic, finding its customary horizons at the boundaries of Italy's congeries of independent and semi-dependent city-states.[25] This civic character of Italian humanism no doubt lent it considerable intensity, but it also narrowed it. As the literary-educational pattern which we have been calling humanism slowly moved across the Alps, it was itself transformed by the northern men of letters whom it had formed. As a consequence of this development in the early years of the sixteenth century, the humanists of Germany, the Netherlands, France, England, and, belatedly, Spain were linked together in a way that transcended in its scope and aspirations the earlier humanism of the Italian *literati*.

The label ordinarily applied to these northern men of letters is "Christian humanists," but the precise nature of the entity thus labeled is not so easy to specify. Scholars doubtful of the utility of the label and of the very existence of the link have made much of the differences of doctrine which seem to separate the men sometimes called Christian humanists. Suggestions that John Colet was not by conviction a humanist at all,[26] accounts of the controversy between Erasmus

---

[24] Woodward, *Vittorino*, pp. 25, 45–46, 170–73.

[25] This point is emphasized in Hans Baron's *The Crisis of the Early Italian Renaissance*, 1 vol. in 2 (Princeton, 1955).

[26] Eugene F. Rice, Jr., "John Colet and the Annihilation of the Natural," *Harvard Theological Review, 45* (1952), 141–63. Professor Rice's essay appears to me to be based on two doubtful assumptions: (1) that the views Colet set forth in his lectures fairly early in his intellectual career underwent no modification throughout his life, and (2) that humanism is most usefully defined as a structured philosophical position on certain doctrinal questions. The first assumption is unverified and may be unverifiable. The second involves a matter of judgment as to what sense of "humanism" will best serve the purposes of coherent, intelligible, and unambiguous discourse; and in this my judgment is at variance with that of Professor Rice. In effect his argument disregards the sense of fellow-feeling that emerges from the correspondence carried on between Erasmus and Colet from 1499 to within a few months of the latter's death.

and Lefèvre,[27] lengthy and trivial lists of matters on which Thomas More's judgment at one time or another diverged from that of Erasmus[28]—individually and cumulatively these and other bits of data are offered to prove that little or no substance lies behind the label "Christian humanist." And if one insists that Christian humanism must refer to a series of rationally related propositions concerning the character of the cosmos, the nature and destiny of man, and the more arcane details of Christian theology, then indeed the term has no referent in sixteenth-century history. But there is no warrant for requiring that the entity called Christian humanism be this particular sort of entity. There was, in fact, a double bond among the Christian humanists—a personal bond of comradeship and a spiritual bond of shared sentiment and activity. At the center, linking both of these bonds together, stood the single great figure of Desiderius Erasmus.

The bond of comradeship can be clearly discerned in Erasmus' vast correspondence and in the surviving fragments of the multilateral correspondence of his host of friends in Germany, France, the Netherlands, and England. In 1515 a man who knew him well describes Erasmus' way of interlinking the lines of friendship of which he was the center. "His greatest pleasure is to praise absent friends to friends present. Since he is greatly loved by so many men, and that too in different parts of the world, because of his learning and most charming character, he tries earnestly to bind all men together with that same affection which all have for him alone. And so he constantly mentions each one of his friends individually to them all; and to insinuate them into the friendship of all the others, he constantly talks about those qualities each one has that deserve affection."[29]

Lending reinforcement to the personal bond linking the Christian humanists was a bond of the spirit, and in his voluminous literary output Erasmus propagated that spirit. Above all else he believed that God had sent His Son into the world and made Him flesh so that by Christ's words and deeds He might teach men the way of living that was best. Erasmus was the kind of Christian who focuses his faith on the preaching, teaching Jesus more intensely than on the dying, rising man-God, so that Incarnation and Crucifixion become the supreme guarantee of the precepts of the Savior. Deeply versed in the literature of Rome and later of Greece, Erasmus joined in the reverence of

[27] For full references to Erasmus' controversy with Lefèvre see Eras., *Ep.*, 3, 5, n. 32, and 12, 17 under "Apologiae: Ad J. Fabrum Stapulensem."

[28] Pineas, *Renaissance News*, 13, 298–300.

[29] *Corresp.*, p. 28 (the letter to Dorp). This and subsequent translations from the letter are those of Marcus A. Haworth, S.J., as they appear in E. F. Rogers' *St. Thomas More: Selected Letters* (New Haven, 1961), pp. 6–64. Cited hereafter as *Selected Letters*.

earlier generations of humanists for the teachers of classical antiquity.[30] But for him they are only the dawn of understanding whose bright noon is the philosophy of Christ. Christ's Grace is in His Word; and His Word is in the New Testament and in the guidance it offers to those who would lead the good life. The immediate function of education as Erasmus saw it, and of his own work, was to provide men with the readiest possible access to the teaching they most need if they are to lead lives in accordance with the rule of life their Savior gave them. Through men so taught the world could be transformed. For Erasmus education in the philosophy of Christ offers a sick world the best promise of the reformation in the Church, the renovation of Christianity, and the restoration of man to the place in the scheme of things, to the dignity and worth, for which God has created him.[31]

The most exact and succinct statement of Erasmus' views, views which he shared in varying degree with the remarkable cluster of European scholars and men of letters who were bound to him and to each other by a sense of sharing in a noble venture of the spirit, occurs in his *Paraclesis* to the New Testament. This work was perhaps the crowning glory of the most fruitful years of Erasmus' life, the years between his return to England from Italy in 1509 and his final departure from England in 1517. This period saw the publication of *The Praise of Folly*, of *The Education of a Christian Prince*, of a revised and greatly expanded edition of the *Adages*, of the great edition of the *Letters of St. Jerome*, and of Erasmus' new Greek edition and Latin paraphrase of the New Testament. During these years, as we have seen, much of his work as an educational reformer was finding practical fruition in educational institutions—schools, colleges, universities. In those years, then, the opinions of Desiderius Erasmus on the ultimate end of the kind of education which he wished to render accessible to every man, so that each man might receive as much of it as he could absorb, were fast making their way in the world. During part of this period he lived in London and in the house of his friend Thomas More.[32] What were More's opinions on these matters in 1515–16? Did they coincide with those of Erasmus?

[30] What immediately follows is drawn mainly from Erasmus' *Paraclesis* to his edition of the Greek New Testament (Erasmus, *Opera omnia*, ed. Jean Leclerc, 10 vols. in 11 [Louvain, 1703–1706] 6, *3–*4v.)

[31] On this point see Otto Schottenloher, *Erasmus im Ringen um die humanistische Bildungsform* (Reformationgeschichtliche Studien und Texte, *61*, 1933), p. 113.

[32] Chambers, *Thomas More*, p. 101; Eras., *Ep.*, 2, 94, 317.

9. Christian Humanism

The years of the most intense and fertile development of Christian humanism coincide with the years of most intensive communication between Erasmus, its most active propagator, and More. And near the end of those fruitful years, in 1515–16, More wrote *Utopia*. These facts suggest a possible, indeed a probable, connection between the book and its author on the one hand and Christian humanism as it was being propounded in those years by Erasmus on the other. Yet two very persuasive expositions of *Utopia,* each deserving serious and careful consideration, tend to separate it from the Christian humanism of Erasmus and to assimilate it to modes of understanding either opposite or unrelated to his. The first exposition proceeds by counterposing two opposite methods of attaining knowledge—the analytical method of the medieval schools and the rhetorical method of the humanists.[1] The former moves by means of logical argumentation from presumably irrefragable premises to putatively ineluctable conclusions. It is substantially metaphysical and formally dialectical. By its very nature the scholastic method fragments whatever literary texts it uses—whether Cicero or St. Paul—employing bits and pieces of them as premises or supporting statements or conclusions for its sequence of syllogistically connected trains of reasoning. The rhetorical (or historical) method of the humanists, on the other hand, takes a literary text and by studying it at once internally as a coherent expression of its author's intention and externally in connection with its setting in time and space, with its historical milieu, aims to achieve a sympathetic understanding of the work as a whole and of the whole intention of its author. For this purpose a most careful study of the language of the text is indispensable, so that philology and history replace dialectic and classification as the instruments of investigation. For the literature of pagan antiquity this kind of study began in the age of Petrarch. It was the great achievement of the northern Christian humanists, beginning with John Colet, to apply the methods hitherto focused on classical literature to Scripture itself. Now there is none of this sort of thing in *Utopia*, no philological investigation, no *explication de texte*, no historical orientation. There is, however, especially in the Discourse, a considerable amount of what can be construed as systematic logical exposition. Therefore, it is argued, far from being a humanist work, *Utopia* is More's most medieval effort.

This argument has been presented with far more erudition and persuasiveness than the above inadequate summary conveys. Never-

[1] P. Albert Duhamel, "Medievalism of More's *Utopia*."

theless it is not entirely convincing. In the first place the very mode of demonstration by which the argument for the scholastic character of *Utopia* is put forward is itself a trifle scholastic; it would better satisfy a medieval logician than a Renaissance humanist. It tends to break the text of the Discourse on Utopia to bits and reshuffle those bits into a structure dialectically adequate, rather than to examine the work as the expression of a living man at a moment in his life, and to discern the meaning and intention of the work in terms of the interplay between a personality and its historical milieu. Moreover, the argument rests on a conception of Christian humanism which would exclude not only *Utopia* but also Erasmus' *Colloquies, The Education of a Christian Prince*, even *The Complaint of Peace* and *The Praise of Folly*, since they are not *explications de texte*, while, perhaps a trifle oddly, it would find room for Luther's *Lectures on the Epistle to the Romans*. Under the circumstances the dissociation of *Utopia* from Christian humanism seems less likely to be the consequence of More's intention than of an arbitrarily meager image of Christian humanism in the mind of the scholar who makes the dissociation.

But as soon as one places *Utopia* in its chronological setting, in its relation to More's own activities and those of his friends, the likelihood that at that point in time More's habits of thought assumed a scholastic cast begins to evaporate. In England, with the patronage and encouragement of the circle who were More's warm friends, Erasmus was engaged on the task that above all others defined the Christian humanist's method and goal, the emendation of the Greek text of the New Testament and the provision of a new Latin paraphrase.[2] More's mission to the Netherlands in 1515 did not take him beyond the bounds of the Christian humanist circle, for Cuthbert Tunstal was one of his colleagues, and he spent time during his stay with Jerome Busleyden and Peter Giles.

To get an idea of the degree to which common outlook, common purpose, and common sentiment bound More and Erasmus together in 1515, we need to turn first not to the brilliant and remembered *Utopia*, but to More's long, wordy, and nearly forgotten letter to Martin Dorp, a professor at Louvain. Apparently urged on by fellow theologians there, Dorp in an exchange of letters with Erasmus[3] had taken exception to some of the satire, especially that against theologians and the theology of the schools, in *The Praise of Folly*. He had also expressed alarm at the implication, latent in Erasmus' editorial work on the New Testament, that, on occasion, a towering medieval

[2] On good evidence Allen ascribed the impetus behind Erasmus' edition of the New Testament to his association with John Colet (Eras., *Ep.*, 2, 182). For the encouragement of Warham and Fisher, see ibid., 2, 268.

[3] Eras., *Ep.*, 2, 10–16, 90–114, 126–36; *Selected Letters*, pp. 6–8.

theological structure might rest on a scriptural foundation no more firm than a copyist's error. To combat both these views More took up his pen, rushing to the defense of his friend in what he wryly called a laconic note—a letter-apologia of more than 15,000 words.

The letter is a vigorous defense of two positions, one embodied in *The Praise of Folly*, the other in the edition of the New Testament. Those positions were the key points in the propaganda of Christian humanism as Erasmus conceived it. The first position was that one of the best and most effective ways to combat stupidity, fatuousness, and even in some instances evil itself was through satire. The second position, as we have already seen, was that to bring about a revival of religion and a reform of society men needed to know the teaching of Christ, and that to achieve this knowledge the study of His words and those of the Apostles, as they were first spoken and written, was indispensable. Exhaustively and exhaustingly in his letter to Dorp, More offers a detailed defense of satire and of the philological study of Scripture. The length of his apologia measures the depth of his conviction: he had had his introduction to the Christian humanist method of studying the New Testament from John Colet more than a decade before,[4] and he made evident his high valuation of satire as early as 1506, when jointly with Erasmus he translated several of Lucian's dialogues. He may have been able to dash off the long letter to Dorp in jig time because, besides being saturated with the subject, he had seen Dorp's first letter and Erasmus' answer well before he composed his apologia. The letter to Dorp is a hasty, rambling composition, but it expresses a long-ripening, coherent, and firmly held judgment.

More's concern with the Erasmus-Dorp controversy and his composition of *Utopia* were continuous if not indeed coeval. But this increases the difficulty of thinking of *Utopia* as a work predominantly scholastic rather than humanist in character. It requires us to suppose that while one part of More's mind was most intensely focused on the sort of thing that most concerned Christian humanists in his letter to Dorp, the other part of his mind dealing with *Utopia* fell or had just fallen into a pattern of thinking which at that very time he was holding up to ridicule and contempt. For in his letter to Dorp one of the stratagems by which More defended Christian humanism was a devastating and unqualified attack on school philosophy from Peter Lombard on. The intellectual profit to be derived from the supposition above stated is hardly adequate to compensate for the excessive and unnecessary stress to which it subjects our credulity.

The same observation applies to a second way of thinking about

[4] Lupton, *Colet*, pp. 62–74, 95; Duhamel, "Medievalism of More's *Utopia*," and "The Oxford Lectures of John Colet," *The Journal of the History of Ideas*, 14 (1953), 493–510.

Utopia and its author which emphasizes their medieval orientation and dissociates them from Erasmus. The Utopian commonwealth, the argument goes, was patently a heathen, not a Christian, state. To anyone reared as More had been in Catholic orthodoxy there was an obvious distinction between the four pagan virtues, which were accessible to heathen reason, and the three Christian virtues, which were not. By basing his *Utopia* on the distinction between Temperance, Courage, Wisdom, and Justice on the one hand and Faith, Hope, and Charity on the other, More both follows the medieval tradition and gives point to his satire on contemporary abuses in Christian Europe. "The underlying thought of *Utopia* always is, *With nothing save reason to guide them, the Utopians do this; and yet we Christian Englishmen, we Christian Europeans . . .* ! The virtues of heathen Utopia show up by contrast the vices of Christian Europe. But the Four Cardinal Virtues are subsidiary to, not a substitute for, the Christian virtues. More has done his best to make this clear. It is not his fault if he has been misunderstood."[5]

Yet in *Utopia* itself one vainly seeks any such distinction.[6] If More indeed did his best to make this point, he did it so badly that for four hundred years no one recognized it as being his point. To suggest such an unfortunate and crucial failure of communication imputes to the author of *Utopia* an incapacity to make himself clear about his main argument, which is not at all evident when he deals with subsidiary arguments. Fortunately, there is an alternative: it is that what stood to the fore of its author's mind as he wrote the *Utopia* may not have been the contrast of the virtuous heathen and the wicked professed Christian. This turns us again to the question of historical milieu. And once again the region of More's historical milieu which is pertinent to our present inquiry is the one we have designated Christian humanism.

What preoccupation of Christian humanists, especially of Erasmus and of More himself, at the time the latter was writing *Utopia*, most satisfactorily explains the unmistakable and invidious comparison which More insistently makes between the Christian realms of Europe and

---

[5] Chambers, *Thomas More*, p. 127.

[6] The only place it is even suggested in the published volume of *Utopia* is in Busleyden's letter to More. After the former's death, Erasmus, in preparing the Basel edition of 1518, removed the letter from the front, where it had stood in the Louvain edition, to the back, perhaps a covert editorial comment. In any case Busleyden neither draws a distinction between the natural and theological virtues nor suggests that Utopia exhibited the former but not the latter. He simply picks up More's own occasional references to parallels between Utopia and Plato's commonwealth and draws out an exact parallel in the distribution of excellences among classes, which does more credit to his understanding of the *Republic* than to his understanding of *Utopia*, where no such class distribution of virtues is stated or implied. Indeed, the whole passage smacks of a humanist showing that he too had read Plato.

his imaginary commonwealth? In raising this question we again follow the method of the humanists themselves rather than that of their opponents, the philosophers of the schools. It would not be much use, after the scholastic fashion, to try to contrive the particular set of logically interrelated doctrinal propositions to which, if they were put to the question, most Christian humanists might assent. For such assent would tell us little about the matter of paramount interest to us (and to them): what *at a given moment* did they feel a serious Christian should especially concern himself about? What did Christendom *at that moment* most need to worry about? The moment or time span to which our inquiry is directed is 1515–16.

The question that Erasmus believed was paramount in those years was at once great and simple: "What is it to be a Christian?" Concerning that question he had two powerful convictions. The first was that the answers to it represented in much of the teaching and most of the common practice of his day were worse than wrong, that they were an outrageous parody of the truth, perpetuated by men narrow of mind and blinded by self-interest. The second was that the true answer was already in a large measure accessible and that it could be made more readily accessible. Erasmus believed that it was his vocation, with the help of his ever-growing circle of friends through all Christendom, unremittingly to strive to discredit the wrong answers to the question "What is a Christian?" and to give men the best chance possible to know the right one.

These two convictions Erasmus most strikingly juxtaposes in the adage *Dulce Bellum Inexpertis* ("War has charm for those without experience of it").[7] In early editions of the *Adages* from 1508 on, the *Dulce Bellum* had received less than forty words of comment. In the edition of 1515 it becomes the subject of a vigorous invective essay of about 11,000 words. Although particular major facets of Erasmus' way of thinking receive fuller and more coherent expression elsewhere, in no work does the relation of those facets appear more clearly. The ills of his world, Erasmus believed, resulted from a deadly interplay of wrong thinking and bad acting. The wrong thinking was in part the result of the principal ends that the universities of Erasmus' day, and for centuries before his day, had set for the education they provided. Those ends were the assimilation of knowledge to the patterns provided by the corpus of Aristotle's philosophy and the Roman *Corpus Juris*. The propagators of this kind of education were the professors of theology and law in the universities of Christendom. In effect the

---

[7] What follows is drawn from the adage as edited and translated into French by Y. Remy and R. Dunil-Marquebreucq, *Collection Latomus, 8* (Brussels, 1953). Based on the text of the *Opera Omnia* of Leclerc, this modern edition indicates the variants of the 1515 edition in its critical apparatus.

philosophy of the schools accommodated the teaching of Christ to the doctrines of Aristotle, to theories of Roman lawyers, and by extension to the notions of all sorts of pagan writers. To achieve this accommodation the faculties of the universities had literally torn the word of God to tatters. When it did not engage professional logicians in noisy but sterile logomachy, this process led them to something worse. It set them to seeking ways to bring the teaching of the Son of God, who set Himself over against the ways of the world, into accord with Aristotle's philosophy and Roman law, which accepted the world, never looking or thinking beyond it.

For those who lived by their rules, Aristotle and the Roman jurists aimed only to make life within a worldly framework as satisfactory and orderly as could be. Following Aristotle, the school philosophers taught that no society where all things were common could flourish; to attain perfect happiness men must have the goods of the body and of fortune. And masking Roman law under the cloak and name of equity, civilians and canonists supported the schoolmen, allowing force to be met with force, approving the pursuit of gain and even moderate usury, and declaring war, if just, to be a splendid thing. To seek to bring such teaching into agreement with that of Christ was to mix fire and water. The pursuit of honor, the pursuit of riches, the pursuit of power became acceptable, and with them greed, pride, and tyranny. And so the teaching of Christ, dismantled bit by bit, was scattered with scarcely a trace in a world that called itself Christian.

But ideas have consequences. What is Christianity in a world that disregards Christ's teaching? In such a world, what does a man mean when he professes to be a Christian? When one takes the heart out of Christianity, all that is left, all that can be left, is a dead body. To simulate life in such a body it must be put through ever more exacting and ever more numerous formal and mechanical motions. What are the motions? Pilgrimages, worship of relics, hagiolatry, fasts, rites of all sorts, degenerating at the worst into sheer superstition and magic-mongering. And who beat the drums for this vain parade? The beneficiaries, of course: the monks with their collections of relics, the ignorant friars, the lordly bishops. It cannot be otherwise. Once the teaching of Christ is rationalized away, there is nothing left but external acts of sacerdotally certified and clerically sponsored busy-work.[8]

The price of the reduction of Christianity to a mockery of what Christ came for is high; it is also inevitable: it is the war of Christian against Christian. The mystical body of Christ becomes a battleground; Christians burn and loot; they rape and murder other Christians. For

---

[8] This is the burden of a mass of Erasmian satire, especially *The Praise of Folly* and the *Colloquies*.

war is the culminating corruption of corrupted man, the colligation of all his evil propensities. The teachers of Christendom had given over their true vocation in order to become apologists at retail for each particular kind of worldliness, provisioners of counterfeited Christian licenses to allow base men to do what they would, and therefore the final wickedness of war was sure to follow. In the face of war among Christians, the ultimate treason to the Prince of Peace, those teachers were not merely silent; they actually sanctioned that treason. If they did not quite dare to make war as such into a positive good, they so managed matters as to relieve every warrior, from the hated mercenaries to the insatiable soldier-princes, of any qualms of conscience for a course of conduct as congenial to the vile appetites of those murderous men as it was disastrous to the Christian commonwealth and contrary to the Savior's teaching and example.[9]

Though the learned of Europe had long engaged in what Erasmus took to be a conspiracy to misguide men as to what it meant to be a Christian, he had no doubt about what being a Christian meant. To be a Christian was not first and foremost to assent to a creed, or to participate in a particular routine of pious observances; to be a Christian was to *do* as a Christian; to be a Christian was a way of life. To help them to discover this way of life men had of all guides the best —the very Son of God, Jesus Christ Himself. He still taught men how to be Christians, as He had taught His disciples hundreds and hundreds of years before, by His words, preserved in the Gospels and expressed in the letters of the Apostles. He also taught by His own life, for Christ was the first and perfect Christian. What men needed then was not new teaching; it was to find again the best teaching of all; and having found it to make it their way of living. The most important work a man of letters could do was to rescue the Gospel from the theologians and canon lawyers who had torn it to shreds and thus prevented men from knowing it. Erasmus believed he had notably advanced this work by editing and translating the New Testament. The philosophy of Christ which he speaks of often in the *Paraclesis* has nothing to do with the philosophy of the schools. It rests more on feeling than on syllogism; it is life rather than discourse, inspiration rather than erudition. And the simple man inspired by the Gospel is a far better teacher of that philosophy than the learned worldlywiseman. For the philosophy of Christ belongs to the heart not to the head; it is a matter of spirit and action rather than of ceremonies and maxims. What men do, not what

[9] Erasmus' antipathy to war was a recurrent theme in his writing for decades. It crops up in the *Adages, The Praise of Folly,* and *The Complaint of Peace,* in his series of formal letters and treatises of advice to princes, and in his familiar correspondence. See Robert P. Adams, *The Better Part of Valor* (Seattle, 1962).

they say, what they practice, not what they profess, make them Christian; and the best Christian is he whose doings, whose whole life, comes nearest the teaching and example of the Master.

We need not inquire whether on the critical or on the constructive side Erasmus' judgment was sound and his history accurate, whether school philosophy, Roman law, and formalism in religious observance were related to one another and to the early sixteenth-century world as Erasmus believed them to be. For present purposes it is enough to recognize that at the time of their publication Thomas More accepted without a single explicit qualification the main positions which Erasmus took in the two crucial works just examined—the *Dulce Bellum Inexpertis* and the *Paraclesis*. Indeed to say that More accepted Erasmus' positions is to understate and perhaps to misstate the matter in at least two ways. In the first place he did far more than passively accept the positions; in the second place to describe those positions merely as those of Erasmus implies a view of their origin which might be hard to sustain.

From 1515 to 1520 More not only "accepted" Erasmus' views; he was their most pertinacious and combative defender, in one instance indeed more combative than Erasmus himself. Aside from *Utopia* and an unfortunate and tiresome squabble with the French humanist Germain de Brie, More directed his literary efforts for five years into a defense of his friend, or rather into an all-out assault on his friend's detractors. During these years he wrote four important letters. In the one to Oxford University, he threatened the Oxford "Trojans," those who opposed the introduction of the curriculum espoused by Erasmus, with the displeasure of the Archbishop of Canterbury, of the Cardinal-Archbishop of York and Lord Chancellor, and of the King himself.[10] From a distance of nearly half a millennium it looks like using three very big mallets to crush a gnat. In the three other letters—to Dorp, to Edward Lee, and to a monk[11]—More makes fierce assaults, very energetic and as little edifying as such things are likely to be after four and a half centuries, on those who doubted the wisdom or the worth of Erasmus' work on the New Testament. The letter to Dorp gives More a chance to savage the school theologians, the letter to a monk gives him a chance to do the like to the regular clergy—for a long time two favored targets of Erasmian satire. With great zest More seizes both chances. The sophistic pedantry of the dialecticians,[12] their wanderings in a confused labyrinth of *quaestiunculae*,[13] their absorption in "the

[10] *Corresp.*, pp. 118–19.
[11] Ibid., pp. 27–74, 137–54, 165–206.
[12] Ibid., pp. 37–38.
[13] Ibid., p. 33.

petty casuistry of the moderns,"[14] which is to Scripture as a kitchen maid to the queen,[15] are the objects of his unmeasured and unqualified contempt. And the life of the professed religious of his day fares no better. Lately much has been said about More's admiration of the monastic life, and what has been said is part of the truth; but in his letter to a monk he shows small respect for the notion that "to reside forever in the same spot and, like a clam or sponge, to cling eternally to the same rock is the last word in sanctity."[16] The occasion of this tirade was monkish criticism of Erasmus for his perpetual wanderings over the face of Europe, and More seizes on the opportunity to appraise the character and work of the chief of Christian humanists. It is an appraisal which should give pause to recent scholars who have tried to impute major differences in outlook to the two friends as early as 1515.

The lazy, More says, would no doubt rather squat with the monks than roam with Erasmus, who "does more work in one day than you people do in several months. . . . He sometimes has done more for the whole Church in one month than you have in several years, unless you suppose that anybody's fastings or pious prayers have as deep and wide an influence as his brilliant works, which are educating the entire world to the meaning of true holiness." Erasmus "defies stormy seas and savage skies and the scourges of land travel, provided it furthers the common cause." He bears "sea-sickness, the tortures of tossing waves, the threat of deadly storms, and faces the ever-present danger of shipwreck." He plods "through dense forest and wild woodland, over rugged hilltops and steep mountains, along roads beset with bandits." He is ever "tattered by the winds, spattered with mud, travel-weary, worn out by hardships." And the body that Erasmus subjects to these torments "is growing old and has lost its strength from hard study and toil." Clearly Erasmus must have long since succumbed to these hardships "had not God preserved him for the benefit of an ungrateful people. No matter where his journeys take him, he always comes back bearing wonderful gifts for everyone else, while he gets nothing but shattered health and the insults of wicked men, occasioned by his beneficence." Erasmus is forced to travel in the interest of his studies, "that is, for the common good. . . . As the sun spreads its rays, so wherever Erasmus is, he spreads his wonderful riches." Dedicated wholly to the service of others, he expects no personal reward here below. Surely there is a more than accidental parallel between this account of the tribulations of Erasmus in his valiant propagation of

[14] Ibid., p. 48.
[15] Ibid., p. 50.
[16] Ibid., p. 201; *Selected Letters*, p. 137. The quotations which follow are all from this same passage, *Corresp.*, pp. 201–203; *Selected Letters*, pp. 137–40.

the philosophy of Christ and Paul's tale of his hardships in behalf of
the gospel of Christ, "in journeyings often, in perils of waters, in perils
of robbers . . . in perils in the city, in perils in the wilderness, in perils
in the sea . . . in weariness and painfulness . . . in hunger and thirst
. . . in cold."[17]

Returning again to the relative value of the monk's service to God
and of the service Erasmus was rendering, More continues, "God will
prefer his speech to your silence, his silence to your prayers, his eating
to your fasting, and in short everything you proudly despise about
Erasmus' way of life God will value more highly than all that you find
most sweet in your own way of life." The tree may be known by its
fruit and the fruit of Erasmus' ceaseless toil and travel has been the
publication of more works "abounding not merely in learning but in
solid piety than any other man has written for many centuries."[18] And
the advances made in sacred as in secular learning are due as much
to the unflagging efforts of Erasmus as to "anyone else in the past
several centuries."[19] This is why in every land in Christendom men of
true intellectual and moral worth seek to outdo one another in their
thanks to Erasmus for what his work has done for them.[20]

The scholarly proficiency and the unremitting, almost ruthless, dedication by means of which Erasmus achieved his enormous output were
unique. But the ideas and beliefs that inspired that output were probably less the achievement of Erasmus' individual genius than the
product of the mutually fructifying interplay of a number of like minds.
A very important phase of that interplay had begun with Erasmus'
first journey to England in 1499, which initiated his long association
and friendship with a small but able group of English humanists. More
had a part in it from the beginning; and one of its consequences over
two decades seems to have been an ever closer congruence in the
outlooks of the two men. Even before 1506 a friend of theirs had
remarked on a likeness of "mind, tastes, feelings, and interest such that
twin brothers could not more closely resemble one another."[21] At the
center of this common ground shared by the two men was the conviction that to be a Christian was first of all to live like a Christian, to
take as the model of day-to-day conduct the words and acts of Christ.

During the very year when Erasmus quoted the above comment on
the similarity of their outlook, More in his dedicatory letter to his
translation of Lucian observed that in *The Cynic* that satirist was
praising Christian living, those Christian virtues of "simplicity, tem-

[17] II Corinthians 11:26–27.
[18] *Corresp.*, pp. 166–67.
[19] Ibid., p. 141.
[20] Ibid., p. 191.
[21] Eras., *Ep.*, 1, 423. The observation was made by Richard Whitford.

perance and frugality that make up the straight and narrow path which leads to life."[22] There is no distinction here between pagan virtues and Christian. All virtues that men must practice in order to live righteously are Christian virtues. The distinction that concerns More is not one between types of virtue but between kinds of men—the men who live the rigorous disciplined life commanded and exemplified by Christ and the men who—whatever their assiduity in lip service to orthodoxy— live like pigs and hyenas.

Nine years before he wrote *Utopia*, then, More, like his friend Erasmus, saw Christianity as a way of life. Whatever moves men toward that way of life is Christian. And if it comes from Lucian, who was not a Christian, it is no less Christian for that. This indeed follows from the Christian humanist propensity to see Christ primarily as a teacher, as the most effective of all teachers of virtue, who perfectly embodied in action what others, whether pagan or Jew, had offered as precept. In the sphere of conduct particularly, the boundary between the region of nature and the region of grace is not very sharp. This is especially so if Christ's mission was, as Erasmus and perhaps More believed, the renewal of a nature once wholly good but corrupted by evil custom beyond the power of mere men to restore it.

In 1515 More and Erasmus and many of their friends were full of the excitement of new discovery—the discovery, they believed, of a method of understanding the message of Christianity and the life and teaching of their Lord Jesus far superior to the method current in their own day. Into a world gone stale and sour they hoped they could bring a sense of the good and the true, which would freshen and sweeten it. The method of understanding espoused by the humanists was new, but not the understanding itself. The method—philological investigation and "rhetorical" apprehension of Christ's teaching—had to be new because the old method, so the adherents of the New Learning contended, had buried both understanding and the thing to be understood under a pile of sophistical scholastic debris and futile formalism. The thing to be understood was, of course, as old as, in some matters older than, the Apostles, and as new as tomorrow. It was the eternal word of God's revelation of His Truth, His Will, and His Love to men.

Our inquiry about the relation between More and Erasmus and about the substance of Christian humanism has revealed that in 1515– 16 the two men stood in complete agreement on precisely those matters which at the time both regarded as of primary importance—especially on the need to deploy the talents and the erudition of humanists in order to remold the world in conformity to Christ's rule. Was this Christian humanist outlook which More so fully shared with Erasmus

[22] *Corresp.*, p. 12.

reflected in *Utopia*, and particularly in that contrast, sometimes implicit, sometimes explicit, between Europeans and Utopians which pervades the book? Under the circumstances it would be odd if it were not. Yet it was not, if the question that the contrast raises is merely: How can Christians behave so badly when heathen Utopians behave so well? That question smacks a little too strongly of the medieval schools. But the contrast may raise another question, at once shocking and more in line with Christian humanist habits of thought: as between the Europeans and the Utopians, *which are truly Christian?* Such a question would bring *Utopia* into positive and central relation to the defense and propagation of Christian humanism which was More's primary commitment when he wrote the book. For in wrestling with the question about Europeans and Utopians in the context More provides, one also by inference wrestles with the question: What, truly, is it to be a Christian?

There is a reasonable amount of evidence that these questions were among those with which More intended to confront the reader in *Utopia.* Comments by both Budé and Erasmus indicate that they sense such an intent. Budé calls Utopia *Hagnopolis*, a holy community (12/6). He describes Utopia as a place where, as by a miracle, men have achieved Christianity without revelation. In a marginal note Erasmus calls it a holy commonwealth (146/17). In those notes, too, he observes how the Utopians surpass European Christians in several matters characteristically Christian—Utopian rejection of astrological superstition (224/13–15), Utopian belief in immortality (224/5 f.), and the sanctity of the Utopian priesthood (226/19 f.).

In its content and occasionally even in its language the Discourse on Utopia keeps before the reader the problem of balancing the nominal Christianity of Europeans against the way of thinking and acting of the Utopians. The Utopians not only possess in the highest measure the virtues More had described as Christian a decade earlier —simplicity, temperance, frugality; they also have faith in a God in whose goodness and mercy they trust. Along with that faith goes *spes*, hope for life eternal. And along with faith and hope goes *charitas*, or love. The Utopians repay their benefactors with *charitas* and share a *mutuus amor charitasque*, while magistrates and citizens deal with one another lovingly like fathers and children (164/26–30, 194/2, 224/8). The institutions of Utopia are not only *prudentissima*, the most prudent; they are also *sanctissima*, the most holy (102/27–28). And their social order established the rules of life which Christ had taught as the right way for men. According to Erasmus' *Dulce Bellum*, in Christian Europe, Aristotelian theologians and Romanist lawyers had reasoned away those very rules in order to permit the pursuit of profit, usury, private property. Nowhere does More make the community of spirit

between true Christians and Utopians more explicit than at the point
of the story where one would expect the contrast to be sharpest—the
point where Hythlodaeus and his band convert many Utopians to
Christianity. For beside Christ's miracles and the martyrs, what draws
the Utopians to Christianity is His teachings and character (216/33–34).
The *contrast* of Christian teaching with what they know by reason is
not what moves so many Utopians to accept baptism in the faith, nor
does More say anything about such a contrast. Quite to the contrary,
they become converts because the teaching of Christ accords with their
most cherished beliefs. It is of special weight with them that "His
disciples' common *way of life* had been pleasing to Christ and that it
is still in use among the truest societies of Christians" (219/6–8). The
italics are mine, the emphasis is More's. It is the emphasis of the Christian humanists. The teaching and the way of life are what count above
all else. In their teaching, the Utopians are very like Christians; and
in their way of life they are far closer than any European Christian
people to the way of the first and best Christians of all. Their whole
society indeed exemplifies the chief Christian virtue—*charitas*. More
than any other Christian institution the family embodies giving without demanding an equivalent in return. And this is the very essence
of *charitas*, of that Christian love of which Christ's giving of His life
for sinners is the supreme symbol and perfect example. Fulfilling the
Gospel command of Christian brotherhood—*mutuum date nihil inde
sperantes*: "Give, seeking nothing in return"[23]—in Utopia "they make
up the scarcity of one place with the surplus of another. This service
they perform without payment, receiving nothing in return from those
to whom they give." And so, More concludes, driving his point home,
"the whole island is like a single family" (149/3–4). If in the light of
all this one wonders today whether the Utopians were not better Christians than the formal Christians of More's time and place, it seems
likely that More's contemporaries wondered the same thing, and that
this is what More intended should happen.

From the description of the conversion of the Utopians More might
have meant to suggest that even before Hythlodaeus instructed them
in Christian teaching and baptized them with water, the Utopians
already enjoyed what Catholic theologians call the baptism of desire.
This, however, imputes to More in 1516 a stronger preoccupation with
the niceties of school theology than the evidence seems to warrant. It
is more likely that he was reaching for a less technical distinction—
that between those who know God in the bottom of their heart and
those who merely acknowledge Him with the top of their head. The
latter avowed their faith and performed the ritual motions formally

[23] Luke 6:35.

required of a Christian, but they denied Christ in every other act of their lives. The former, not having heard Christ preached or seen the sacraments administered, did not know how to produce any of the outward and visible signs of an inward and spiritual grace, but that grace was nevertheless in them and showed itself in their relations to their fellowmen. The great commandment was not two separate injunctions but one. Truly to "love the Lord thy God" and not to "love thy neighbor as thyself" was impossible; thus their own deeds gave the lie to all the Christian professions of the princes and great ones of Europe. But the reverse was also true. Men could not truly love their neighbors without having God in Christ at the bottom of their heart, no matter with what superstitious nonsense the top of their head might be stuffed. And such a people loving God and their neighbors were the Utopians. Surely for men not heavily committed to any formal school of philosophy—and none of the Christian humanists seems to have been so committed—the most pertinent fact about the Utopians was not merely that they discoursed like reasonable pagans but that they lived like very good Christians. When they heard about Christ for the first time, they experienced not so much revelation as recognition. For the first time they recognized with the top of their head the truth that had long been in the bottom of their heart, that had inspired their actions and their institutions, and that made Utopia the best of commonwealths.[24] If this is so, then in 1515 More like Erasmus was preoccupied with the central problem of the Christian humanists, "What, truly, is it to be a Christian?" And *Utopia* reflects his preoccupation. The conclusion which *Utopia* powerfully suggests without flatly stating it is that Christianity was not a mere occasional flurry of formal deeds demanded by authority but a way of life that emanated from every heart where Christ had found a home.

The peculiar twist More gives to that problem—the Utopians living in the New World had been out of the range of the spoken and written Word—testifies to his early perception of what was to become a difficult psychological problem for the Christian world. The untold millions of men who had never heard the Gospel preached were only slowly emerging into the consciousness of Christians in the wake of the great discoveries and explorations of the quarter century since the first voyage of Columbus. Increasing contact with and awareness of these millions were to impose on Christians a crisis of creed and conscience altogether different from that raised by contact with overtly anti-Christian Moslems in the Middle Ages. For these new millions were not anti-Christian, at least not in the beginning; they were non-

[24] Whatever insight the above discussion may possess I owe to John Baillie, *Our Knowledge of God* (New York, 1959), pp. 47–104.

Christian. In *Utopia* More had started to nudge Western men into a posture that might have spared non-Europeans much suffering. Such a posture might also have spared Christian churches from assuming, toward the unconverted, attitudes that were to impede and in places wholly frustrate the Christian mission of conversion and that were one day to help drive Western men of sensitive conscience from the Christian fold. But it was not to be.

Before we turned to the task of defining the relation of Thomas More at the time he wrote *Utopia* to his friend Erasmus and to that part of his historical milieu, Christian humanism, which found its embodiment and fullest expression in Erasmus, we raised the question whether More had in mind any possible successor to the ruling aristocracies of Christendom, whose political bankruptcy he so vigorously (and prematurely) proclaimed in his book.[25] To this question we now return. Did More believe that there was in Europe a group of men suitable to serve as its rulers? If so, what was this group? How do we find these men?

One way to find them is to start with a dream—a dream of the author of *Utopia*. To try to solve a problem in social history by the analysis of a dream is not a procedure likely to commend itself very often to a sober historian; it is the sort of thing he is likely to expect from the more desperate varieties of social scientist. But in this case we confront special circumstances. *Utopia*, after all, is fantasy; and—many of the difficulties in interpreting the book result from this—fantasy itself dwells where the boundary between dreaming and waking, imagery and actuality, is not a sharp line but a broad, indistinct twilight region. Indeed we cannot be sure whether the dream of Thomas More which we are about to look into was a true dream or a daydream, another bit of sheer fantasy. He tells Erasmus of his dream in a letter of December 1516. When More wrote Erasmus, he was still waiting "for our *Utopia*, with the feelings with which a mother awaits the return of her boy from foreign parts."[26] His letter goes this way:

> You have no idea how thrilled I am; I feel so expanded, and I hold my head high. For in my daydreams I have been marked out by my Utopians to be their king forever; I can see myself now marching along, crowned with a diadem of wheat, very striking in my Franciscan frock, carrying a handful of wheat as my sacred scepter, thronged by a distinguished retinue of Amaurotians, and, with this huge entourage, giving audience to foreign ambassadors and sovereigns; wretched creatures they are, in comparison with us, as they stupidly pride themselves on appearing in childish garb and feminine finery, laced with that despicable gold, and ludicrous in their purple and jewels and other baubles. Yet, I would not want either you or

[25] See above, p. 57.
[26] Eras., *Ep.*, 2, 502.

our friend, Tunstal, to judge me by other men, whose character shifts with
fortune. Even if heaven has decreed to waft me from my lowly estate to
this soaring pinnacle which, I think, defies comparison with that of kings,
still you will never find me forgetful of that old friendship I had with you
when I was but a private citizen. And if you do not mind making the short
trip to visit me in Utopia, I shall definitely see to it that all mortals governed by my kindly rule will show you the honor due to those who, they
know, are very dear to the heart of their king.

I was going to continue with this fascinating vision, but the rising Dawn
has shattered my dream—poor me!—and shaken me off my throne and
summons me back to the drudgery of the courts. But at least this thought
gives me consolation: real kingdoms do not last much longer.[27]

With every due allowance for the fanciful element in the letter,
something about More's yearnings emerges from this unusually distinct dream or vision. For to the heart's desire of a man what better
guide can there be than his daydreams? When More let his imagination range freely it did not reveal ascetic flight from the world or a
purely contemplative immersion in scholarship to be the ultimate
desire of his heart; More saw himself most completely fulfilled as a
ruler, or prince. But he saw himself as a prince in Utopia; it was with
the rulers of his own imaginary commonwealth that he identified himself. And this meant that, save for the fact of ruling, he would in every
way differ from the rulers of Europe, the leaders of the cosmopolitan
military élite, the primary target of his most savage satire.

What manner of men were these rulers of Utopia of whom he would
be one? The letter itself tells us something about them. They are contemptuous of finery and wealth; and they themselves wear only the
simple habit in which all Utopians dress. The emblem of office borne
before them is not the sword, the symbol of power, destruction, war;
it is the sheaf of wheat, symbol of peace, prosperity—and work. Simplicity, sobriety, industry, love of peace—the virtues of the rulers of
Utopia begin to seem a bit bourgeois after all! Until, of course, we
recall that the medieval bourgeoisie had not undergone purgation by
Calvinism, that in the centers of urban life in More's day—the Netherlands and Italy—the town rulers were distinguished neither for their
austerity nor for their addiction to the ways of peace. The list omits
two indispensable bourgeois traits—craftiness and appetite for gain.
The Utopian magistrates with their sobriety and appetite for hard work
are modeled not on the money-grubber but on the scholar; the end
of their way of life is not to maximize gain or profit or wealth, but to
maximize leisure—*otium* in the good sense of time free for study and
contemplation. *Industria* and *studium* (104/15, 128/2) have as their
ends not the accumulation of riches but *cultus* and *humanitas* (112/5),

[27] Ibid., 414; *Selected Letters*, p. 85.

culture and humanity, *libertas* and *cultus animi*, spiritual freedom and culture (134/19). The very pastimes of Utopians are steeped in the pursuit of learning, and possession of it is the prime qualification for office (128/4–5).

The rulers of Utopia did not buy office or inherit it or receive it as a favor from a king as was the common European practice. Indeed anyone caught soliciting office was forever banned from it (192/29–30). Their fellow citizens elected them to office for life because they were the best men in the land (122/14–15)—the best not because they were the strongest, the richest, or the craftiest, or because they had had great and renowned forbears, but because they were chosen from a select group of men. For their excellence, and by the recommendation of the priests and the secret vote of the lesser magistrates, the members of this group, which was about one-thousandth of the population,[28] were exempted from the common Utopian requirement of six hours of labor a day. During good conduct and when not required for government service, this very small band of men devoted itself wholly to study (130/32 f.). It was therefore for extraordinary merit attained in the life of learning that the highest offices were awarded in Utopia, the place which beyond all others would have satisfied Thomas More's freest fantasy of the best life a man could have on earth.

In the Europe of his own day, were there any men who for More represented living analogues to the rulers of the Utopian commonwealth? There were indeed, and our previous investigation of the relationship between More and Erasmus allows us to infer who they were. We need not, however, rely altogether on inference, for in a letter More comes close to identifying them for us explicitly. While still nervously awaiting the publication of his book, More wrote Erasmus:

> I am anxious to find out if it meets with the approval of Tunstal, and Busleyden, and your Chancellor; but their approval is more than I could wish for, since they are so fortunate as to be top-ranking officials in their own governments, although they might be won over by the fact that in this commonwealth of mine the ruling class would be completely made up of such men as are distinguished for learning and virtue. No matter how powerful those men are in their present governments—and, true, they are very powerful—still they have some high and mighty clowns as their equals, if not their superiors, in authority and influence. I do not think that men of this caliber are swayed by the fact that they would not have many under them as subjects, as the term is now used by kings to refer

---

[28] Forty persons per family $\times$ 6000 families = 240,000 persons per city $\div$ (500 persons exempt from labor minus 200 syphogrants, 20 tranibors, and 13 priests, ambassadors, one prince) equals about 1000 persons per 1 scholar not engaged in public service (122/9–19, 130/27–29, 196/2–4, 226/20). There is no evidence that More himself ever performed this computation.

to their people, who are really worse off than slaves; for it is a much higher honor to rule over free people; and good men, such as they, are far removed from that spiteful feeling which desires others to suffer while they are well off themselves.[29]

When More thought of ruling and rulers in connection with *Utopia*, among the names which came to his mind were those of Busleyden, Tunstal, Jean Le Sauvage, Chancellor of Prince Charles—and himself. The first three men were already serving their rulers in important offices; he was under pressure from his King to do the like. In Utopia such men would not be servants of rulers, but rulers themselves "in authority and power." Here indeed are the true analogues in Christendom to the rulers of Utopia. Or rather, to align the fantasy with the facts, the rulers of Utopia are the analogues of such men as Busleyden, Tunstal, Le Sauvage, and More—analogues, that is to say, of the Christian humanists. More felt that in his day one group of men was suited for rule in Europe. It was the group which shared his convictions on those matters that at the moment he deemed of paramount importance. This is hardly surprising, but perhaps a little prideful.

10. Councilors and Prophets

The Christian humanists, then, are the appropriate men to govern the Christian realms of Europe; but is it appropriate that they should undertake the task of governing them when they are called to it? This is a different question and a very difficult one; yet it had long been implicit in the position of the Christian humanists. They were not philosophical observers analyzing the conditions of the world they lived in but committed men, wishing and hoping to change those conditions. They believed that the renovation of society depended on the proper education of its ruling class in the humanities. There are, however, two possible ways of attaining this prime condition: either through the education in the Christian humanist ethic of the ruling class of Europe, or through the displacement of the existing ignorant ruling class by men already possessed of the education needed for the renewal of civilization. It does not appear that during the first two decades of the sixteenth century the northern humanists formulated this dilemma with complete clarity. Had they done so, they would have had to come to closer grips with the problem it posed than most of them seem to have done. Their failure to do so accounts for an

[29] Eras., *Ep.*, 2, 372; *Selected Letters*, p. 80.

unresolved ambiguity in the attitudes of men like Colet,[1] Budé, and Erasmus toward the aristocracy, toward the princes, and even toward themselves and their mission.

The relationship between the northern humanists and the princes of Europe was, at the least, ambivalent. Most of the princes—at any rate those not too deep in the backwoods to be even faintly attuned to current intellectual fashions—had some sense of the decorative value of men of letters to a court and of the pleasure and prestige which accrued to rulers from their boughten homage. For such decoration and homage, however, the price must not run too high. It must not interfere with necessary expenditures on serious matters like horses, mistresses, palaces, and wars. With a literary churchman the problem was usually resolved by rewarding him out of funds of the ecclesiastical establishment not directly available for the more serious matters above mentioned. Such men of letters, for example, often got benefices which the clerics in the court bureaucracy had not got around to snapping up or had not thought it worthwhile to snap up. Literary laymen, of course, presented a more difficult economic problem; but then in the early sixteenth century north of the Alps they were not yet very numerous in courtly circles.

On the other hand, the princes were at once the hope and the despair of men like Erasmus. The power of Europe was in their grasp, all the more plainly so since for half a century at least the Papacy had abdicated its pastoral mission, which was its serious source of efficacy, in order to play sordid political games with and against the princelings and republics of Italy. If there was really to be Christian reform, support from the great rulers of the West was indispensable, and actual initiative on their part was probably necessary. Reformers need to believe that the necessary and the indispensable are also possible. One of the tragic yet grimly amusing episodes of the early sixteenth century is the duel, intermittent but always renewed, that goes on between Erasmus' hopes for the princes of his day and the nasty cruel facts about those princes as they forced themselves on a mind not wholly immune to the impact of reality.

Under the circumstances it is natural that the words and actions of Erasmus and his spiritual fellows were rarely the precise expression of clear-cut, fully thought-out views on contemporary society and politics. Frequently those words and actions expressed only the fluctuations of the hopes and fears of their authors. To follow the correspondence of Erasmus from the early 1500's to the early 1520's is to

[1] The evidence on Colet's relations with Henry VIII is not adequate, but what there is seems to indicate that the Dean of St. Paul's was thoroughly taken in by the King. Lupton, *Colet*, pp. 188–98; Eras., *Ep.*, *4*, 524–26.

be made continually aware of the range of those fluctuations; and his more formal literary works simply confirm solidly what his letters express so vividly—his unwillingness to settle for either of the obvious alternatives—to educate the military aristocracy or to displace it with men educated along the lines he believed in. If he had looked straight at the problem of re-educating the military aristocracy and its princely chiefs along the lines that he and his fellow humanists deemed sound, he might have come strongly to suspect that just so much of humanist education would prove acceptable to that aristocracy as would help it to adapt itself to a changed world, while it retained its military pre-eminence and habitudes and its dominant position in Christendom. And if he found this alternative repugnant, he would have had to consider the ways and means by which men nurtured on the values he deemed indispensable for human welfare could displace the military aristocracy. He would also have had to give thought to what would happen to those values when Christian humanists began to pursue power and place within the structure of the sixteenth-century political order, that is in the councils and courts of princely military dynasts.

Because he never sharply defined in his own mind the difficulties which beset the course of humanist reform, Erasmus never assumed a firm position with respect to them; instead, his stance at a given moment depended almost entirely on his mood. Thus in 1501, in the *Enchiridion Militis Christiani*, he set forth succinctly for the instruction of a knight the mode of life that his kind of humanism required of an aristocracy. In 1520 he republished the same work for the edification of his vastly increased body of readers. In the latter edition he does not even hint that, time and again between 1501 and 1520, he had made the military aristocracy the butt of his satire and the object of his scorn for their hopeless addiction to brutality and to the most brutal of all pastimes—war—or that for all the effect it had, he might as well not have ridiculed them at all.

As with the military aristocracy, so with its many heads, the princes. Again Erasmus composes treatises on the proper education of rulers, liberally seasoned with flattery in hopes of making his advice more palatable to the princes to whom it is addressed. And again there is the bitter denunciation of those princes and their warlike appetites in Erasmus' series of tracts wholly or in part devoted to the exaltation of peace and the condemnation of war—the *Praise of Folly*, the *Complaint of Peace*, and the great anti-war adages, especially the *Dulce Bellum Inexpertis*. And throughout those years his letters erratically flutter between opposed moods: on the one hand rapt enthusiasm for Henry VIII, Francis I, and the future Charles V, proportioned to their momentary inclinations toward peace or even toward patronage of humanists and especially of himself; on the other, black despair as one, another, or all those princes go right on stumbling recklessly into war with all the insouciance of the White Knight falling off his horse. Repeated again and again without producing any effect on society and without awareness on the part of its author that social changes more radical than any he ever contemplated were needed to produce the effect he aimed at, Erasmus' *querela pacis* begins to sound querulous indeed.

As he did with respect to other matters, the author of *Utopia* came more firmly to grips than any of his contemporaries with the humanist's political dilemma. The central theme of Book I of *Utopia* is precisely an exploration of the problem of the Christian humanist confronted with counseling a (nominally) Christian prince in More's time. For in this context Hythlodaeus may be taken as a sort of ideal type of Christian humanist: he personifies the literary interests, the educational views, and the moral and religious commitments of the group, free of all the limitations that the circumstances, ambitions, and temperaments of actual living Christian humanists imposed on the perfect expression of those interests, views, and commitments.[2] More's exploration of the humanist's political dilemma is the most profound and the most effective that any man of his time achieved partly because of the form he employed in dealing with it. He posed the question in a most extreme way: "Ought a man like Hythlodaeus—that is, a Christian humanist—involve himself *at all* in the affairs of a prince?" And in dealing with the question so posed in *Utopia* he switched his literary form completely from discourse to dialogue, thus enabling him to generate in his readers some sense of the moral tension to which that question subjected a man of More's convictions.

If we consider More's situation in 1516 we can recognize that for him the problem of counsel had several dimensions. One of those dimensions we have already dealt with. The problem, as we have seen, became a highly personal one to him because at a moment of crisis in his own career he was being solicited by his prince to become an adviser. But although More's personal situation made the problem of counsel more poignant to him in 1516 than it ever had been before, and although it may have had a considerable effect on his actual ultimate decision, it figures behind the Dialogue in *Utopia* rather than in it; it probably sharpened More's perception of the problem, but

[2] Because Erasmus succeeded in achieving a position which permitted him a greater freedom of expression than most men of his age enjoyed, some scholars have identified Hythlodaeus with him. But on many issues Erasmus was far more pliable and ready to compromise than More's imaginary Christian humanist.

it is not entwined with his actual definition or treatment of the problem in the book.[3]

The problem had a second dimension, one that has perplexed many men before More's time and since. Imagine a man who is not committed to the general proposition that the life of contemplation is better than the life of action. Imagine him to be an intellectual and therefore committed to thinking problems through to the most adequate solution he is capable of. Imagine he has in fact been pursuing this course, and then has opened to him the opportunity to occupy a place of considerable importance in the council of a ruler. What should he do?[4] The spontaneous response tends to be that he should seize the opportunity to put his talents to practical use, that indeed he owes it to his fellowmen to do so. In the Dialogue of Counsel this position is taken by Giles and More (86/6–10). Hythlodaeus, the Christian humanist, is both an intellectual and an expert, not only a man of cultivated intelligence but one who has spent much of his life observing the laws and customs of many nations with the practical purpose of discovering those that are desirable and applicable in civilized lands (52/24–31). Of the many kinds of men who seek office his is the kind best prepared to serve at the same time both the ruler and the ruled.

To the argument at this intellectual level Hythlodaeus has an intellectual reply. It is that Giles and More do not understand what goes on in the councils of the great. The independent expert enters such councils at the cost of what his main worth depends on—his independence. His concern as a councilor is to offer the most competent advice he knows. In the language of present-day social science he is "job-oriented"; he wants primarily to cope with objective difficulties at a maximum level of competence. But the councils of the great are "status-oriented"; the aim of councilors is not to do a job but to secure or advance their own positions as councilors. This latter end is most readily effected not by telling the ruler what he needs to know but what he wants to hear. And what rulers particularly enjoy hearing is that they should do whatever they please.

In such circumstances, advice that is not drastic but mere good sense, which should be spoken anywhere, will not be followed at all. It will, More admits, "fall on very deaf ears doubtlessly" (97/39). And if simple good sense is rejected out of hand in the councils of rulers, why should an independent expert waste his time in such places? In *Utopia*, then, there is none of the fluctuation between ebullient hope and utter despair characteristic of Erasmus' attitude on the possibilities inherent

[3] Hythlodaeus immediately dismisses the considerations of family obligation raised by Giles (54/19–27).

[4] This problem has been posed by Robert K. Merton, "Role of the Intellectual in a Public Bureaucracy," *Social Forces,* 23 (1945), 405–15.

in the relation between the Christian humanists and the powers that be. Even More, supporting the position Hythlodaeus rejects, hopes only that by "handling matters tactfully, what you cannot turn to good," you may make a little less bad (99/39–101/2).

Hythlodaeus' view is more somber still. As a consequence of the entry of a Christian humanist into princely councils he foresees not merely the frustration of the job-oriented expert trapped and sinking in the ooze of sycophancy and self-seeking maneuvers that is the perdurable milieu of the councils of the great; he foresees for the humanist a destiny far worse. What he foresees is worse because of something that is part of the Christian humanist heritage, something that makes the Christian humanists other than, perhaps more than, independent and expert intellectuals. To grasp the meaning of this third dimension that More gives to the problem we need to detour once again into the area of religion and ask what is distinctive about the religious stance implicit *throughout Utopia* and what its foundations in the past were. The emphasis here is on *"throughout Utopia"* rather than on the sections formally devoted to religion and philosophy. When More treated those topics specifically he may have done so with an awareness of doctrinal issues and an attention to correctness of theological posture heightened by the nature of the subjects themselves. Paradoxically we may be less intimately in the presence of More's immediate religious concern when he deals with religion and philosophy than elsewhere in *Utopia*. For in many passages of the book he assumes a distinctive Christian stance without any special self-consciousness; like a seasoned spiritual athlete, he has so trained himself that the stance has become second nature to him.

To describe the posture which More manifests diffusedly throughout *Utopia* as "biblical Christianity" is to invite the retort that all Christianity is and has always been biblical. Indeed the Bible is a book of many voices; and at different times and even at the same times different men have thought they heard coming from it remarkably divergent messages. In contrast, however, to predecessors and contemporaries who found in Scripture an apocalyptic or mystical message, and to others who found there clues for a systematic metaphysics and theology, in *Utopia* in 1515–16 More displays a Christianity evangelical and prophetic in that the main source of its ethic is the moral teaching of Jesus and of those great seers who were also the conscience of Israel. Every rediscovery of the Gospel has latent in it a condemnation of life as it is lived by most men in the world most of the time, for the New Testament's first prophetic voice is a voice crying in the wilderness, "Repent, repent!" It generates doubts about that perennial re-accommodation of Christ's word to the ordinary appetites of man, which gradually substitutes rational prudence for Christian righteousness as the accepted rule of daily life for prosperous Christians. The accommodations current in More's England were, as we have seen, those effected by theologians and canonists with the help of Aristotle and Roman civil law. Of such maneuvers for smoothing away the rough parts of the Bible message Hythlodaeus says bitterly, "If all the things which by the perverse minds of men have come to seem odd are to be dropped as unusual and absurd, we must dissemble almost all the doctrines of Christ" (101/23–26).

From such adulteration of the Gospel what gain is there save to the wicked, whom it enables to be bad in greater comfort? It was because he believed them to be contorters of Christ's teaching that Erasmus waged his endless war on school theologians and canon lawyers.[5] If the Christian humanist confrontation of the world with the Gospel standard was to be more than a rhetorical exercise, it must not end in the accommodation of God's teaching to human appetites but in the judgment of those appetites by God's rule.

Once again we can best apprehend a peculiarity in *Utopia* and in the outlook of its author by noting a deviation of the work from the writings to which its formal debt was greatest, the writings of Plato. In this case the peculiarity we seek to apprehend is the impact of biblical Christianity on the ethic that saturates the book. Plato, "that wise sage," says Hythlodaeus, refused "to make laws for those who rejected that legislation which gave to all an equal share in all goods," because he foresaw that the only way to assure the general good was to maintain *"equality in all respects"* (105/5–10). More takes this story from no work of Plato but probably from Diogenes Laertius' *Lives of the Philosophers*, written more than five hundred years after Plato's death. What the *Lives* actually and tersely says is that Plato refused to become legislator for the founders of a new city because "they were opposed to *equality of possessions.*"[6]

Although the statement in Diogenes Laertius came a little short of what More extracted from it, still it was closer to what he wanted to say than anything he could have found in Plato. It is difficult to believe that More did not know this. He was certainly well enough acquainted with the *Republic*, perhaps well enough acquainted with the *Laws*, to realize that neither treated equality in a way wholly suitable to his purpose. In the *Laws*, the alternative Plato posed was not between equality and inequality but between a total merging or obliteration of personalities and inequality. And since the former condition is either for "the gods or the sons of gods," but not for mere men, he opted for

[5] See above, pp. 69–71.
[6] Diogenes Laertius, *Lives of Eminent Philosophers*, trans. R. D. Hicks, 1 (2 vols. London, 1950), 298–99.

the latter.[7] In the *Republic*, of course, there is the strictest "equality in all respects" and completely "equal sharing in all good things"— but only for the ruling military élite. The total communism of the guardians, the experts at ruling, serves to widen and deepen the gulf that separates them from common working men and traders, who are not as they and who live by a different law, in which the community of life and goods has no place.

In *Utopia*, on the contrary, there are no grades of possessing as in the *Laws*, and equal sharing is not for the rulers alone, as in the *Republic*, but for all citizens alike. Equality is not merely a political device to correct malfunctions in governance; it is also a moral weapon to destroy unrighteousness. For the worst of inequality is not just that it allows most goods to fall into the grasp of a handful of rich men; the worst of it is that those rich men are the worst men, "greedy, unscrupulous, and useless" (105/16), who by active contrivance reap where they sowed not, and seize what should not be theirs. It is they who by their vanity, gluttony, and avarice devastate a whole country- side (66/10–11). It is they who keep serving men in idleness till they grow old and then turn them out onto the roads to starve or to steal. And it is they who as judges pollute the very sources of justice by hanging the men that by their own wickedness they have driven to crime. The iniquity of inequality is that it feeds what it feeds on— the unrighteousness of the rich. More's fiery denunciation of the evil wrought by rich men in his day speaks powerfully to us still across the centuries—and its power does not derive from mere humanistic, rhetorical display. Nor does it have much in common with the spirit of fourth-century Greece and the intellectual and political predilec- tions of the Athenian aristocrat Plato. But, bridging a gulf of more than two thousand years, it establishes contact between Thomas More, Renaissance humanist man of letters, and Amos, a rough shepherd of Tekoa in the hill country of Palestine, who also heard in his heart God's condemnation of the great men of his day. These men in their palaces "despised the law of the Lord," and in ancient Israel as in Tudor England "turned aside the way of the humble . . . sold the just man for silver, and the poor man for a pair of shoes."[8] In the days of Amos as in More's day the rich made their devices for exploiting the poor into laws, and as judges inflicted them on the men they had ruined (240/26–28). Or, as Amos said more poignantly, they "turn judgment into wormwood, and forsake justice in the land."[9]

Of all the places in *Utopia* where More's quick and experienced

---

[7] Plato, *Laws* (trans. R. G. Bury), 739–40 B.
[8] Amos 2:6–8.
[9] Amos 5:7.

sympathy with the sufferings of the victims of the rich and powerful still stirs us after over four hundred years, the most moving is surely his account of the victims of eviction by enclosure. They were driven from their poor cottages—old folks, children, and all—forced to sell their household goods for even less than their pitiful value, left to wander the roads begging, and finally, while seeking vainly for work, jailed as vagrants by the same sort of men who threw them off the land. And all this misery was inflicted by the same insatiable gluttons who made all houses and all plowland into a wilderness in order to run fields together (66/11–12). Again More tells his sixteenth-century tale of oppression to an ancient refrain: "Woe to you that join house to house and lay field to field . . . shall you alone dwell in the midst of the earth?"[10] And the indignant response of the Christian humanist to the attempts of the wicked to square God by an expensive punctilio in ritualistic observances echoes yet another ancient refrain: "To what purpose is the multitude of your sacrifices to me? saith the Lord . . . Bring no more vain oblations; incense is an abomination to me . . . Your appointed feasts my soul hateth . . . I am weary to hear them . . . When ye make many prayers, I will not hear: *your hands are full of blood.*"[11] So Isaiah spoke in the name of the God of Israel to the "respectable people" who "justify the wicked for gifts, and take away the justice of the just from him."[12] To such sepulchers, outwardly white and righteous but full of all uncleanness within, the prophets had announced the real demands that a righteous God made of mankind. "Wash yourselves, be clean, take away the evil of your devices from my eyes: cease to do perversely. Learn to do well: seek judgment, relieve the oppressed, judge for the fatherless, defend the widow."[13]

Thus if we ask what generated the spiritual fervor (never far beneath the occasionally playful surface of *Utopia*) with which More judged and condemned his own age, we cannot be fully satisfied with references to *Piers Plowman* and medieval social ethics, since we do not know whether More even knew Langland's poem and we do know that he held in considerable disesteem the quasi-official ethics of the Middle Ages and its formulators—the philosophy of the schools and the professors of theology. Indeed to go rooting about in obscure corners of More's milieu for the source of his fervor is to seek in the darkness for what stands in the light. That the one and only God was a righteous God who loved justice and taught it, and who required justice in men and hated evil and injustice, was the profound conviction of the great prophets of Israel. Of More's knowledge of Scripture

---

[10] Isaiah 5:8.
[11] Isaiah 1:15.
[12] Isaiah 5:23.
[13] Isaiah 1:16–17.

there is no doubt. His sensitive conscience and his own intimate knowledge of the details of man's inhumanity to man in his own land in his
own day prepared him to feel the full force of the most eloquent
judgments men ever passed on human injustice and wickedness, judgments which, More was sure, were the judgments of God Himself.

From *Utopia* through Christian humanism and biblical Christianity
back to the prophets of Israel—there is mediation here but no breach
in continuity of spirit. If in what concerns the right relations of men
and communities More expressed the prophetic element in Christian
humanism with a unique force, it is because for some reason—in part
perhaps the range of his human experience and contacts—he felt them
with a unique intensity. But the prophetic in More and in the Christian
humanists was the source of that third dimension to the dilemma of
counsel, a dimension which received very forceful though not very
explicit expression in the Dialogue. The trouble with and for the
prophets is that they are hostile to the current *effective* fabric of
imperatives, not the fabric to which men say they ought to conform
their acts, but the one to which they make some attempt actually to
conform them. With the maintenance of this fabric, its repair, adjustment, extension, and modification, a host of curators are always very
busy—lawyers, teachers, preachers, philosophers, and poets in More's
day; sociologists, educationists, editorial writers, columnists, psychoanalysts, and guidance counselors in ours. It is the very essence of the
function of these curators that they care for, help take care of, the
current fabric of imperatives.

The members of the body social who get a comfortable share of the
social product partly because of the way the fabric works, that is, the
rulers of the earth, frequently require the services of men with special
skills in verbal manipulation. Now, prophets are also concerned with
the fabric of imperatives and for their vocation they also need a considerable verbal dexterity. But they are rarely of use to the powerful
of the earth because their vocation is not the care and repair of the
actual and effective fabric of imperatives but its destruction and replacement; and that is very rarely indeed what existing rulers want.
That some prophets appeal from the operative fabric of imperatives
to one professed by the rulers in moments of tradition-bound rhetoric
such as prayer and worship makes them no more useful to the mighty
or less dangerous. On the contrary, it increases the peril that they will
induce the many non-rulers who already also profess those values to
take them seriously. Experience indicates that prophets are most effectively killed with kindness, a kindness no less lethal because it is
sometimes quite genuine.

The immediate weakness of the unarmed prophet is notorious. He
either avoids direct action in behalf of the transvaluation of values

to which he is committed, or he attempts such action and is destroyed. About three years before More wrote the Dialogue of Counsel, Niccolò Machiavelli wrote a bitter and contemptuous epitaph for the most successful and unsuccessful prophet-without-arms of his time and place, Girolamo Savonarola, *"Profeti . . . disarmati ruinorno."*[14] As unarmed prophets before and after them have done, the Christian humanists sought to displace the effective fabric of imperatives of their day with the professed fabric—the fabric which they sought and believed that they found in Scripture, the fabric which in their view had been twisted and contorted beyond recognition by lawyers and philosophers of the universities to suit the appetites of the great and the powerful. But few of them were ready to follow the path which Savonarola had trod, a path scarcely made more attractive by the flames of the pyre at the end.

If to preach when no one listens is hard, the condition of the Christian humanists about 1515 was yet harder. For they preached, and the world listened, and many assented—and went right on doing what they always had done. The humanists were dedicated to changing the world, but the sum of visible change was a prodigious increase in the number of printed pages covered with words they had written. And as the apparent futility of crying "Repent!" in a plush-lined wilderness was borne in on them, doors swung wide to them, and they were invited to take their place on the very stairs to the thrones of the powers of this world, those princes from whom, More says in the Dialogue, as "from a never-failing spring, flows a stream of all that is good or evil over the whole nation" (57/17–18). The Christian humanists were asked to come to court—Tunstal, Pace, Budé, Jean Le Sauvage, a host of other and lesser lights. They were asked and they came. The temptation to enter was the greater because it could be given the aura of obligation, of service to the common cause. Into the minds of the mighty they could put "straightforward and honorable courses" (57/16). To do so, More adds, "is the duty of every good man" (87/10–11). If they could enjoy the sweets of preferment and at the same time perform their highest duty, how could they refuse to come to court? So they came, and now Thomas More himself was asked to come.

He was asked to come, as we earlier had occasion to note, at a most remarkable moment, at the moment when his own handiwork, the Discourse on Utopia—his own effort to think through the conditions of a decently ordered society—had become a part of his own historical milieu. Perhaps it was this improbable concatenation of circumstances that enabled him to see with extraordinary vividness and for a little while what the humanists who had taken service before him failed

[14] Niccolò Machiavelli, *Il Principe*, chapter 6.

to see or refused to believe, what he himself perhaps soon ceased to believe—that the prophet who serves the powers of this world may live on as a man but he dies as a prophet. It was not easy to understand why this should be so. Erasmus, who intuitively grasped the truth and acted on it, never seems to have thought it through systematically. As his friends entered the service of their princes he was torn between joy and sorrow—joy that Europe had princes so conscious of the merit of those who shared his faith and hopes, sorrow that such men would be "lost to letters." They were lost to something other than letters, something of greater importance, and Hythlodaeus knew it; they were lost to their own cause and their true calling. For at court in the council of a prince there was no place for a prophet.

The prophet is above all a soothsayer, a truth speaker. "If I would stick to the truth, I must needs speak in the manner I have described," cries Hythlodaeus with the authentic voice of a prophet (101/7–8). Not a scrap of the truth tossed into a kettle of lies because it is all the truth that the weak stomachs of the mighty can—or will—digest, but the whole truth. Tampering with the truth, adulterating it, watering it down, is the very condition of service in the councils of the mighty. Again and again Hythlodaeus hammers this point home. And Giles and More do not deny it; indeed they advise it. Speak low, aim low; seek patiently to remedy the vice that custom has confirmed. Utter nothing out of due order, nothing out of fashion (98/24–100/3). Do not try to drive the things of which you are persuaded into the heads of men of a wholly different mind. By such courses of moderation and prudence a man might indeed hope to handle matters so that if he cannot turn them to the good he can at least so order them that they are not very bad. This was sound advice; indeed, for a more or less conscientious statesman the very best. But to the man to whom it was addressed it was wholly beside the point. To Hythlodaeus Christian humanism was not a training ground for pretty good politicians; it was a calling for prophets: "If all the things which by the perverse morals of men have come to seem odd are to be dropped as unusual and absurd, we must dissemble almost all the doctrines of Christ" (101/23–26). To wink at the things Christ taught, to hide that light, the Light of the world, under a bushel, was to do precisely what the Christian humanists had attacked the canon lawyers and the philosophers of the universities for doing. To stifle and muffle God's Word in the councils of princes is not the vocation of the Christian humanists; that vocation—and here Hythlodaeus goes straight to the Gospel itself—is to preach the Word from the rooftops. Thus Hythlodaeus, the ideal type of Christian humanist, saw clearly the cost to the Christian humanists of entering the service of princes. They would thereby both lose their title and forfeit their capacity to be the prophets of the Christian Revival.

11. *Utopia* and the Christian Revival

In the end the Christian humanists who had followed Erasmus did not become the victorious prophets of the Christian Revival. But here the phrase "Christian Revival" reminds us that once again we have come to a point where we need to broaden our perspective on More's historical milieu in that area which throughout his adult life was most important to More himself—the area of religion. I have somewhat arbitrarily chosen the term Christian Revival to describe a particular constellation of religious happenings to parts of which historians have given several names. The part which precedes 1517 has been called the Prereformation and the Religious Revival. Part of what followed 1517 has been called the Protestant Reformation or simply the Reformation, the Protestant Revolt, and the Protestant Revolution; the other part the Catholic Reformation, the Catholic Counter-Reformation, or the Catholic Counter-Revolution. And this may not be an exhaustive inventory of the current nomenclature. To add yet another name to the many already in use may seem a supererogatory contribution to an already more than adequate confusion. The addition, however, may be warranted because historians have no covering phrase to describe the intensification of religious sentiment and concern that began long before 1517 and extended long beyond, that in its full span had room for Martin Luther and Ignatius Loyola; the Reformed Churches and the Jesuits; Cardinal Ximenes and Girolamo Savonarola; Paul IV and John of Leyden; Thomas Cranmer and Edmund Campion and Michael Servetus.

Here we are concerned only with that portion of the Christian Revival which preceded the writing of *Utopia*; but even in this period the span of the Revival included far more than what historians ordinarily mean by the term Christian Humanism. Indeed one of the pervasive historical phenomena of More's time and of the preceding century was a powerful but diffuse upsurge of religious sentiment. Naturally a historian whose center of interest lies in a particular place will seek to account for the phase of the upsurge which forces itself on his attention by linking it to what was going on at that time in that place. Thus the religious renovation associated with Ximenes and the Catholic kings in Spain is sometimes connected only with personal and local events, including the stimulus of the conquest of Granada.[1] And reaction against what they suppose to be the worldly excesses of the Italian Renaissance has been taken by some historians to explain

---

[1] As by Roger B. Merriman, *The Rise of the Spanish Empire*, 4 vols. (New York, 1918–34), 2, 86–97, 154–55.

the improbable ascendancy of Savonarola in Florence. When, however, we discover a number of other well-marked symptoms of a renewal of religious concern roughly concurrent in time but different in style and not coincident in place with the movements led by Savonarola and Ximenes, we may suspect that each movement expresses in a form suitable to a particular place a more widespread impulsion. The upsurge of religious sentiment at the end of the Middle Ages seems too much of an ecumenical affair adequately to be accounted for by what was going on uniquely in this or that parish.

That upsurge was also far too diverse in its manifestations to be circumscribed by precise and simple doctrinal definition. Up to 1516 none of its manifestations was marked by a profound concern with Christian doctrine, which was on the whole accepted as authoritatively defined. The character of the religious upsurge varied from place to place partly because the religious life of Christendom was paralyzed at the center. As a result of its organizational continuity the Papacy had still enough power to prevent occasional church councils from instituting effective reforms and at the same time threatening papal authority. But the defeat of the conciliar reformers of Constance and Basel in the first half of the fifteenth century had exacted its price. Even well-intentioned popes—Nicholas V and Pius II—were unable, or unready, or unwilling to move decisively to reform their own court, and until that court was reformed no papal initiative could effectively be transmitted to the rest of the Church, and no local initiative would be universalized through and throughout the ecclesiastic structure. And, of course, in the half century after the death of Pius II, when the tiara went to such choice specimens as Sixtus IV, Alexander VI, and Julius II, the Papacy did not suffer from a glut of good intentions. The traditional route of reforming impulses from their place of origin to Rome and thence with official blessing and assistance to the rest of the Church—the route they had taken from the time of the Gregorian reforms to the time of St. Dominic and St. Francis—this route was blocked. So, although the winds of Christian revival blew strong in the very late Middle Ages, they had no unifying direction. Before 1510 no leader gained a following outside a limited region; and no one tried to achieve unity of thought and action among the many groups touched with a new religious concern. Because their immediate aim usually was not the reconstruction of formal theology but the toning up of the spiritual life,[2] friends living in the same place and sharing the powerful impulse toward religious renewal might yet diverge considerably in their formal theology and their metaphysics. This may have been so in the case of Erasmus and John Colet, and

[2] Rice, *Harvard Theological Review*, 45, 141–63.

it was almost certainly so in the case of Pico della Mirandola and Savonarola.[3]

Here we can do little more than mention scantily a few signs of the religious ferment in the decades before More wrote *Utopia*. We have already referred to Cardinal Ximenes de Cisneros and the reinvigoration of religious life in Spain. Despite footdragging by some of the monastic houses, Ximenes imposed reform on the religious orders, restoring the severe rules of monastic life and rescinding the dispensations from them enjoyed in many convents. In this he had the support of the Catholic kings, as he did also in his creation of a great center of higher studies in religion, literature, and languages at Alcalá. The most magnificent achievement of that center was the preparation, even before the publication of Erasmus' New Testament, of the Complutensian Polyglot, a great work of erudition in which in parallel columns the Vulgate appeared with the text of the Old Testament in Hebrew and Greek and the New Testament in Greek. Along with this monument of Christian erudition the Spanish presses printed a large amount of devotional literature in the vernacular. Although this literature held up as exemplary the life of the monastic ascetic, it seems to have circulated mainly among lay people.[4] Ximenes not only approved the development of lay piety, he helped stimulate it. He encouraged the circulation of the devotional writings of Savonarola, who, brought to death at the stake with the aid and complicity of the most corrupt of popes, lost thereby none of the sanctity which had surrounded his life. In the year after the publication of Erasmus' edition of the New Testament, Ximenes invited him to Spain.[5] Thus the orthodox Franciscan Cardinal-statesman of out-of-the-way, upland Castile is a link between the fierce Dominican prophet-preacher of Florence and the outwardly mild cosmopolitan scholar and reformer whose birthplace was Rotterdam and whose homes were the intellectual capitals of the West—Antwerp, Louvain, Brussels, Basel, Rome, Venice, Paris, Oxford, Cambridge, London.

In the heartland of Renaissance Italy, in the spiritual capital of the new intellectual movement, Savonarola had preached an intensified Christianity—a faith that rejected outward show. He attacked both the vanity of personal adornment and rich dress which failed to hide the empty sinful souls beneath, and the vanity of religious pomp which failed to conceal hearts cold to Christ. He sought to make Florence a holy city, in which Christ would truly reign through His teaching

[3] See Ernst Cassirer, "Giovanni Pico Della Mirandola," *Journal of the History of Ideas*, 3 (1942), 123–44; and Roberto Ridolfi, *The Life of Girolamo Savonarola* (New York, 1959), pp. 97–100.
[4] Bataillon, *Erasme*, pp. 47–55, especially pp. 52–53.
[5] Ibid., pp. 77–83; cf. Eras., *Ep.*, 2, 559, n. 9.

and law, and from which a renewed faith would penetrate all Christendom. In the end and in a few years Savonarola failed; too many
wearied quickly of being citizens of the New Jerusalem. Savonarola's
eventual failure is less surprising than that even for a little while he
succeeded, and that so many in the most cultivated city in Europe
(he often preached, it was said, to fifteen thousand people) responded
to the friar's teaching from the depths of their being. It was not only
the poor whom Savonarola attracted. His call to ascetic life brought
some of the gilded youth of Florence to renounce the world. He afforded consolation to Lorenzo himself on his deathbed. And Poliziano,
the polished poet and pet of the Medicean court, was buried in the
Dominican habit. An even more eminent member of Lorenzo's circle,
Pico della Mirandola, was the man responsible for bringing Savonarola back to Florence. Pico, a child prodigy of vast if ill-sorted erudition, had long sought for routes to a closer union with the Divine
——through Neoplatonism, through oriental religious lore, through number mysticism. He had also been drawn to the ascetic renunciation
required by the monastic life. Yet despite his own inclination, despite
Savonarola's expostulations, and even his threats, Pico held back. Like
Poliziano he renounced the world only *in extremis*, when willy-nilly
he was about to leave it forever.[6]

The attraction which drew Pico and a worldly generation of cultured
Florentines toward an otherworldly ethic had earlier worked on simpler
folk far away in the region of the lower Rhine. There men—and
women, too—had organized themselves in groups which, though not
subjecting themselves to the formal requirements of a monastic rule,
lived a common life of piety, study, devotion, and charitable works,
and shared all their possessions as a sign of Christian love. Such were
the Brethren of the Common Life, whose activities for a century
provided a spiritual leaven which worked among the people of the
Netherlands and over a wide area of northern Germany. Here, as later
in Spain, works of devotion originally written for men who had left
the world and entered a religious community, directing them toward
the perfect Christian life, became the reading and the inspiration of
devout laymen. From this milieu came the most successful of all such
works, the *Imitatio Christi*, ascribed to Thomas a Kempis. Written for
the Brethren of the Common Life by a Brother, teaching joyful renunciation of worldly goods and worldly appetites, it owed its massive
popularity to the vision of a wholly and rightly ordered Christian life,
formed on the model of Christ, that men who remained in the world
found in it.[7]

[6] Ridolfi, *Savonarola*, especially pp. 50–51, 97–100, 126.
[7] See Albert Hyma, *The Christian Renaissance* (New York, 1925), especially pp.
41–98.

In Paris, the home of medieval theology and philosophy, the religious stirrings of the north and of Italy came together. The *Imitatio* was issued there again and again after 1490; religious houses were reformed, some on the model of the Dutch congregations. Among the reformed houses was the great ancient abbey of St. Germain des Prés, set in order by Guillaume Briçonnet, successively bishop of Lodève and Meaux. Briçonnet was the patron of Jacques Lefèvre d'Étaples, and in the latter many of the ingredients of the religious renewal were super-imposed one on the other, layer by layer, in a way that exemplifies the complexity of the movement without exhausting it. Educated in the school philosophy of his day, Lefèvre turned away from it. In his writing, "one discovers too many elements sometimes scarcely recon-cilable . . . a few scanty reminders of the Ockhamist criticism; the humanism of Guillaume Fichet, Robert Gaguin and Giles de Delft; Italian humanism and the resurrection of classical antiquity; the Aris-totelianism of Ermolao Barbaro, the philosophical and religious speculation of the Florentines, the Platonism of Marsilio Ficino, the metaphysical and oriental encyclopedism of Pico della Mirandola; Flemish and German mystics; Ruysbroeck and the visionaries of the Rhineland, and in this area, too, the spirituality of Nicholas of Cusa; the Erasmian critique, return to the Bible in the Erasmian sense; an active discovery of ancient Christian texts, and work as commentator and translator of the Bible into the French language."[8] And of course underpinning these miscellaneous and massive preoccupations of Le-fèvre stood a profound, practical concern with the discovery of the right way of life for a Christian, with the practice of piety, and with the reform of the Church in the light of God's word.[9]

Such, then, in some of the places where they manifested themselves, were some of the lines of thought, some of the directions which the widespread and diffuse impulse toward religious renovation took in Western Christendom in the fifteenth and early sixteenth centuries. This impulse touched England, too. At the very end of the fifteenth century, as we have seen, the thaw began there. Enough Englishmen returned from schooling in Italy to form one of those small groups without which the newly acquired interests of its members might have died for lack of sympathetic understanding. In the group were two or three men with enough command of Greek to teach it; and a few of those who were taught, notably Thomas More, became closely linked with their teachers. In the group, too, was John Colet, who had ab-sorbed some Neoplatonic views from the Florentine Platonists, but who also, and more important, had glimpsed new possibilities in the rhe-

---

[8] Augustin Renaudet, *Humanisme et Renaissance*, Travaux d'Humanisme et Renaissance *30* (Geneva, 1958), p. 202.
[9] Ibid., pp. 201–16.

torical as against the dialectical approach to understanding the human condition.[10] The view that what men said in antiquity was addressed not solely to the discursive rational intellect but to the whole man had extraordinary force when Colet turned it away from pagan writings to the Gospels and the letters of Paul. So, beginning in 1499, over a period of almost two decades, Erasmus had chosen his closest intimates from among the Englishmen most deeply involved with the religious unrest of the age; and through his mediation the aspirations of the English proponents of spiritual renovation kept abreast of—indeed in some measure provided a standard for—reformers on the continent.

A few traits of the widespread religious ferment that we have cursorily surveyed require particular attention because they appeared in several of the centers whence strong impulses toward religious renewal emanated, and because they bear on our present inquiry. One trait we have already noted. The urge toward religious renewal strongly appealed to many European intellectuals. In Spain, France, Germany, Italy, and England, men steeped in the literature of antiquity were in the forefront of the revival. In Florence, despite the indifference of Savonarola to their intellectual concerns, the sophisticates of the Medici circle were powerfully attracted by his prophetic preaching of repentance. Another pervasive theme was ascetic renunciation. This took several forms, the most traditional being that of a restoration of a former strictness in the established religious orders. So Ximenes encouraged the Observants against the Conventuals in his own Franciscan order and all other orders in Spain,[11] and a similar drive for reform, less powerfully supported, made some progress in France.[12] So, too, Savonarola's first effective action in Florence was the reform of San Marco.[13] This renewed austerity in the religious orders was not merely an internal affair. It evoked an enthusiasm in laymen which involved far more than the undemanding approval of spectators for exemplary Christian conduct on the part of others. The religiously inclined laymen were themselves moved toward the disciplined lives which they admired in the monks and the friars—witness the community around Briçonnet at Meaux,[14] and, most impressively, the Brethren of the Common Life and their followers.[15] Rejecting the slack rein with which the Church guided the lives of worldlings, many laymen imposed on themselves a stern control and discipline. Such were Pico and

[10] See Lupton, *Colet*, pp. 52–55, 62–74; and P. Albert Duhamel, "The Oxford Lectures of John Colet."

[11] Bataillon, *Erasme*, pp. 5–8.

[12] Renaudet, *Preréforme et Humanisme* (Paris, 1953), pp. 205–46, 316–37, 563–76.

[13] Ridolfi, *Savonarola*, pp. 66–76.

[14] Renaudet, *Humanisme*, pp. 213–14.

[15] Hyma, *Christian Renaissance*, pp. 41–98.

More—Pico who scourged himself, giving "alms of his own body," who sold his principality and gave most of the proceeds to the poor, and who held earthly things in contempt;[16] More, who as chancellor of England wore a hair shirt.[17] Both were strongly drawn to what the Roman Church held to be the highest calling for men disposed as they were—the monastic life.[18]

They hesitated on the threshold of the convent, however, and ultimately declined to pass across it. In this they exemplified a curious, significant, and very widespread trait of the religious ferment. In a sense the movement was anti-monastic and anti-clerical, in a sense anti-ecclesiastical. A man, even a cleric, could be all these things and still remain dedicated to the Church as the community of the faithful, the mystical body of Christ. Before 1517 the men of the Revival were not anti-clerical in an absolute sense or in principle. No one openly and few covertly aimed at the destruction of the monastic orders, of the sacerdotal priesthood, or of the established ecclesiastical structure. But many were contemptuous of and hostile to the way religion was actually practiced in their time, and the active agents and beneficiaries of that way were the monks, the priests, the clergy as organized in existing ecclesiastical institutions for the mediation of salvation to Christians. At worst, for many of the most sensitive and engaged Christians of the day, the Church's traditional apparatus of mediation was not important; at best, it was not enough to satisfy their aspirations toward a life in the world permeated by a spirit of religious vocation. Pico was not the only layman who lived as if "he labored only for the love of God and profit of His Church," as if he "had dedicated unto Him all his works."[19]

The widespread laic character of the religious revival paradoxically finds its most striking exemplification in a man who himself was for most of his adult life a professed religious and for all of it a priest—Desiderius Erasmus. The monk Erasmus spent many years seeking a papal release from his monastic vows; against the religious orders, he charged that they found, in regulations and ceremonies, the essence, the sign, and the test of sanctity, thus exalting empty observance before mercy and love. For him there was only one way of Christian life, that of following the teaching of the Gospel. He did not formally reject the traditional Catholic ascetic tradition, but he clearly deemed it unessential. In 1514 he stated his views to Servatius, prior of the convent at Steyn, where he had himself entered the monastic life. Monks, he wrote, censure others and minister to their own pride on the basis

[16] More, *Workes*, sigs. a₃–a₃v.
[17] Roper, *Life*, pp. 48–49.
[18] Ibid., pp. 6, 80–81.
[19] More, *Workes*, sig. a₃v.

of rules that re-establish a Jewish legalism in Christianity. "How much more in accord with Christ's teaching it is to regard the whole world as one household or as it were one convent, think of all mankind as brethren or fellow canons, to hold the sacrament of baptism as the highest order of religion and not to examine where a man lives but how well he lives."[20] Yet as his friend More pointed out, few monks gave themselves more fully to the service of God than Erasmus did. If he came close to enunciating the doctrine of the priesthood of all believers, he also upheld for the laity a rule of daily conduct no less exacting than the conduct demanded of the priests. And it was in such daily conduct that in Erasmus' eyes men came closest to Christ their Redeemer. Curiously another monk, but one deeply attached to the traditional monastic life, shared Erasmus' contempt for the empty sterile formalism into which the practice of Christianity had fallen. In prison after a trial conducted with exemplary crookedness by an appropriate emissary of the Borgia pope, Savonarola wrote his exposition of the Fifty-First Psalm *Miserere*, setting forth the Christian need above all, "to feel within one's self the birth of a pure heart . . . which is the work of God, and the only gift worth giving to a God indifferent to ceremonial offerings."[21]

Thus a sense of the shortcomings of the clergy reinforced the laic character of the Christian revival. The deeply felt yearning of earnest lay Christians for an intimate, direct, and personal confrontation with the Divine led them consciously or unconsciously to a relative devaluation (not a repudiation) of much of the Church's paraphernalia for reconciling men with God. This devaluation might extend only to such minor formal devices as pilgrimages and cults of relics. In extreme cases it might reach as far as the objective efficacy of the sacraments themselves. The quest of pious laymen for routes of access to God other than those officially policed and controlled by ecclesiastical organizations led them up diverse paths. The Neoplatonic ladder of love attracted Ficino and his followers,[22] including for a time at least John Colet.[23] Contemplation even more mystically oriented won some following. And as has often been the case during periods of enhanced religious sensitivity, pietism and quietism penetrated the Brethren of the Common Life. But many of the religiously awakened did not find that the sort of link with God provided by sectarian pietism or inner-light mysticism met their needs. They were men acutely conscious of the necessity for Christian revival not as the inward experience of a

[20] Eras., *Ep.*, *1*, 567–68.
[21] Bataillon, *Erasme*, p. 53.
[22] P. O. Kristeller, *Il Pensiero filosofico di Marsiglio Ficino* (Florence, 1953), pp. 274–310.
[23] Lupton, *Colet*, pp. 79–83.

few but throughout the whole body of Christ on earth, the whole Church, the entire *Respublica Christiana*. However differently Ximenes, Savonarola, and Erasmus may have conceived the *regnum Christi*, they not only prayed that God's kingdom might come and that His will be done on earth as it is in Heaven; they also believed that in this matter God helped those who helped themselves. And so all three in their different ways and in the light of their divergent conceptions acted with all their resources to bring the rule of Christ, His will as they understood it, nearer to realization on earth.

In the powerful currents of religious reform of his day, More was deeply involved, and never more deeply than in 1515 when he was composing the Discourse on Utopia. In one of its aspects the Discourse is thus the fruit of More's meditations, begun long before he conceived and wrote *Utopia*, on the necessary conditions of a society in which Christ's will was man's rule, on the necessary conditions of the *regnum Christi*. So in 1515 in the matter of the *regnum Christi*, as in so many other respects, More shared the concern of his friend Erasmus. Yet in this matter at this time the differences between the two friends were considerable. It is possible to discern these differences very clearly, for within a few months of the writing of the Utopian Discourse Erasmus wrote *The Education of a Christian Prince*. It afforded him an opportunity, if he chose to take it, to set forth his conception of the right ordering of a good society.

Contemporary and recent works with which to compare Erasmus' tract abound.[24] Indeed, leaving aside its plea for Christian peace, that tract, distinguished from the rest, if at all, only by the amenity of its style, tends to vanish into the endlessly tepid puddle of hortatory treatises addressed to Christian princes. When Erasmus turns from his two central preoccupations, the restoration of Christian letters and the maintenance of Christian peace, his social observations are invertebrate; they are unconnected, particular responses to social malaises, because he has only a very slight awareness of the interpenetration of social institutions and social structures.

On the other hand, to find an earlier literary work with which to compare *Utopia* one must go back almost two thousand years to Plato's *Republic*. We have already been at considerable pains to point out the divergences of *Utopia* and the *Republic*, but we had to be at such pains because of the unmistakable likenesses between the two books. The significant fact in this context is that there is no similar felt need to point out the difference between *Utopia* and any book written

---

[24] See A. H. Gilbert, *Machiavelli's Prince and Its Forerunners* (Durham, N.C., 1938), especially the bibliography at pp. 238–45; and Erasmus, *The Education of a Christian Prince*, trans. L. K. Born (New York, 1936), pp. 94–130 for studies of the earlier and contemporary literature.

between the fourth century B.C. and 1515. The differences are obvious
to the hastiest reader.

To his meditations on the problems of the *regnum Christi*, More's
Netherlands mission brought a new dimension, almost literally. It let
More see in depth, in perspective, and in mutual relation problems
which his contemporaries saw in the flat and as a disjointed series. In
1515 More saw European society as a whole, and this enabled him to
achieve his vision of the best commonwealth, Utopia. For Utopia is
a sort of anti-Europe, a reverse-Europe, whose institutional organization at all levels above the family is the opposite of that of Europe.
Whether he made sense of Utopia because he had already made sense
of Europe or whether, as the sequence of the composition of *Utopia*
suggests, it was the other way about, More does achieve a clarity of
vision about the world he lives in unsurpassed by any contemporary
but Machiavelli and perhaps Guicciardini, and a range and depth of
insight into that world of which neither of his Italian contemporaries
was capable.

And yet in *Utopia* he does not ultimately ascribe the troubles of the
world to impersonal forces, to the underlying patterns of history, to
chance, or to human error and the natural insufficiency of human understanding—not once, not ever. His way of explaining and understanding
contemporary social pathology bears the imprint of the evangelical
and prophetic outlook which he shared with other men affected by the
Christian Revival: for him social ills resulted from sin. And, among the
sins, sloth, greed, and pride above all infect More's world, as it is set
forth in *Utopia*—the sloth of the idle retainer and his more idle master
(62); the monstrous greed of the usurer, the fat abbot, and the enclos-
ing landlord (64–66); the insatiable pride of the rich and the powerful,
diplayed in rich clothing, in gems and baubles, but above all in a
passionate and ruthless pursuit of social place (166/23–168/24.). For
man's pride glories in the subjection and servility of others; it knows
no limit and no satisfaction because it is the result of no natural need
(242/26 f.). It grows hungrier from what it feeds on because it is rooted
in the ultimate and infinite emptiness of the sinful soul turned away
from God. It is the shame of Christians that despite the clear teaching
of Christ, which they profess to follow, they have erected their so-called
commonwealths on foundations made of the very stuff that human sinfulness, and especially pride, feeds on—the glorification of force and
violence, rewards for successful chicanery, tolerance of individual and
private aggrandizement at the expense of the common good and the
public welfare. Actual Christian societies are therefore faulty in their
foundations, in the very structure of their laws; to try to raise the
regnum Christi on such a footing is to build on sand. Such is the
explicit judgment passed in *Utopia* on the world More lived in; and

it is a judgment not explicitly made by any of More's intellectual comrades-in-arms.

Under such circumstances pious exhortation and instruction are ineffectual, since they run completely counter to men's deeds and the laws which sanction them. Nowhere in *Utopia* does More suggest that propaganda for reform directed at individual consciences is of itself enough to raise Europe from its slough. When law, by sanctioning iniquity, renders it easy for bad men to satisfy appetites offensive to God at the expense of their fellowmen, mere words are not enough to counter its force. The only sure foundation of a righteous society is the bond of law. Thus it is in Utopia. There the human propensity to sin, instead of being fattened by the very rules of the commonwealth, is starved and weakened by those rules. No man can seek a false prestige for himself by personal adornment, because all clothing is the same and unadorned. No man can waste the substance of society on what a later writer was to call conspicuous leisure and what More with greater directness calls idleness, because by the laws of that holy commonwealth he who does not work does not eat. No man can lord it over others by making them his servants because in Utopia no adult freeman, indeed no slave, has a man for a master or a lord, not even for a landlord. Service, bond or free, military or civil, is rendered to or for the commonwealth only.

Finally, consider that institution of Utopia which not only is most striking to the casual reader but which was most striking to some of the shrewdest of More's contemporaries, the institution which he himself singled out as the chief difference between Utopia and all European societies—Utopian communism. Of all the measures to crush the monster Pride it is the most important and most effective, because it goes to the root of the evil, which is man's chronic sense of insecurity, insufficiency, and anxiety. In Europe, men's endless pursuit of money and their ruthless victimization of their fellows resulted largely from the sin of pride; but the institutions of Europe often enough encouraged men to act in such evil ways and did little serious to discourage them. To acquire more than one's fellows had acquired was legally possible and socially advantageous; from this fact followed the worst of the social malaises that afflicted Christian Europe. Utopian communism made such acquisition socially absurd and legally impossible; from this followed the potentiality for a decent society. Thus attacked at its roots, Pride is a sin that "can have no place at all in the Utopian scheme of things" (139/10).

As we have already seen in another connection, the overall effect of the structure of Utopian law is the elimination of all social organisms intermediate between the commonwealth on the one hand and the patriarchal family on the other. What is left are two institutions, one by definition public, the other by nature providing minimal scope to individual idiosyncrasy. Men live, eat, travel, work, study, and play (if the no doubt elevating but rather stuffy recreations permitted in Utopia can be called play) according to public regulation, in public places, under public authority. They drink, brawl, gamble, and fornicate nowhere, at least not without danger from Utopia's harsh laws. In Utopia there is no "pretext to evade work" (147/22), and men live all the time under everyone's eyes. Truly there is no place to hide in the land Budé called Hagnopolis, the City of Saints.

Utopia then is a society at once religious and austere. Its austerities, however, are not those of a withdrawn community of spiritual athletes performing special feats of self-mortification to win thereby from the divine spectator some transmundane guerdon for themselves or for their spiritual beneficiaries. The austerities of Utopia are imposed on all Utopians by the laws of a commonwealth, not the rules of a cloister. They are also the laws *for* a commonwealth, neither arbitrary nor useless. The laws for a holy commonwealth, of course; their rigor is the indispensable prop of social righteousness; the asceticism of Utopia is an asceticism of this world, an *innerweltliche askese*, directed toward making sure that, on earth by mortal men as in heaven by saints and angels, God's will be done and His Name thereby glorified.

In such a holy commonwealth the problem of the Dialogue of Counsel vanishes. The Christian humanists of the early sixteenth century were caught, as we have seen, on the horns of a dilemma, the dilemma of the prophet to whom the greatest danger turns out to be honor in his own country. Most of them acknowledged the duty and responsibility of an active life; but their range of choice in carrying out their duty was narrow and, to the more conscientious among them, painful. They could serve the commonwealth as unattached intellectuals with the pen only, or they could enter the council of a prince, where the power of decision lay. Once there, they would have to "approve the worst counsels and subscribe to the most ruinous decrees," since to give "only faint praise to evil counsels" is to be counted "a spy, and almost a traitor" (103/6–8). But in Utopia the Christian humanist would have the duty, which then would be the privilege, too, of serving by ruling the kind of society that it was his prophetic mission to set before Christians as a goal and an example. In that society Christ's law of love of God and neighbor prevailed, and public service meant something better than active participation in "a kind of conspiracy of the rich, who are aiming at their own interests under the name and title of the commonwealth" (241/27–29). Earlier we saw that in a vision More imagined himself a prince in Utopia, and found the vision good, because Utopia was ruled by cosmopolitan intellectuals, in effect by humanists like himself. But More found the vision good not only because of who ruled but also because of what the rulers ruled—an austere laic commonwealth whose ordinances struck at the roots of sin, a commonwealth where Christ's teaching of equality, righteousness, and love toward God through love toward one's neighbor was the custom of the land and its law. Thus *Utopia* expressed the highest aspirations not only of early sixteenth-century men of letters but especially of Christian humanists. It also figured forth some of the hopes of that Christian Revival which was an important element in its historical matrix.

More ingeniously conceived a mode of organizing human affairs which would resolve many of the spiritual dilemmas of his day, of his friends, of his own, which would incorporate within itself a broad band of the spectrum of religious renewal as the most ardent reformers of the age envisaged that renewal. Having performed this rather remarkable imaginative feat, More put it in a book. There was nothing much else to do with it. So slight was the likelihood that the only people—the princes and the popes—who could do anything forceful to bring the *regnum Christi* closer to actuality would do anything, that some have doubted the seriousness of *Utopia*, especially since a little after the book was published its author took a course quite contrary to the one Hythlodaeus prescribed. In hopes, no doubt, of ameliorating the evils of his day along the lines that he suggested in his stories about the Achorians, the Polylerites, and the Macarians in the Dialogue of Counsel, More entered the service of his prince. In a fashion almost too pat, his experience vindicated Hythlodaeus' wisdom; his hopes were quite baseless. Under a rather heavy veneer of humane learning and geniality Henry VIII was the very model of the predatory leader of a predatory semi-military ruling class; he was magnificent, splendid, spendthrift, idle, envious, treacherous, rapacious, and stupidly and stupefyingly vainglorious. His chief minister and alter ego, Wolsey, made up for Henry's idleness by his own tireless activity; in all other respects he shared in full measure his master's traits of character.[25]

As a councilor of his prince during the decade before Wolsey's fall, More was an intimate witness of much that he most detested in the doings of Europe's rulers—notably the judicial murder of the Duke of Buckingham and the fruitless and inordinately costly war against France. As speaker of the House of Commons in 1523, he helped Wolsey bully and cajole a large grant from Parliament for a military venture which he must have detested; and he received, for his "faithful diligence" in helping his master extort money from his subjects, a reward of £200.[26] The English got only humiliation and heavy finan-

[25] A. F. Pollard, *Wolsey* (London, 1929), *passim*.
[26] *LP 1515–16*, 3, No. 3267.

cial loss from Henry's misbegotten enterprise against France. After Francis' disaster at Pavia, however, the French paid Henry's councilors off for their good offices in truce negotiations with the Emperor. Sir Thomas was in the book for a pension of 150 crowns.[27] Whether in these douceurs, the common rewards of the servants of kings, the delicate spiritual sensorium of More caught a whiff of blood money, one cannot say. There is no evidence that he refused to accept payment. In any case he may have felt more poignantly than when he wrote it the force of Hythlodaeus' remark that although in a prince's council it might barely be possible to keep "your own integrity and innocence, you will be made a screen for the wickedness and folly of others" (103/12–14). He learned soon enough in person what his own literary creation could have told him: what happens to a would-be prophet who puts his faith in princes. The route to the *regnum Christi* did not pass through the courts of Renaissance rulers.

12. Utopia and Geneva

As we have just seen, More's perception of the requirements of a holy commonwealth, more astute than that of his contemporaries, projected his vision beyond theirs. He was able to see farther than they because his eyes were not dazzled nor his mind perplexed by the brilliant and confusing light that the courts of Renaissance princes emanated. He thought deeply about what was necessary to bring about a fundamental spiritual change in Europe, a change in the quality of life that would realize his aspirations and Christ's teaching. *Utopia* set forth More's conception of the preconditions for achieving such a change.

But in *Utopia* he did not suggest a strategy for establishing those preconditions. Rather, as we have seen, he revealed two daunting obstacles which any such strategy must encounter and had but little chance to overcome: first, the inability of reformers to serve with good conscience as advisers to the rulers of Europe; and second, the rooted characteristics of Europe's institutions, especially its institutions of property. Scarcely a decade after More's death, a Christian humanist reformer, in some ways very unlike More, in others somewhat like him, obliterated the first obstacle, circumvented the second, and established in a town in the heart of Europe a holy community almost as austere as Utopia. By the end of the sixteenth century, under resolute pressure the town had become "peaceful, well-ordered, pious, literate, learned, poised, cultured, when before it was nothing but a

---

[27] *LP 1515–16, 4,* No. 3619.

big uncivilized village."[1] The transformed "village" was Geneva; the reformer was John Calvin.

The curious similarities between Utopia and Geneva have been unduly obscured by the undeniable differences between More and Calvin, between the Roman Catholic martyr and the hero of the Reformation. Calvin, of course, wrought under limitations with which More did not have to concern himself; his materials were considerably more intractable. More worked with pens and paper, Calvin with men and a social order. It is easier to impress one's aspirations with pens on paper than with men on a social order; men are more balky, a social order less readily receptive to new imprints. Consequently, compared with some of Utopia's iron ordinances, the law of Calvin's Geneva was mild. Idle pastime and evil resorts, prohibited in Utopia (146/6–21), were regulated in Geneva. In the Swiss city no law reduced to bondage a citizen who twice left town without permission, as Utopia's law did (146/6–9); nor was criminal intent punished as heavily as criminal act (192/4–6), as it was on More's blessed island. And real flesh being somewhat harder to tame than paper flesh, the Utopian penalty for adultery—bondage for the first offense, death for the second (190/7–15)—was, despite Calvin, too stern for Calvin's Geneva, where, as late as 1556, a citizen reckoned that rigorous proceedings against adulterers and fornicators might cost the town half its population. Unlike King Utopus, Calvin did not fall heir to what every radical reformer dreams of—a submissive and ductile people like the conquered Utopians. Only slowly and with frequent setbacks was he gradually able to mold the tough, late-medieval institutions of the Genevan urban patriciate into something closer to his heart's and therefore (as he saw it) to God's desire.

Yet the similarity both in detail and in spirit between Utopia and Geneva is noteworthy, even when the instruments and institutions for working out the details and for maintaining the spirit diverge. This similarity is evident in the rules of More's "best ordered commonwealth" and Calvin's New Jerusalem with respect to dress, leisure, and privacy. Sumptuary legislation dealing with dress was an old medieval story. But in the Middle Ages the purpose of such legislation was to maintain social hierarchy, in effect to maintain the status value of aristocratic conspicuous consumption by denying bourgeois crows the right to noble peacock feathers.[2] Utopia and Geneva, too, had rules

---

[1] H. Bordier, *L'École historique de Jérome Bolsec*, p. 15, quoted in Émile Doumergue, *Jean Calvin, les hommes et les choses de son temps*, (7 vols. Lausanne and Neuilly-sur-Seine, 1899–1927), 6: 116.

[2] The first general English statute regulating apparel was 33 E III c. 8–15. For the history of such regulation see Frances E. Baldwin, *Sumptuary Legislation and Personal Regulation in England*, Johns Hopkins University Studies in Historical and Political Science, 44:1 (Baltimore, 1926).

about what the inhabitants might wear, but they differed markedly and in a similar way from the medieval rules. The Utopians wore plain undyed grey garments (132/29–134/10). For a Utopian there was nothing else to wear; the law allowed no finery, not so much as variety in the color of clothing, not even to the magistrates. Similarly and at considerable risk, on the rather odd issue of slashed breeches for the local soldiery, Calvin faced down the chief of the citizen militia, who was also the spearhead of the patrician opposition to the reformer.[3] Geneva's law and Utopia's, Calvin's attitudes and More's, stood squarely and precisely opposed in purpose to medieval sumptuary legislation and precisely identical to each other. The Utopians despised men who felt that the more splendidly they dressed, the higher the honor due them (166/23–33). Or as Calvin succinctly put it, slashed breeches, as other unnecessary adornments, ministered to pride. Therefore "it is against God and of the devil, and a disorder such as ought not to be tolerated at any price."[4]

As on the matter of dress, so on the question of leisure, the views of More and Calvin were much alike. In both Utopia and Geneva mere idleness lay under a ban (146/15–21). The aristocratic-courtly conception of a *pastime*, something to fend off *accidia* or boredom, was offensive to both the English humanist and the Geneva pastor. Time was God's gift to men, not to be destroyed, but to be used to glorify Him through righteous useful doing in the world, whether with hands or with mind. In both Utopia and Geneva the courtly pastime is replaced by the scholar's recreation, that respite which does not kill time but saves it by refreshing a man's forces for the activity or study to follow (126/32–128/27).

As with dress and leisure, so with privacy. In Utopia with its extended families (134/22–136/1), multiple-unit houses without locks on the doors (120/2–12), and common meals (140/17–144/18), privacy had little place. Nor was this an accident. The open and common way of life in Utopia was designed to maintain a common standard of conduct, to foster a common ethic. In the ecclesiastical ordinances for his New Jerusalem, Calvin created a new kind of church officer whose authority over morals obliterated the customary line between private affairs and public life almost as effectively as Utopian institutions did. The lay-elders had the duty *"to watch over the life of everyone,* to admonish in a friendly way those who fell short or led ill-ordered lives." Such elders were to be chosen for every section of the city *"in order*

[3] Eugène Choisy, *La Théocratie à Genève au temps de Calvin* (Geneva, n.d.), p. 90.
[4] Ibid., p. 90.

to have an eye everywhere"[5] (italics mine). In a startling way Calvin's language echoes More's description of Utopia. There, too, men have no "license to waste time nor pretext to evade work, . . . no lurking hole . . . *being under the eyes of all*" (147/21–26).

By making sin very public indeed, Calvin succeeded in achieving some of the ends of Utopic society without resorting to Utopian means—community of property, destruction of the market, abolition of money. As a most practical man with a series of very knotty problems to solve in his relentless drive to create in Geneva a model Christion commonwealth, Calvin did not consider means as far beyond his reach as the Utopian social order was. He had a system, however, which in a measure served the same purpose. And that system is curiously prefigured in detail in *Utopia* itself. Describing the Utopian clergy, Hythlodaeus says they

> are censors of morals. It is counted a great disgrace for a man to be summoned or rebuked by them as not being of upright life. It is their function to give advice and admonition, but to check and punish offenders belongs to the governor and the other civil officials. They, however, do exclude from divine services individuals whom they find to be unusually bad. There is almost no punishment which is more dreaded: they incur very great disgrace and are tortured by a secret fear of religion. Even their bodies will not long go scot free. If they do not demonstrate their speedy repentance, they are seized and punished by the senate for their impiety (227/37–229/8).

In Geneva, Calvin created an instrument of ecclesiastical discipline much like the Utopian one. The institution he created to suit his purpose was the Consistory, the assembly of ministers and lay-elders. The weapon was excommunication with restoration to the holy community contingent on public repentance. And as in Utopia the cutting edge was the threat of action by the civil magistrates against those who long failed to repent. Using its disciplinary power the Consistory "intervened to re-establish peace and union in families, to recall individuals to their duty; it took in hand . . . reforms favorable to the weak and the lesser folk, it summoned and censured the lazy and the idle, over-hard fathers and creditors; it was pitiless to usurers, monopolists and engrossers. It combatted the coarse manners of the age, the brutality of men."[6] Thus the expression of brotherhood was achieved not through community of property but by the spiritual communion of those who shared in the holy sacrament of the Lord's Supper and

[5] B. J. Kidd, *Documents Illustrative of the Continental Reformation* (Oxford, 1911), p. 595.
[6] Choisy, pp. 244–45.

by the exclusion from it of the unworthy. Through the disciplinary instrument provided by the Lord's Supper, too, the Reformed Church at Geneva was able to express the profound leveling implicit in the Calvinist sense of God's majesty and man's depravity and in Calvin's doctrine of the calling. So worthless and shriveled was sinful man beside the greatness of God that the scale of earthly rank was as nothing to Him or to the ministers of His Word. To those entrusted with earthly authority who glorified God by earnest service in their calling praise was due, as it was to all men who served God well; to men who did otherwise, whatever their rank, censure was due; and with no respect of person or station the Consistory brought to book the great men of the city as well as the less. Thus by means short of Utopian Calvin came close to achieving in his City of Saints an equality of austere men not unlike that of More's Utopia.

And of course, like Utopia, Geneva was dedicated not only to education but to the principle that sound education helped to make righteous citizens. This is not surprising, since Calvin was an admirer of Erasmus and a Christian humanist. In his inaugural at the founding of the Academy of Geneva, Theodore Béza, the first rector, chosen by Calvin, spoke to the students who, "instructed in the *true religion* and *the knowledge of good literature*, have come in order to *work for the glory of God*."[7] It would be hard to find in so few phrases a more perfect expression of the religious aspiration which the Utopian commonwealth reflected.

Except, of course, that the religion Béza called true and loved, More, had he known it, would surely have called false and hated. Between Utopia and Geneva, between More in 1516 and Calvin, after all, lies the thundering torrent of religious revolution. All the better reason then, lest we lose our bearings in a flood that destroyed many landmarks, that we recognize continuities, however unexpected, indeed however unlikely, at first glance they may seem. Those continuities exist as elements in a vast stratum of events—the Christian Revival, a stratum that lies on both sides of that conspicuous historical watershed, 1517. Amid the upheavals of the following century we need to discern the continuity provided by the Christian Revival. That continuity renders intelligible some of the varieties of human conduct during the Age of the Reformation, varieties otherwise hard to understand. They become intelligible as partial consummations of some of the durable aspirations of the Revival. It thus may seem improbable that the nearest men came in the sixteeth century to actualizing More's dream of a sober, disciplined commonwealth ruled in its daily life by the teaching of Christ was the Calvinist capital at Geneva. But it is a

[7] Choisy, pp. 212–13.

fact; and grasping it helps explain a considerable group of other facts about the history of Europe in the sixteenth century.

Of these facts the largest in import is the survival and resilience of Protestantism in the century after the death of Luther. In the generation between the posting of the ninety-five theses on indulgences and Luther's death the religious movement that took his name had lost most of its momentum in the heart of Europe and advanced only in murky struggles in the backward northlands. In the course of that same generation the Roman Church began to rally its forces of defense and soon went over to the counterattack. When Mary Tudor became Queen of England in 1553, there was not a single great Protestant realm in Europe, only a few low-grade German and Northern principalities with princes all too likely to make a deal and return to the Roman obedience if the going got rough, as it looked like doing. Yet in 1600, for better or worse, Protestantism was very much alive and kicking; it did not fold up in face of the Catholic Counter-Revolution; and that it did not do so was unmistakably the result of the initiative of the followers of Calvin.

What were the resources of the Calvinists that enabled them to resist the Catholic counterattack so effectively? No doubt they had a certain amount of luck, but no more than their share, and in almost all the more obvious equipage of combat they were absurdly deficient compared with their Catholic adversaries. Their military resources were trivial. All the best generals had been on the other side—the Duke de Guise, Alva, Parma. Far and away the best soldiers, too— the Spanish tercios. Also far and away *most* of the soldiers. Since the Calvinists did not control the political apparatus in a single considerable European state, their military recruiting was always hand-to-mouth. And of course compared to the enemy they were bone poor. Even when Elizabeth was dragged kicking and screaming into Europe's religious wars, the gross financial resources available to the Calvinists came far short of those commanded by the Pope, the Catholic League, and Philip II. Before the half-hearted accession of Elizabeth to support of their cause the Calvinists had been *gueux*, indeed, Sea Beggars, Land Beggars, beggars every way. And finally the Calvinists were enormously outnumbered. At a very rough guess in Western Europe there were from ten to thirty Catholics for every Calvinist, and perhaps even more.

Under such adverse circumstances, how were the Calvinists able not only to hold their own but to enjoy a more secure position in 1600 than they had in 1564 at Calvin's death? Part of the answer is suggested by a letter sent in the 1560's from a Catholic governor of a province in the Netherlands to his masters in Brussels. With something between petulance and patience he explains to the Council in Brussels why he is not enthusiastically and as per order uprooting heresy in his territory. Unfortunately, he observes, all the ablest people in the province are heretics—which makes matters difficult. The heretics in question were, of course, Calvinists.[8] Any explanation of the survival of Protestantism that leaves out of account what the governor was, however imprecisely, pointing to is deficient. In the later sixteenth century, compared with other religious creeds, Calvinism had a very high proportion of adherents who combined keen intelligence with deep dedication and zeal, and among such adherents was a high proportion of laymen. And this suggests that Calvinism somehow drew on a reservoir of talents that had hitherto remained untapped. The reservoir consisted of men of a kind that had begun to come to the fore in the Christian Revival. Well-read in classical literature, deeply pious, convinced that there was a hideous gap between what Christ demanded of Christians and the way professed Christians lived, these men were sure that to narrow that gap was part of the duty of a true Christian. The difficulty for such a man lay in the fact that though he believed himself called by God to action, he did not find channels into which he could pour his energies in the conviction that he was making the full and right use of the talents God gave him. Drawn to the monastic life by its theoretical rigor and discipline, by the renunciation of avarice and sloth and pride which it demanded, he was repelled by the actualities of that life in his time—the rules relaxed, the monks resistant to reform, study at a halt, idleness and tedium instead of learning and labor. And though to take the vows of an order did not necessarily prevent a man from working for God's kingdom on earth, still by subjecting his freedom of action to a religious superior of dubious zeal, it well might do so. Nor outside Italy did the universities, still in the main devoted to the old Aristotelian-scholastic learning, which to such a man was not merely old but bad, offer great attraction. Rightly or wrongly, like More, he found the scholastic questions empty and stultifying. He was driven by zeal for the Christian commonwealth, for deploying such powers as God gave him toward drawing men toward the *regnum Christi*. Consequently, as More observed, he did not regard it as the pinnacle of human achievement and godly doing to "squat with the monks," in the ill-warranted belief that "to reside forever in the same spot like a clam or sponge, to cling eternally to the same rock is the last word in sanctity."[9]

Of course some men of the Christian Revival did go to the cloister

[8] Hours of searching through notes taken fifteen years ago have failed to come up with the source of this observation or the identity of the observer.

[9] *Corresp.*, p. 201.

and some to the schools, but perhaps not without qualms of conscience and the sense they had left half their work behind them in a world in which they belonged.

There was another way to go—the way of the court. "Mere" humanists, proficients in the classical languages with little Christian concern and no commitment to reform, paddled merrily—and some indeed wallowed—in courtly pleasure and courtly rackets hitherto mainly the perquisites of the legists and the military élite. But to the men most deeply engaged by the religious resurgence there was bound to be about the courts of most Renaissance princes the stench of a moral pigsty rather than the odor of sanctity. The better the man, the worse his lot at court; it was not a place for one with a demanding conscience. Others with such a moral constitution had learned the same lesson before the Renaissance, and more were to do so after. In earlier centuries medieval authors, quite unaffected by deep religious feelings, had produced a considerable literature on the falseness of court life and recommended retreat to the country to avoid its pitfalls.[10] Some men touched by the Christian Revival doubtless pursued this course; but it too had its frustrations—the frustrations of village Hampdens or mute inglorious Miltons ready to serve the Christian commonwealth with all their heart, all their soul, and all their mind, but finding nothing in their rustic retirement to engage half their talents. Few Christian reformers were endowed with either the temperament or the intricate egoism of Michel de Montaigne.

From the 1540's on, a number of men whose response to their historical milieu was similar to the one that inspired *Utopia* found in Calvin's Geneva the resolution in action of dilemmas that More resolved only in imagination in his well-ordered commonwealth. They came to the Savoyard town in thousands from France, from the Netherlands, from Italy, from Spain, from Germany, from England, from Scotland. And there they believed they found what they sought, "the most perfect *school of Christ* that ever was in the earth since the days of the apostles,"[11] "the miracle of the whole world" where men of many nations "being coupled with the only yoke of Christ . . . live . . . lovingly and friendly, and monks, laymen, and nuns . . . dwell together like a spiritual and Christian congregation."[12] What gave Geneva its magnetic attraction for men who had felt the impulse toward a Christian Revival, John Knox explained very succinctly. Christ was truly preached

---

[10] E.g., Alain Chartier, *Tractatus de vita curiali*, written about 1427, and early translated into French as *Le Curial.* G. R. Owst, *Literature and Pulpit*, pp. 310–11.

[11] John Knox, quoted in John T. McNeill, *The History and Character of Calvinism* (New York, 1957), p. 178.

[12] John Bale, quoted in McNeill, pp. 178–79.

elsewhere as well as there, "but manners and religion to be so sincerely reformed, I have not yet seen in any other place."[13] It was the "manners . . . sincerely reformed" that drew monks and nuns from their cloisters, well-to-do laymen from town and country "to live in poverty"[14] in Geneva in enjoyment of "the holy discipline."

In the Middle Ages successive waves of religious fervor, the impulse toward dedication, toward living wholly for God and by His rule, flowed into new or revitalized forms of monastic life, and an *ausserweltliche askese*, an otherworldly asceticism. In the sixteenth century, as a consequence of the holy discipline in Geneva, many of those waves flowed into the *innerweltliche askese* of a City of Saints in this world.[15] The layman official in the councils or consistory of Geneva had no need to feel the compunction which afflicted the author of *Utopia* over a life spent in serving the wicked appetites of vainglorious princes. He could find fulfillment in the austere joy of ruling in a holy commonwealth, in a realization, partial at least, of More's own dream of being a prince in Utopia.

This emancipation from scruple of pious Calvinist laymen brought the full range of their abilities into action in the political arena. In the later sixteenth century it spread from Geneva to the lands where Calvinism penetrated, especially to France, the Netherlands, England, and Scotland. It was able to spread because Geneva remained an example to Calvin's followers of how a community could be transformed by the holy discipline. In France Calvinist laymen provided zealous support for Henry of Navarre, in the Netherlands for William of Orange, and in England for Elizabeth. Henry eventually became a Roman Catholic. William, baptized a Roman Catholic, raised Lutheran in his nonage, and Roman Catholic thereafter, did not become a Calvinist until 1573, when he was forty, with what degree of conviction it is hard to know. And Elizabeth never made any bones about her opposition to the Genevan Church order. Yet men touched by the Calvinist aspiration to execute God's will, as they saw it, on earth could heartily serve Henry and William and Elizabeth, because God not only walked in mysterious ways, but occasionally He chose rather odd instruments, His wonders to perform; and, again as they saw it, Henry and William and Elizabeth were clearly such instruments. Through them the society of saints might yet bring Christ's kingdom on earth. Therefore able and religious laymen, among whom Francis Walsingham, Philippe de Mornay, and St. Aldegonde are perhaps the

---

[13] John Knox, quoted in McNeill, p. 178.
[14] John Bale, quoted in McNeill, pp. 178–79.
[15] Max Weber, *The Protestant Ethic and the Spirit of Capitalism*, tr. T. Parsons (London, 1930), pp. 95–128; Ernst Troeltsch, *The Social Teaching of the Christian Churches*, 1 vol. in 2, tr. O. Wyon (New York, 1931), pp. 602–17.

most eminent, men who might have turned away from political action under other circumstances, provided invaluable aid to their princes during Europe's religious civil wars in the later sixteenth century.[16] Most remarkable was a cluster of Elizabeth's councilors—Mildmay, Chancellor of the Exchequer; Sadler, Chancellor of the Duchy of Lancaster; Knollys, Treasurer of the Household; Wilson and Walsingham, Secretaries of State. They brought to the Queen's service a sobriety, honesty, and zeal not common in princely courts, accompanied by a continuing and unpunished personal alliance with the elements in the country intent on subverting her too-worldly religious settlement. This almost accidental materialization in More's country of a situation in which men similar to him not in creed but in moral temper were drawn toward the service of their ruler did not last. Even before the accession of the Stuarts, the curious symbiosis had broken down. Lay religious zeal gradually went out of Court when Archbishop Whitgift won his struggle against the Puritans. The dilemmas of *Utopia* reasserted themselves again—the dilemma of the intellectual in a bureaucracy, the dilemma of a Christian servant of worldly power, the dilemma of the prophet and the prince.[17] Those dilemmas were in the cards for men with their hearts and minds set on the attainment of the Christian commonwealth, on having God's will done on earth as it is in heaven, who tried to reach that goal through service in the courts of Renaissance princes. Indeed More had already well read those cards in 1516, when he wrote *Utopia*.

> At court . . . one must openly approve the worst counsels and subscribe to the most ruinous decrees. He would be counted a spy and almost a traitor, who gives only faint praise to evil counsels. Moreover there is no chance for you to do any good because you are brought among colleagues who would easily corrupt even the best men before being reformed themselves. By their evil companionship either you will be seduced yourself or, keeping your own integrity and innocence, you will be made a screen for the wickedness and folly of others (103/5–14).

The conjuncture of the aims and aspirations of zealous Calvinists directed toward the *regnun Christi* with the aims and aspirations of rulers with eyes hard fixed on the earthly kingdom was both fortuitous and short.

[16] Whether and how the post-Tridentine forms of Roman Catholic piety affected the service and servants of Catholic rulers during the Counter-Reformation are interesting questions to which unfortunately, through ignorance, the author is unable even to suggest answers.

[17] For an attempt to explore these dilemmas see above pp. 82–93 and Hexter, *More's "Utopia,"* pp. 111–38.

For a while, however, Calvin's Geneva and international Calvinism provided psychic fulfillment for a number of men steeped in the spirit of Christian humanism. And the curious similarities of Utopia and Geneva help us understand how this could have been. As we have seen, however, in one most important matter, Utopia was not at all like Geneva. Calvin tried to infuse into all citizens a sense of their obligation to serve God and do His Will unremittingly, and to this end he forced a remodeling of the Church in doctrine, government, and discipline. But it was the Church alone he sought directly to remodel. In Geneva and wherever else Calvinists planted a Reformed Church they simply accepted in the main the existing structure of rules about property and power. They sought to permeate that structure with the spirit of the Holy Community generated by the Church. More, too, recognized how essential it was that good teaching permeate the structure of society. But not for a moment in *Utopia* does he accept the notion that merely by good teaching (or good preaching), or even by ecclesiastical discipline and censure, a corrupt commonwealth can be transformed into a good one. Such a transformation is only possible through a transmutation of the *forma reipublicae*, the structure of the commonwealth (236/31), of the *maximum totius institutiones fundamentum*, the principal foundation of the whole structure (244/18), of the *vitae . . . instituta*, the institutions of life (244/4), of the *reipublicae fundamenta*, of the foundations of the commonwealth (244/5). For these sixteenth-century Latin phrases the nearest present-day English equivalent is "the social order," and the nearest present-day English equivalent for the transformation More wrote about is "social revolution."

13. A Window to the Future: The Radicalism of *Utopia*

Utopia transcended its milieu in another way, however, a way that justifies speaking, with appropriate reservations, of its modernity. Before we try to discover the etiology of that modernity let us consider a few of its more obvious symptoms. "Utopian" has become a common adjective in English both in the ordinary and in the syntactical sense of "common": it is used frequently and rarely capitalized. Nor was "utopian" in its current common sense the invention of Karl Marx in the nineteenth century; it seems to have been first used in this way by the poet Donne in the sixteenth, and from that time on it remained imbedded in the language. Indeed, "utopia," a "portmanteau"

word put together from Greek roots for a book in Latin by an Englishman, is a common noun and "utopian" a common adjective in every
major European language and in some languages that are not European. In this respect it has enjoyed a success unshared by any other
term coined by an author for a particular occasion.

Moreover, *Utopia* is the only Latin work by an Englishman that—
in translation, of course—is still read by anybody besides professional
scholars. How much *Utopia* has been read is worth considering; for
the number of its readers has been out of the ordinary. From the day
of its publication to the present, for fully four hundred and fifty
years, not a quarter century has passed but *Utopia* has been reprinted
in one European language or another. This is surely a rare achievement. One suspects that it is true of no work by an English writer up
to More's time, quite probably true only of Shakespeare's plays and
More's *Utopia* in More's own century, and true of very few works by
English writers since. It is also worth noting that *Utopia* in English
translation was reprinted at least 92 times in the 72 years between
1868 and 1940, when the bibliographer stopped counting; and that
it has been constantly available in cheap editions for at least the past
eighty years.[1]

More's work created a genre. Within a century of the publication
of *Utopia* the conjuring up of imaginary societies became established
as an appropriate exercise for European *literati*. The process has gone
on sporadically ever since. Yet no utopia has captured the imagination
of men quite as successfully as the first one, and this is not an accident.
Later utopians have usually started with an interest in contrivances
for creating what at the time they conceive as a mechanically satisfactory internal adjustment of the parts of society under current, an-
ticipated, or purely imaginary states of technological development.
Since technology has continually outrun the efforts of man's social
imagination to bring it to heel and since the conceptions of satisfactory
adjustment tend to be various among persons and transitory between
generations, utopian literature tends to be ephemeral. In contrast,
underlying the details of the first Utopian commonwealth are More's
profoundly felt convictions about the nature of man. Those convictions
may not be wholly free of ambiguity or even of internal contradiction,
but they are deeply imbedded in the traditional soil of Western culture.
Consequently, unlike so many of the free-floating commonwealths created by later projectors of utopias, and despite the remarkable freeing

[1] For the early editions to 1750, see W. R. Gibson and J. Max Patrick, *St. Thomas
More: A Preliminary Bibliography* (New Haven, 1961), nos. 1–44. Editions after
1750 are partially listed in Frank and Majie Padberg Sullivan, *Moreana* (Kansas
City, 1946).

of More's imagination, the first Utopia has an air of substantiality about it. More's Land of Nowhere is down-to-earth.

The modernity of *Utopia* lies neither in the philosophy nor in the religion of the Utopians. For the many generations of the readers of *Utopia*, as for More himself, the philosophy of the Utopians was after all not much more than a *tour de force*, which More imposed on himself by his decision to feed into the Discourse on Utopia Amerigo Vespucci's casual remark about the Epicureanism of the American aborigines. The result is a sort of broken-backed hedonism, relying, in a way that would have shocked Epicurus and Lucretius, on divine sanctions and fear of postmortem punishment. It is not particularly persuasive; it did not capture the imagination of More's contemporaries or of subsequent generations;[2] and it retains an interest mainly for literary historians attracted by the problem of unraveling a rather intricate bit of humanistic intellectual fancy-work. A carefully trimmed version of the formal religion of the Utopians, which cut out the bits about ritual, polytheism, religious orders, sacrifices, and priests, and played up the parts about the deism (somewhat vague) of the Utopians and their religious toleration (somewhat restricted), evoked occasional interest and enthusiasm when, after the religious wars and Louis XIV, butchering and harassing heretics lost their attractions for many Europeans. But in More's century and under stresses far stronger than More knew in 1515, there were devoted Christians who, far less ambiguously than the author of *Utopia*, advocated religious toleration.[3] By all but scholars, the words, indeed the very names, of these men have been forgotten; and surely More's highly equivocal comment on the place of toleration in the religion of the Utopian commonwealth would have been forgotten too had he not dropped it in a book that has survived and continued to fascinate the generations for quite other reasons.

To arrive at the curious position he attained on the margins of modernity More had to break through inhibitions patent in the minds of most people of his time. Those people accepted a condition of society in which power and wealth were heavily concentrated in the hands of men who participated or acquiesced in the ethos of a warrior élite. As we have seen, More found this breakthrough relatively easy because the convergence of his intellectual interests, his own temperament,

---

[2] None of the men who wrote letters in conjunction with the early editions of *Utopia* considered Utopian philosophy worthy of comment. This is in contrast to the several who remarked on its political and economic institutions.

[3] See W. K. Jordan, *The Development of Religious Toleration in England from the Beginning of the English Reformation to the Death of Queen Elizabeth* (Cambridge, 1932,), pp. 303–65.

and his friendships prepared his mind for its escape from the warrior ethos. But those same intellectual interests had predisposed toward their own version of aristocracy men concerned, as More was, with the revival of antiquity. After all, the humanists were men of letters in a world where mere literacy of the most rudimentary kind was rare. And like most men they tended to set a high value on those things which they shared with few others and had taken great pains to acquire. Indeed we have already seen that part of the charm which his brain-child had for More derived from the eminent place in Utopia occupied by an intellectual élite.

Another short cross-glance from *Utopia* to the *Republic*, however, indicates how fully More escaped the aristocratic and hierarchical impulsion that might have resulted from his high valuation of his own intellectual preoccupations. For insofar as it deals directly with what are usually called political problems, the *Republic* is concerned, to the exclusion of nearly all else, with the selection, care, and training of political experts, and concerned scarcely at all about what we might call the overall juridical structure of society. Given the Platonic iden-tification of knowledge with virtue, this is quite intelligible. Once the experts govern, the laws will be good by that very fact; so details are unnecessary. In contrast, most of More's description of Utopia deals with the rules of living—the laws and customs in which all Utopian citizens participate and by which, more than by men, they are governed. In this matter it was More's Christian faith that enabled him to break some of the restraints laid on him by his own intellectual commitments. For the convinced Christian, even if he is a man of letters, the most important things for men must be those which God requires of all of them, and More would never have dreamed of sug-gesting that what God requires of all depends on the possession of special intellectual gifts granted only to the few. When, saturated with the Christian concern which prevailed in the circles of his nearest friends, More came to consider how the best commonwealth ought to be organized, this concern enabled him to counterbalance his predis-positions in favor of a literary élite, his interest in the rulers, with an even more intense interest in the ruled. He was clearly drawn to con-sider very carefully the conditions under which ordinary men might actualize their highest potential. Not their highest potential for self-expression certainly. Nor even their highest potential for self-fulfillment perhaps. But at least their highest potential for righteous living, which may not be so far from self-fulfillment after all.

The modernity of *Utopia* lies in the institutions of the Utopian com-monwealth; it is there that More clearly transcends his historical milieu, there that he stands on the margins of modernity. The conditions for righteous living in Utopia were achieved by means of its institutions, and its central institution is Utopian communism. What fascinated and still fascinates so many people about *Utopia*, what has kept the book selling, what is new and modern about it, is precisely the communism of the Utopians. This assertion, however, opens the door wide to an onrush of objections and denials. Surely in the sixteenth century there is nothing new about communism. We find it in Plato's *Republic*, and in *Utopia* More acknowledges his debt to that book. We find it in that "common way of life . . . pleasing to Christ and . . . still in use among the truest societies of Christians" (219/6–8), that is, in the apostolic Church and the better monasteries where its presence, says Hythlodaeus, made it easier to convert the Utopians to Christianity. We also find communism in the later Stoic conception of man's natural condition, which included the community of all possessions. This conception was taken up by the early Church Fathers and by canon lawyers and theologians in the Middle Ages;[4] and More was far too well-read not to have come across it in one or several of the forms thus given it.

But although the idea of communism was very old in More's day, it is not with that idea as such that we are concerned. We are concerned not with the genus communism or with other species of the genus: Platonic, Stoic, early Christian, monastic, canonist, or theological communism; we are concerned with Utopian communism— that is, simply communism as it appears in the imaginary commonwealth of Utopia, as More conceived it. Perhaps one way to sharpen our sense of the modernity of Utopian communism is to contrast it with the principal earlier types of communistic theory. We will achieve a more vivid sense of what it is by realizing what it is not.

The contrast in substance between Utopian communism and the communism of the *Republic* is especially notable because of the very odd formal relationship between *Utopia* and the *Republic*, More and Plato. The enthusiasm for Plato as against Aristotle was well-rooted among many Renaissance philosophers of the generation or two before More's own. More himself surely knew about the Platonic Academy in Florence with whose most eminent scholar, Marsilio Ficino, his friend and confessor John Colet had corresponded. He even translated the biography of one of the most famous members of that group, Pico

---

[4] The history of this conception of property from late antiquity through the thirteenth century can conveniently be traced by following the references in the chapters on Seneca and the chapters and sections on property in R. W. and A. J. Carlyle, *A History of Medieval Political Theory in the West*, 1 (Edinburgh, 1903), 23–24; 2 (1904), 41–49, 136–42; 5 (1928), 14–20; and chapter 14 of E. Surtz, *The Praise of Pleasure* (Cambridge, Mass., 1957), pp. 226–28.

della Mirandola. But although well-acquainted with the *Republic* the Renaissance Platonists showed little interest in the political theme of that work or in the ordering of Plato's imaginary commonwealth. What drew them were those parts of the *Republic* which could be made to fit their Neoplatonic preoccupations and their desire to set Christianity on a Platonic rather than an Aristotelian philosophical foundation.[5] And this preoccupation is very remote from a concern with the best condition of a commonwealth. This view of Plato is quite evident in John Colet. Colet, deeply moved by the sinfulness of humanity in contrast to the righteousness of God, spoke out sharply against some of the social iniquities of his day.[6] But for all the connection he made between his social views and the *Republic*, or for that matter any of the dialogues preoccupied with man as a political animal, he need not have known Plato at all. On the other hand, it would take a very fine mesh indeed to sift out of *Utopia* any discernible residue of Renaissance Neoplatonism. Yet in the book More explicitly refers to Plato five times, more often than to any other man of letters. Four of his five references are to Plato's political views, and all those four are to the *Republic*. But—and this is an extreme oddity—while three of the four political references report the substance of their source with reasonable accuracy, a fourth does not. In that fourth reference Hythlodaeus says that if he told the advisers of princes about "the kind of things which Plato creates in his republic or which the Utopians actually put in practice in theirs . . . such institutions . . . might appear odd because here individuals have the right of private property, there all things are common" (101/12–18). As we have seen, this is simply not so: in Utopia private property is indeed altogether abolished; in the *Republic* it is indeed not.

In Plato's *Republic* communism is—to speak anachronistically—a communism of Janissaries. Its function is to separate from the ruled mass, among whom private ownership prevails, the governing warrior élite. Moreover, it is too readily forgotten that in the *Republic* what gave the initial impetus to Plato's excursus into the construction of an imaginary commonwealth was his quest for a canon for the proper ordering of the individual human psyche; and it is to this problem that the *Republic* ultimately returns. In More's *Utopia* communism is not a means of separating out a warrior élite from the lumpish mass. Utopian communism applies to all Utopians. And in the economy of the book it is not peripheral but central. As specified in its title, the concern of *Utopia* is directly with the *optimo reipublicae statu*, the

[5] Kristeller, *Ficino*, and the same author's *Renaissance Thought*, pp. 57–60.
[6] John Colet, *An Exposition of St. Paul's First Epistle to the Corinthians*, tr. J. H. Lupton (London, 1874), pp. xx–xxi.

best ordering of a civil society or commonwealth; and it is again and again made clear that Utopian communism provides the institutional array indispensable to that best ordering.

To derive Utopian communism from the Jerusalem community of the apostolic age or from its medieval successors-in-spirit, the monastic communities, is as misleading as to derive it from Plato's *Republic*: in the *Republic* we have to do with an élite of physical and intellectual athletes, in the apostolic and monastic communities with an élite of spiritual and religious athletes. The apostolic community was literally an élite: personally chosen by Christ himself. And the monastic communities were supposed to be made up of volunteers selected only after a novitiate which would test their religious aptitude for monastic rigors. But Utopians were not selected for citizenship in Utopia; they were born there.

Nor can More's emphasis on Utopian communism as the very root of the matter be ascribed merely to his involvement in Christian humanism and the Christian Revival. It is true, of course, that a spiritual impulse which moves men to listen open-eared to the Gospels has latent in it radical possibilities. But to find in the Gospel one of the sources of inspiration for the radicalism of *Utopia* is by no means to exhaust that radicalism. The effect of the Gospels taken seriously is to deracinate old habits of thought about the way life should be lived; but to one concerned with the civil life of men it does not provide unambiguous guidance or any clear mandate. Men who in the name of the Gospel have rejected the way of living of their daily world have arrived at the most diverse conclusions as to what the Gospel requires them to put in its place. More was surely moved to his criticism of his own world by his share in the concern of his day with biblical Christianity. But the bare fact of the matter is that no one else involved in Christian humanism or the Christian Revival achieved the sort of modern conception of society which manifests itself in Utopian communism.

Finally, the conception of the *natural* community of all possessions which originated with the Stoics was firmly fixed in tradition by More's time, although it was not accepted by all the theologian-philosophers of the Middle Ages. It moved its communism back to the safe distance of the age of innocence, but it did not serve to contrast the existing order of society with a possible alternative order, because, for the Christian, the age of innocence was not a possible alternative once man had sinned. The actual function of patristic-civilian-canonist-scholastic communism was set forth by St. Gregory almost a millennium before More wrote *Utopia*. "The soil is common to all men; when we give the necessities of life to the poor, we restore to them what is already theirs. We should think of it more as an act of justice than compassion."[7]

Because community, not severalty, of property is the law of nature, according to this view, no man can assert an absolutely unalterable right to private possessions. Indeed, every man is by nature and reason and therefore by conscience obligated to regard himself as a custodian of what he possesses. He is a trustee for the common good, however feeble may be the safeguards which the positive or public law of property provides against his misuse of that share of the common fund wisely or unwisely entrusted to his keeping. In contrast to this Stoic-patristic view, *Utopia* implies that the nature of man is such that to rely on individual conscience to supply the deficiencies of public law is to embark in a sieve on the bottomless sea of human sinfulness. The Utopians brace weak conscience with strong legal sanctions. In a properly ordered society the massive force of public law performs the function which in natural law is ineptly left altogether to a small voice so often still.

In all the ways shown above, Utopian communism differs from previous conceptions in which community of possessions and living play a role. Neither from one of these conceptions nor from a combination of them can it be deduced; it remains an integral whole, original—a new thing. Utopian communism is one of the few new things in *Utopia*; much of the rest is medieval or Christian humanist or part of an old tradition of social criticism. But to say that at a moment in history something is *new* is not necessarily to say that it is modern; and for this statement the best evidence comes within the five years following the publication of *Utopia*, when Martin Luther elaborated a new vision of the nature of God's encounter with man. New, indeed, was Luther's vision, but not modern, as anyone knows who has ever tried to make intelligible to modern students what Luther was getting at.

Although Utopian communism is both new in 1516 and also modern, it is not modern communism or even modern socialism, as they exist or have ever existed in theory or in practice. Consider the features of Utopian communism: generous public provision for the infirm; democratic and secret elections of all officers including priests; meals taken publicly in common refectories; a common habit or uniform prescribed for all citizens; even houses changed once a decade; six hours of manual labor a day for all but a handful of magistrates and scholars and careful measures to prevent anyone from shirking; no private property, no money; no sort of pricing at all for any goods or services, and there-

---

[7] Gregory the Great, "Regulae Pastoralis Liber," pt. 3, chap. 21; *Patrologia Latina*, ed. J.–P. Migne, 77 (1896), 87.

fore no market in the economic sense of the term. Indeed by the standards of economists—capitalist or socialist—the Utopian commonwealth
is quite hopeless. It is not properly geared to maximizing utilities, to
satisfying men's wants. On the contrary, so many things that a good
many people want are banned in Utopia that Calvin's Geneva looks
a bit frivolous and frisky by comparison. We have already had a clue
to the reason for the deficiencies of Utopia as an economy. More's
interest was not in the most effective organization of economic resources for the satisfaction of human wants because he was not concerned with the best economy or with the satisfaction of wants, and
probably he had no clear conception of an economy distinct from the
other relations of men in a community. He was primarily concerned,
as he said on the title page of his book, with the best condition of a
commonwealth, with the common well-being. And this well-being
could be attained not by seeing that men, often corrupted and certainly
corruptible, had what they wanted, but by seeing that those same
men, often good, and certainly improvable, had what they needed
for their welfare.[8]

So, although Utopian communism diverges substantially from any
communist tradition of thought or action with which More was acquainted, it also differs in detail and outlook from present-day socialist
and communist economic theory and economic practice. It is not the
details, however, that make *Utopia* modern; it is the bent of the spirit,
the attitude of mind which informs and gives structure to those details.
What that bent and that attitude were we will understand better if
we examine more carefully the manner in which they differ from the
bent and attitude of the communist theory, familiar to More, with the
longest continuous tradition. That was the theory which reached Christianity by way of Stoicism through the Church Fathers of late antiquity.

As one examines closely what the Fathers had to say about communism one is struck by something beside the substance of their views.
The two obvious gross facts about those views—so obvious that they
have tended to be overlooked—is that, first, they are scattered and,
second, they are meager. When the Fathers deal with the communism
which they suppose existed in a state of nature, it is rarely in conjunction with other arrangements that they assume existed in that
state—equality of all men, universal liberty, and so on. They tend to
come at the question casually and obliquely, if at all, in conjunction
with some other matters of larger and more present concern—the sin
of avarice, for example. Most of them probably believed that, like
slavery, private property was at once the result and the corrective

[8] Since I wrote the above, the way of life of the Chinese as prescribed by Chair-
man Mao has forced itself on my attention. It sounds uncomfortably like Utopia
in a number of significant respects.

for sin after humanity had fallen through the disobedience of the first man. Yet this fact usually has to be inferred from the general tenor of their remarks: rarely do the Fathers make wholly explicit and unambiguous the relationship between communism and the state of innocence on the one hand, and private property and sin on the other.

Moreover, the Fathers' observations on communism before the Fall are so sketchy and vague that one can never gather from them the faintest conception of how it worked. Perhaps they felt that in a region so scantily populated and so abundantly endowed by Nature as the Earthly Paradise, detailed arrangements were otiose. But the more certain and significant reason for the meagerness of the Fathers' observations on the organization of a society in which possessions were held in common was, as we previously indicated, that not even as an act of imagination did they conceive of such a society as an alternative to the one in which they lived.

In the Church Fathers' view of the matter, then, as a consequence of human sinfulness, men are at once punished and safeguarded by, among other things, the severalty of property; and communism and a number of other desirable human arrangements have slipped beyond the grasp of men because of that sinfulness. *Utopia* does to this view what Karl Marx did to Hegel; it turns it upside down. Private property is not a partial prophylaxis to human sinfulness—quite the contrary. Though not perhaps the unique cause, private property and the dense mass of inequalities which are ancillary to it are the most blatant occasions of human iniquity; they provide the rich black rottenness in which man's sins most abundantly flourish. And the way to deal with the evils which flourish under a regime of money and markets, private property, and inequality is simply to destroy that regime; without destroying it there will be no for the ills it engenders. Although a certain amount of patchwork may keep a sick society from falling into utter decay, patching one part often weakens another, and really "there is no hope . . . of a cure . . . as long as each individual is master of his own property" (105/37–39). Here we get to the heart of what is modern about *Utopia*. It has as one of its central preoccupations not the amelioration of a sick society but the conditions indispensable to a sane one. Moreover, a nature essentially different from the ordinary nature of ordinary men emphatically was not one of the conditions of a sane society. The occidentals "are inferior" to the Utopians, says Hythlodaeus, "neither in brains nor in resources" (109/18–19). The Utopians themselves had once been a "rude and rustic people," (113/5) who lived in "mere cabins and huts, haphazardly made with any wood at hand, with mudplastered walls" (121/32–34). The basis for the transformation of this barbarous folk to "such a perfection of culture and humanity as makes them now superior to almost all other mor-

tals" (113/6–7) was a drastic, a radical transformation of their institutions. That transformation drew out of the private sphere and into the
domain of public law matters that in More's time were left to the
desires and decisions of unregulated or lightly regulated individuals
and groups—costume, meals, care of the aged and infirm, education,
work and the hours of labor, the distribution of goods, the allocation
of what a later generation was to call the factors of production, even
the consumption of leisure.

The contrast between this way of looking at human affairs and the
way most widely current in the Middle Ages and still widespread in
More's own day could hardly be sharper. In that earlier perspective
men through their misdoings had lost the capacity for a rational ordering of their affairs, so that for their present scarcely civil condition
there was no real remedy on earth; and they had better accept the
bad that was, in fear of the worse that might be. This older perspective
Martin Luther shared with St. Augustine.[9] In the perspective of *Utopia*,
however, the irrational ordering of their affairs provided the incentive
for men's misdoing; but they could escape from their present scarcely
civil condition if they would undertake a resolute, rational, and radical
reordering of their affairs. This is the point of view precisely set forth
by Hythlodaeus. In More's sixteenth-century world, he says, self-
seeking is as rational as concern for the common good is in Utopia.
In a corrupt society, corrupt action is reasonable; in a decent society,
decent action is reasonable. In its intense perception and presentation
of community of goods as a conceivably viable alternative to private
property and in its insistence that communism, not private property,
is prophylactic against human wickedness, *Utopia* stands on the margins of modernity.

Another indication of the peculiarity of *Utopia*, of its deviation from
the traditional norm, is provided by its diametrical contrast to the
common medieval Christian attitude toward the broad spectrum of
doings and ways of living which continuously or sporadically have
strongly attracted large numbers of men. Professor Tawney summarizes
the medieval view as follows: "Society is an organism of different
grades, and human activities form a hierarchy of functions which differ in kind and in significance, but each of which is of value on its
own plane, provided that it is governed, however remotely, by the end
which is common to all."[10] This is a most spacious and accommodating
attitude toward human affairs; it enabled the custodians of medieval
values to accept a very wide range of activities as proper to man, if

[9] As emphasized by Ernst Troeltsch, *Social Teaching of the Christian Churches*,
pp. 110–12, 118–20, 515–76, especially 540–54. See also J. W. Allen, *A History
of Political Thought in the Sixteenth Century* (London, 1960), pp. 19–23.

[10] R. H. Tawney, *Religion and the Rise of Capitalism* (New York, 1947), p. 26.

only some way could be found to construct for those activities sets of rules which did not manifestly run counter to divine law.

In effect, during the medieval centuries the social function assumed by the Christian Church, acting primarily through the clergy, was to Christianize society as it found it.[11] By and large, with only occasional and unsystematic eruptions of queasiness, it simply accepted the hierarchical order, the domination of society by a warrior élite, chivalry, serfdom, romantic love, a market economy. By subjecting all Christians to auricular confession and to the sacrament of penance, the ecclesiastical hierarchy sought to infuse all existing legitimatized relations with a Christian spirit; and by setting forth penitential rules based on experience and on a detailed casuistry it brought each new sort of human activity as it emerged under the surveillance and, hopefully, the restraint of Christian morality. In a sense this stance affects with a presumption of rightness, or at least of non-wrongness, the things that at any time men are currently doing and customarily have done. Concerning any human activity the medieval question becomes, "Is there any compelling reason why this should not be permitted in moderation?" On the other hand, the Utopian question is, "Why should a society consistently aiming at the best pursue or permit the pursuit of this activity?" In answering the medieval question it is easy to find room for the chase, the game of chance, the tavern, the gorgeous costume, the jewels, and the gold. In answering More's question it is hard to find room for any of these. In Utopia there are practically no *adiaphora*, practically no things indifferent.

The shift from the medieval stance of initial acceptance of the variety of human desires to the Utopian position which tests the admissibility of every desire by its congruity with the needs of a society rationally conceived generates radicalism of the modern kind. But Utopian communism does not tie in with any of the varieties of scientific socialism originating in Marx or with the anarchists' apocalyptic. Rather it anticipates the radical egalitarianism which flared up fitfully in the Enlightenment. This egalitarianism gained force during the French Revolution among the Jacobins and later in England among the utilitarians. During the nineteenth century, radical egalitarians came to recognize that other kinds of equality became meaningless when traversed by the fierce inequality of the rich and the poor. They concluded that the effects of such inequality could be destroyed only by eradicating the inequality itself, by applying curbs of law in the interest of justice to the force of power and wealth. Thus modern

---

[11] Ernst Troeltsch, *Social Teaching of the Christian Churches*, pp. 246–56, and especially for chivalry, note 114 on p. 399.

egalitarian radicalism arrived at the point where Hythlodaeus began his Discourse on Utopia.

Once we have linked Utopian communism with its proper modern analogue, the way in which *Utopia* projects its vision into a later age becomes clearer. Nevertheless it is a quite curious way. Erasmus has often been identified as a precursor of the *philosophes* of the Enlightenment. In some measure, the inhabitants of Utopia in their outlook *are* Enlightenment *philosophes*. The fund of moral conceptions common to most of the *philosophes* was after all the residue of centuries of Christianity; it was largely Christian ethics minus Christian mystery. The *philosophes* held as evil almost everything (except unbelief) which Christian ethics deemed sinful, as good almost everything Christian ethics deemed righteous (except faith in Christian dogma). In the main they dredged up a more or less plausible non-Christian rationale to provide shoring for a Christian morality for which they sought no substitute. What the *philosophes* did because they rejected Christian revelation, More had done over two centuries earlier because technically his Utopians could not know Christian revelation. The equation *reason equals nature equals virtue*, the deism precariously perched on rational foundations of doubtful solidity, the feeble and slightly apologetic hedonism wavering between the logical need for a this-worldly base and the psychological need for other-worldly sanctions—all these positions, common to so many eighteenth-century *philosophes*, recapitulate the "philosophy" of the Utopians.

More important, the author of *Utopia* combines certain traits and habits of thought in a pattern that was to become part of the ordinary stock in trade of the modern radical. More's contemporaries, especially the humanists, were inhibited from making a like combination by the very form in which they usually cast their writing on politics. That form is the *Fürstenspiegel*, the Mirror of Princes. The form was venerable, and in innumerable treatises "over a period of ten centuries" from A.D. 500 to 1500, "the most striking and prominent thought that we find is the personal attitude toward rulership and rulers. Every one of the writers lays great stress upon the personal moral virtues of the prince. It is from him alone that good or evil, as he wills it, is visited on the land."[12] The question to which this sort of work addresses itself is, "What should the best prince do?" Given the habitual patterns of thought of almost ten centuries, this question had concealed within it a peculiar limitation. What a good prince did not do, so said the unvarying voice of traditional wisdom for a millennium, was to take the law into his own hands. He administered the law, he amended the

[12] Erasmus, *Education of a Christian Prince*, tr. Born, p. 126.

law, occasionally he even dictated the law; but he did not abolish the law and replace it with a totally different law. Under such circumstances it is no wonder that most of the Mirrors of Princes of the Middle Ages and Renaissance go on at great length about the moral qualities of a good ruler and his proper style of conduct but are stonily silent about the substance of his actions. Consequently, in the context of the Middle Ages and the Renaissance, the question, "What ought the prince to do?" does not lead to the question, "What ought a good society to be?" On the contrary it prevents the latter question from being raised by focusing its entire attention on the personality and wisdom of the prince and giving no heed to the structure of society.

More offers Hythlodaeus the standard humanist prince-book gambit early in *Utopia*: a "truly philosophic spirit" ought to be a royal councilor because "from the monarch, as from a never-failing spring flows a stream of all that is good or evil over the whole nation" (57/16–18). The result might be described as "prince-book gambit declined." The protagonist of the Dialogue, Hythlodaeus, refuses to turn it into a disquisition on the character of the virtuous prince. Of course, given the order of composition of *Utopia*, he was bound to refuse the gambit. The Discourse on Utopia had already made pivotal a question that earlier humanists scarcely asked, "What is the best way to order a commonwealth—a polity-economy-society?" And by a significant inversion the princely *deus ex machina* of Utopia, King Utopus, does precisely what the ideal princes of the *Fürstenspiegel* literature never do and what even Machiavelli's prince never does: instead of maintaining the law that he finds among his subjects, he utterly abolishes it. Thus More breaks out of the circle which limited so much humanist writing about politics to platitudinous trivia and futile moralistic incantation.

Having escaped the confines of the humanist prince-books, More's thinking about the commonwealth was free to assume a new pattern. The components of that thinking, in fact, took a form which strikingly anticipates that of modern radicalism; not only are there a number of identifiable elements common to both, but the colligation of the elements seems similar. Separately these elements are (1) humanitarianism, (2) in connection with problems of human conduct a preference for arguments based on reason against arguments based on tradition or custom, (3) belief in the efficacy of good law and good education as a remedy for the ills of the commonwealth, (4) environmentalism, (5) the sense that drastic change is necessary to deal with current ills. Readers of the literature of the Enlightenment and of English radicalism will surely recognize that a considerable part of the story which that literature has to tell can be organized under these five rubrics. It remains to identify them in Utopia. The humanitarian ele-

ment is of course unmistakable—touching sympathy for men dogged
by the insecurities and anxieties of life in More's own society, pity for
the overburdened working people (238/26 f.), concern for decent provision for the aged and infirm (240/11 f.). Most clearly symptomatic,
however, of More's transcendence of his own milieu is his preoccupation with crime and punishment (240/31 f.). Both in the Discourse
and the Dialogue there is evidence of his concern with a rational
penology—in his description of how the Utopians treat their bondmen,
in his contempt for England's harsh penal law (60/13 f.), in his conception of punishment as a means of both deterrence and correction
rather than of vengeance (78/8–12 f.). Indeed Hythlodaeus' description (74/17 f.) of the organization of penal servitude among the
Polylerites is perhaps the first of those attempts to conceive a wholly
rational penology of which the Panopticon of that radical of radicals,
Jeremy Bentham, was to be the most notorious, though not the last.

In *Utopia* the humanitarian quest for a rational penology is of a
piece with a preference there made explicit for the rational over the
merely customary and traditional. Though his world in matters of property and power habitually identified right with custom and tradition,
More gives short shrift to both. It is well enough to let the "wisest
provisions" of the forefathers be; it is another matter in the face of a
rational proposal for improvement to say, "Our forefathers were happy
with that sort of thing, and would to heaven we had their wisdom"
(59/7–9). This kind of nonsense, rampant among the councilors of
Europe's rulers, is unknown in Utopia. There, any new thing that may
make life better, whether proposed by a traveler or learned from books,
is eagerly seized on and tried. While nature and reason are the sure
guides to the good life, perverse habit hardened into custom leads
to vice (172/1–2). But more significant than detail, the whole project
of the Discourse on Utopia is by its nature an unlimited exercise in
rationality; its underlying presupposition is that the best ordering of
human affairs can be discerned by subjecting all merely human institutions to rational criticism, rational consideration, and rational reconstruction.

The extreme rationality of *Utopia* in respect to the ordering of
society is as distinctly marked on the negative as on the positive side.
Even more curious than what *Utopia* says is its silence. Wholly lacking
throughout the book is any hankering, explicit or implicit, for the good
old days, a hankering that seems to have been pandemic in More's
time and that is so deeply rooted in the stuff men are made of that it
survived into an age dominated by the idea of progress. Indeed it survived among such passionate exponents of progress as William Morris
and Friedrich Engels. Even though the best days were coming, good
days there had been; it was now that was truly awful. In More's own

time the good old days might mean the dream world of chivalry, and obviously he had no time for that. It might also mean, and in More's intellectual milieu usually did mean, Greco-Roman antiquity; but oddly enough there is not a trace in *Utopia* of that worship of ancient civilization (as distinct from admiration for an ancient literature) which was common coin among humanists. For the apostolic community of the first century after Christ, More indeed obliquely indicated his admiration, but in antiquity, as he well knew, that community was not a civilization; it was a group separated off, living in the world but not of it.

The means by which the best society is kept best are good institutions and good education—again a recipe after the heart of Bentham and of the generations of radicals who walked along and widened the path he opened. Thus the indifference of Utopians to gold, their aversion to a money economy, and their abomination of the "madness of men who pay almost divine honors to the rich" have two sources. One is *doctrina* and *literae*, teaching and letters for some schooling is given to all; the other is their *educatio*, their upbringing in a commonwealth whose institutions are removed from such folly (156–58). Their very fighting spirit in war derives its force from the institutions of Utopia, from its radical communism. In other lands concern about their livelihood at home and about the future of their families saps the courage of the bravest. The Utopian in arms has no such worry, and consequently is more ready to fight to the finish (210/14–17). Finally it is the institutions of Utopia that make it at once most happy and most stable; and (so goes the last sentence of the Peroration) as long as its institutions remain sound no external enemy can destroy it (244/ 10–13).

Clearly More, like all good modern radicals, is a social environmentalist. This does not imply in either case a belief that men can so manipulate their social environment as to eliminate the need for external controls and coercion. The anarchists have dreamed such a dream; but very few garden-variety radicals have done so. And More certainly did not; he was both too good a Christian and too widely experienced a man to suffer delusions about human perfectibility. Nevertheless the obvious implication of his sketch of a society made excellent by its laws, institutions, and education is that human happiness can be increased in a very large way by rules and teaching that repress men's evil impulses and foster their good ones, that do not subject them to temptations which are beyond the capacity of ordinary mortals to resist. More is very careful to note that the vast difference between the good way affairs are ordered in Utopia and the ill way they are ordered in Europe has nothing to do with any difference in natural endowment between Europeans and Utopians (108/

16–19). It is in the use to which they put their natural gifts that the Utopians surpass the people of Europe.

In effect Utopia provides an environment in which men's natural gifts flourish, Europe an environment which causes them to grow twisted and rot. For example, in England the law which calls for thieves to be hanged simply gives them an incentive to murder, since if they are caught the penalty will be no greater (74/2–11). The conditions which make thieves are poverty and unemployment; and yet the English "ordain grievous and terrible punishments for a thief when it would have been much better to provide some means of getting a living, that no one should be under this terrible necessity first of stealing and then of dying for it" (61/25–30). Again "you allow your youths to be badly brought up and their characters, even from early years, to become more and more corrupt. . . ." To punish men for crimes "which from boyhood they had shown every prospect of committing" is first to "create thieves and then become the very agents of their punishment" (71/11–17). The remedies proposed to reform the penal law are like the ones built into the institutions of Utopia. They aim to achieve the security of life and of means of livelihood which will take away the temptation to theft. The emphasis is all away from mere sermonizing before the criminal event and mere retribution after, all in the direction of prophylaxis by wise social controls. Since those controls are sound in Utopia and all Utopians have had "an excellent rearing to a virtuous life," they subject their fellow-countrymen convicted of heinous crimes to the harshest bondage (185/26–30). It is because men respond rationally to their environment that Europe is racked with social ills. For "there men talk freely of the common interest—but look after their private interest only. In Utopia, where nothing is private, they seriously concerned themselves with public affairs. *Assuredly in both cases they act reasonably* [italics mine]." The social arrangements of Europe drive sensible men, of necessity, to take care of themselves, and the public be damned (239/1–9). It is the social environment of Europe, its laws and customs, and especially its laws and customs with respect to property and money and war, that lead Christian men to prey on Christian men in a society based not on community but on the thinly masked oppression of the poor by the rich.

The analysis in *Utopia* is radical. It stands at the opposite pole to the best-known piece of social analysis in Tudor literature—Ulysses' apostrophe to the principle of hierarchy in *Troilus and Cressida*. Shakespeare's splendid lines are only the most superb exemplar of the current orthodoxy. That human nature was red in tooth and claw, that by inclination men were wolves to other men, that they continually tended to fall into the savage war of each against each, and that the sole safeguard against such horrors was the maintenance of the serried array of the existing order of society under its current rulers, was the firm conviction set forth to and for those who ruled in Renaissance Europe, to whom it doubtless made good listening. Concerning the convictions of those who were ruled in Renaissance Europe our evidence is scanty. The fundamental social conviction expressed in *Utopia* is that, far from being worth preserving, the social order based on hierarchy is. only worth eradicating; that outside the family the true principle of the good commonwealth is the very opposite of hierarchy; it is equality.

The idea of eradicating, deracinating, pulling up by the roots—the starting point of radicalism—is not only implicit in *Utopia*, it is sporadically explicit. To attain justice, property must be utterly cast down (105/18). In Europe pride is too solidly fixed in men to be ripped out easily (244/2), but the Utopians have extirpated the roots of ambition. When the Utopians abolish the use of money they cut away a mass of troubles and pull a crop of crimes up by the roots. *Subferre, evellere, radicibus extirpare, subferre* again, *rescindere, radicatus evellere*—the vernacular equivalents of such terms are the standard coins of intellectual commerce with the modern radical.

The radicalism of *Utopia* is not a bit of *trompe-l'oeil*, a trick of perspective, the results of staring too long at a sixteenth-century book from some place in the twentieth century. The relation of the order of composition of the parts of *Utopia* to the completed work confirms the radical character of the work. Our analysis of the structure of that work indicated that the Dialogue of Counsel, including the Exordium in Book I, and the Conclusion, including the Peroration in Book II, were written after More's return to London, and most likely in about that order, since the effectiveness of both the Exordium and the Peroration indicates that More had the whole work—Dialogue as well as Discourse—clearly in mind and probably on paper when he set them down. In other words, these sections of *Utopia*, though certainly not written at leisure, were composed after More had a chance to ruminate a bit on what he had already written in the Netherlands. He was free to proceed in a wide variety of possible ways, or, if he chose, not to proceed any further at all, but simply to pack up the job with the Introduction and Discourse. So in a way, what More wrote in London was his own judgment on what he had written earlier in the Netherlands. The Discourse was a work of many facets, both in mood and in substance. In the parts of *Utopia* he wrote subsequently in London, More could continue the variety of mood or assume a particular one, could select some substantial elements of the Discourse to the neglect of others for emphasis by reiteration or development.

With respect to mood, the range is narrower while the intensity is greater in the later-written parts of *Utopia* than in the Discourse. In the Discourse there is wit, considerable whimsy, a good bit of detailed but somewhat fanciful elaboration, many touches of humor, and some disengaged intellectual play, as well as harsh satire and angry social comment. In the parts of *Utopia* written in London there is only a trace of whimsy, no intellectual play, no elaboration of detail for the sheer pleasure of elaborating, and only a few bits of humor. There is wit, but the wit is sardonic, at times even savage. The Dialogue is also a diatribe; and whatever shreds of doubt may remain about More's own attitude toward his imaginary commonwealth of Utopia, the Dialogue leaves none at all about his detestation of the way of life of the ruling class in sixteenth-century Europe. The *festivus*, the gay, aspect of the *libellus* about Utopia is almost wholly confined to the Discourse; the Dialogue, the Exordium, and the Peroration are very sober. In those parts the satire, of which there is a great deal, is rarely playful; it is often grim, even bitter. It is the almost unbroken sobriety and earnestness of the exchanges between Hythlodaeus, More, and Giles and of Hythlodaeus' peroration that give them their extraordinary intensity.

All this suggests that More may well have taken the Discourse more seriously after he thought it over in London than he did while he was writing it in the Netherlands. Or rather that he took more seriously those substantial elements of the Discourse which in the Dialogue, the Exordium, and the Peroration he chose to emphasize by reiteration and development. And what elements were these? Not the philosophy of the Utopians. In what he wrote in London More simply stopped fitting the social commentary of *Utopia* to the peculiar exigencies of a specious Epicureanism. Even in the Exordium and the Peroration, where Hythlodaeus is specifically contrasting Europe and Utopia, decrying the former, lauding the latter, he has nothing to say about the Utopian philosophy of pleasure. Indeed the word *voluptas*, which in the Discourse More skillfully wove into Hythlodaeus' praise of Utopian institutions, occurs scarcely at all in the rest of the book.[13] Nor in the Dialogue, Exordium, and Peroration is there any reference to the religious creeds and practices of the Utopians. More did not take the religions of the Utopians, their diverse beliefs and formal practices, seriously any more than he took their philosophy seriously. In the Dialogue he castigates the appetite for ruinous war among Christian princes; he denounces rulers who were wolves devouring their

---

[13] The distribution of *voluptas* in *Utopia* is rather startling. It occurs 72 times, as often as *homo*, more often than any other noun but *res*. Of its 72 occurrences, 69 are in the Discourse. One of the remaining instances (84/31) is neutral. The contexts for the other two occurrences of *voluptas*, one in the Dialogue (94/31) and one in the Peroration (240/8), render it unmistakably pejorative.

subjects through outrageous exactions rather than shepherds watching over them; he attacks the English penal system for its inhumanity. In effect he inveighs against the sins of the whole ruling class of the West—especially against its sloth, its greed, and its pride. And this he had done, too, in the Discourse.

It is the Exordium and the Conclusion (including the Peroration) rather than the Discourse or even the Dialogue that bring the radical character of *Utopia* into the sharpest focus, all the more significantly because these appear to be the sections of the book that More wrote last. In both, the emphasis is the same; in both the colligation of elements that makes the pattern of modern radicalism holds the center of attention. Mild measures, ameliorations are rejected; they may prevent utter disaster, but they are inadequate. If human nature is to grow straight and clean instead of twisted and foul it must be transplanted into a society which will foster such growth. Such a society is Utopia, where there is no money, no private property, no mine and thine. Without Utopian equality in all things, all the evils that plague a commonwealth by destroying the characters of its citizens will again take possession of the body politic, rendering transitory and ultimately futile all reforms and making the commonwealth once more a mere conspiracy of the rich against the poor. Community of property and abolition of money are *the only means* for achieving true equality. They are also *only the means*; the end is equality. For the final equations are simple and radical: the equitable is the good; equality is justice.

Equality is justice. That is the cutting edge of More's thought in *Utopia*. It frees him of the unexamined assumption, nearly universal in his day, about men's relations to men, the assumption not merely of difference, but of inequality, of status, of hierarchy. It envisages equality not as the lost prize of a golden age forever gone, but as the indispensable condition for a righteous social order. Its orientation is not toward the past but toward the future; and it impels the thinking of More into the future, and toward a particular point in that future—toward modern radicalism. Not toward Marx and scientific socialism. More would have found little congenial to him in the potpourri of economic analysis, German speculative thought, and science worship so conspicuous in the Marxian canon. One quotation from an eminent modern historian is enough to indicate where *Utopia* fits in the crazy quilt of modernity, and to summarize the whole structure of More's radicalism, with each element so distinct and sharp that it needs no further clarification here:

The reality of a class struggle in modern society . . . is . . . insistent and the indignation aroused by the phrase is itself evidence of the fact. But to suppose that such phenomena are preordained and unavoidable—to find their sources in inexorable historical tendencies . . . instead of in the obvious, commonplace operations of folly and greed, which can either be indulged till they bring their nemesis, or chastened and repressed— is not science but superstition. . . . Democracy . . . can be used to correct inequalities. . . . Contrasts of environment, and inherited wealth, and educational opportunity and economic security, with the whole sad business of snobbery and servility which such contrasts produce, are the creation, not of nature, but of social convention. . . . Men have given one stamp to their institutions; they can give another. They have idealized money and power; they can "choose" equality.[14]

[14] R. H. Tawney, *Equality* (New York, 1931), pp. 268–69.

APPENDIX A: The Composition of *Utopia*

There are but two small bits of external evidence which bear directly on the composition or structure of Thomas More's *Utopia* as it was published at Louvain in the autumn of 1516.

1. In a letter from London on September 3, 1516, More wrote to his friend, Desiderius Erasmus, in Antwerp: "I am sending you my 'Nowhere' (Nusquama . . . mitto), which is nowhere well written. I have added a prefatory epistle to my friend, Peter [Giles]. I know from experience that I do not have to tell you to give proper attention to everything else."[1]

2. In his letter to Ulrich von Hutten, written in 1519 in response to the latter's request for a word-picture of More, Erasmus remarks about *Utopia* that More "had written the second part because he was at leisure, and the first part he afterwards dashed off as opportunity offered. Hence there is some inequality in the style."[2]

More's letter indicates that he must have completed *Utopia* by early September 1516. The second quotation alerts us to a probable idiosyncrasy in the way More wrote his little book.

Erasmus' statement about the order of composition of the parts of *Utopia*—second part first, first part second—bears all the marks of being at least roughly true. In the context in which it appears, it would have been senseless for Erasmus to make the observation unless he knew it was so. It is purely gratuitous information. It fits well with strong though indirect evidence that Erasmus knew a great deal about the circumstances of the composition of *Utopia*.

If Erasmus did not know a great deal about *Utopia* before its publication, it is difficult to account for More's letter of transmittal quoted above. What is *Nusquama*? Why is More sending Erasmus the manuscript of it? What does he expect or want Erasmus to do with it? These questions might well puzzle a man receiving out of the blue such a manuscript from a friend. They do not seem to have occurred to Erasmus. Indeed, on the assumption that he knew nothing about *Utopia* at the time, his acknowledgment of the receipt of it is even odder than More's transmittal. He replies on October 2, 1516 (*Ep.*, 2, 354), that "Peter Giles . . . is wonderfully struck by your *Nusquama*," but he does not say a word about what he himself thinks of it. Nor does he ask or wonder what he is supposed to do with it. He simply says, "Every care shall be taken about the Island," that is, of course, about

---

[1] Eras., *Ep.*, 2, 339.
[2] Ibid., *4*, 21. Cf. J. H. Hexter, *More's "Utopia,"* pp. 99–102.

Utopia, and then he sets about getting the book published with an appropriate number of laudatory letters from eminent men.[3]

Of course there is nothing really odd in this exchange. Erasmus did not need to consult More about what to do with the manuscript because that had all been decided before More ever sent it to him. He had already read it, and he had already told More what he thought of it. The correspondence between the two men is simply indirect evidence of these facts. There is no direct evidence because Erasmus had read *Utopia*, discussed it with More face to face, and agreed on arrangements for its publication less than a month before More sent him the manuscript. Since all this presumably took place in More's own house, where Erasmus was a guest during the first half of August, detailed correspondence on the subject was unnecessary.[4]

Thus we need no doubt the general accuracy of Erasmus' statement to Hutten, even if, to fit it to the facts, we have to modify it in view of other evidence concerning the composition of *Utopia*, internal evidence offered by the first edition of the work in 1516. The need for modification becomes apparent when we examine Book II of *Utopia*. There More mentions the dictionary of Hesychius, first published at Venice in 1514 (182/1). Thus More had not started on *Utopia* until after some time in 1514 and had finished writing by September 1516. For part of that time—from early May to late October 1515[5]—he was away from home on a mission for Henry VIII in the Netherlands. Both before he left England and after his return, More was about as busy as a man can be in managing his affairs. But Erasmus says More wrote Book II of *Utopia* at leisure. Between the earliest probable date for the starting of *Utopia* and the latest probable date for finishing it, only during his Netherlands mission does More seem to have enjoyed any leisure. It was probably at this time, then, that he wrote Book II of *Utopia*. Now if we look closely at Book II, we notice that it is not an impersonal treatise but a discourse. Somebody who has been to Utopia and who refers to himself in the first person is talking to an audience. The trouble is that anyone who read *only* Book II of *Utopia* would never find out who was listening or where he was listening, and he would get a clue about who was doing all the talking only at the

---

[3] At this point in the correspondence between Erasmus and More there appear to be no gaps. Erasmus did not reach Antwerp much before September 1. More then wrote him several letters, that of September 3 (Eras., *Ep.*, *2*, 339) and one or two others later in September (ibid., *2*, 346–47). Erasmus acknowledges the latter letters in his of October 2 to More (ibid., *2*, 353–54). In none of these letters is there any indication of other correspondence between the two during this time, in which Erasmus might have been informed or instructed about *Utopia*.

[4] Eras., *Ep.*, *2*, 317.

[5] *Corresp.*, pp. 16, 26, 73 and n.; *LP 1515–16*, No. 1067.

last full page of Book II. The audience is not identified at all in Book II, the speaker only on that last page. Even then the reader would get only the first name of the narrator, apparently, Raphael (244/13). And finally he would not have any notion how the belatedly named Raphael happened to be in Utopia, a rather odd place after all for anyone to be in, or how he happened to be talking to whomever he was talking to.

Of course ordinarily readers do not begin *Utopia* with Book II; they begin at the beginning of Book I. So they have no doubt about who is telling the story—Raphael Hythlodaeus; or who is listening—"Thomas More" and "Peter Giles"; or where—in the garden of the house in Antwerp where "More" was staying. They will also have some notion about the location of Utopia.

All these things are made quite clear early in Book I (48–50). But on the supposition that Erasmus' statement about the composition of *Utopia* is not only generally true but precisely accurate in every detail, we cannot properly seek in Book I for the identity of the persons presumably present and the place they were at in Book II, because on that supposition none of Book I had been written until the whole of Book II was finished. One would then have to suppose that More wrote Book II, complete with narrator, audience, and *mise en scène* while he was in the Netherlands, but that he did not bother to furnish any of them with local habitation or full name until several months later. It is not a likely story, and it becomes all the more unlikely when we recognize that scattered through Book II of *Utopia* there are bits of autobiography, recognizable fragments of a narrator, and that it is therefore highly probable that the narrator to whom the fragments belong had been earlier provided with an identity. In Book II the narrator offers the following information concerning himself:

1. He lived for five years in Amaurotum, the capital of the Utopian federation (116/28).

2. He personally prefers Greek authors to Latin and suspects that, except for the Roman poets and historians, the Utopians would find little in Latin literature to interest them (180).

3. The venture he was on when he encountered the Utopians was connected with "the fourth voyage"—*whose* voyage is not specified (180/26).

4. When he was in Utopia, there were only four men in his party although before there had been six (218/10–11).

Of these bits of autobiographical data the last two make no sense if, following the clue presented by Erasmus, one starts reading *Utopia* at the beginning of Book II—*whose* fourth voyage? *what* party of six? As soon as one begins with Book I, however, the difficulty vanishes, for there we are early introduced to the wandering philosopher Raphael Hythlodaeus, of whom we are told, among other things, that he lived in Utopia for five years (106/15), that he accompanied Amerigo Vespucci on the last three of his four voyages to the New World (50/5), that he prefers Greek authors to Latin ones (48/32–33), and that when Vespucci returned from his fourth voyage, Hythlodaeus had remained behind in the new-found lands in a party of six and gone off on an exploring expedition (50/14–16). All this confirms what the narrator says about himself in Book II of *Utopia*, and indeed is most, though not all, of what he says about himself there. For the foregoing facts there is only one moderately plausible explanation. In Book II More could drop bits of information about the narrator, because he had already introduced him. But if this is so, along with Book II some portion of Book I of *Utopia* must have been written in the Netherlands.

But how much of Book I? Here we ought to respect the *general* tenor of Erasmus' remarks in his letter to Hutten. If possible, the kernel of Book I should be saved for composition in England after More's Netherlands mission, when, no longer at leisure but frantically busy, he wrote *ex tempore per occasionem*.[6] How far need we go through Book I, then, before we can reasonably assign the writing of what remains to the months More was in London before he dispatched his manuscript to Erasmus in September 1516? We need to go at least far enough to introduce Hythlodaeus, and to include some (not necessarily all) of the autobiographical information that turns up again in Book II.[7] Near the beginning of Book I More introduces Hythlodaeus very promptly; he packs into half-a-dozen lines three biographical references that link to those in Hythlodaeus' discourse—the participation in Vespucci's voyages, the explorations of the party of six, and Raphael's preference for Greek as against Latin (48–50). The question then arises: how much beyond these references did More write when he was in the Netherlands?[8]

Once one is alerted to the existence of a problem here, the solution is easy. What we are looking for is a place in Book I where an introduction intended for the Discourse and written in the Netherlands was patched over to permit the insertion of what More subsequently wrote in London—what Erasmus called the first part and what we

---

[6] Eras., *Ep.*, 4, 21.

[7] Not necessarily all, because More was free to let Hythlodaeus make autobiographical references in the Discourse that he had not included when he introduced him. In the Discourse, Hythlodaeus expresses his concern about the problem of getting Christian priests to Utopia to care for the converts (218/10–18), but More does not refer to this matter in the section of the book subsequently written. On the other hand, he does pick up and reiterate Hythlodaeus' reference to his five-year residence in Amaurotum (106/15).

[8] Whether in the first few lines of *Utopia* the mention of Tunstal's elevation to the post of Master of the Rolls in May 1516 (46/14–15) was inserted into a text previously written or whether a few prefatory lines including the reference to Tunstal were so added is hard to say and of no great importance anyway.

may now more accurately designate as part of Book I. There is only one point in Book I which fits our specification. In both books More's problem is to polish off the preliminary materials and get started on the substance of what he wants to deal with. In the two books, however, the substance appears under distinctly different forms—in Book II under the form of a discourse by Hythlodaeus, in Book I under the form of a dialogue among Hythlodaeus, "More," and "Giles." The natural place to look for the patchwork is just before the point where Book I assumes its characteristic form of a dialogue. The dialogue begins with Giles'[9] expression of surprise: "Why, my dear Raphael, I wonder that you do not attach yourself to some king" (55/15–16). Up to this point in Book I all communication among the characters has been set down in the form of indirect discourse. If we closely inspect the text in this area, we discover something a good bit like what we have reason to expect—a piece of literary patchwork. Only seven lines before the remark of Giles just quoted More writes: "*Now I intend to relate merely what he* [Hythlodaeus] *told us of the manners and customs of the Utopians*" (55/5–6, italics mine).

This looks like a firm commitment to start Hythlodaeus' Discourse on Utopia right away, and certainly not like a preface to a long argument about whether Hythlodaeus should become a courtier in Europe. The whole passage preceding it reinforces the commitment of this sentence. Thomas More writes that he is *not* going to relate what Hythlodaeus saw in all places where he went (52/24–26). *Some other time* he may tell about "those wise and prudent provisions which he [Hythlodaeus] noticed anywhere among nations living together in a civilized way." Hythlodaeus had talked about such things (52/1–2, 52/24—54/1); and *on another occasion*, More indicates, he hopes to take up the examples such lands afford for the correction of the errors of European realms. But not now. "Now I intend . . .," and so on (54/5–6). Except, of course, that the dialogue which follows *does not* do what More says he intends; on the contrary, it *does* in part what he says he does not intend. For pages, we hear nothing whatever about Utopia, while we do hear about three other peoples—the Achorians (88–90), the Macarians (96), and the Polylerites (74–78)—whose good institutions are specifically offered as models for Europeans to follow in correcting the defects of their own lands.

[9] In the body of the above essay, no direct attempt has been made to distinguish between "More" and "Giles," the fictitious characters in *Utopia*, and Thomas More and Peter Giles, the actual persons. The reader will note, however, that where the text itself is being quoted or paraphrased, and an opinion *in that context* is referred to as More's, I by no means intend to suggest that Thomas More would necessarily have agreed in actuality with that opinion. On the other hand, in the purely biographical sections, statements regarding Thomas More can be assumed to refer to the historical person.

The passage (54/6–12) by which More slips away from his immediately previous commitment, "right now (*nunc*) . . . to relate merely what [Hythlodaeus] told us of the manners and customs of the Utopians" (55/58), follows hard on that commitment.

First, however, he says he will:

> give the talk which drew and led him [Hythlodaeus] on to mention that commonwealth. Raphael had touched with much wisdom on faults in this hemisphere and that, of which he found very many in both, and had compared the wiser measures that had been taken among us as well as among them; for he remembered the manners and customs of each nation as if he had lived all his life in places which he had only visited (55/6–14).

Then Peter Giles expresses his surprise that Raphael is not serving as councilor to a prince, and a dialogue gets under way.

Once one considers the probability that the interposition of Giles' comment marks the beginning of what More wrote on his return to London, the difference between that section and what he wrote in the Netherlands is evident.[10] The difference is both formal and substantive. Formally, what he wrote in the Netherlands is a loose-knit discourse with a prefatory introduction. What he wrote in England is dialogue in the Platonic mode. Substantially, the former is a discursive description of the Utopian commonwealth. With one digression—a dialogue within a dialogue—to describe the condition of English society (60–84), the latter is a tight-knit dialectic exploration of the problem of counseling princes in sixteenth-century Europe.

So far, then, we have three sections of *Utopia*—an Introduction written in the Netherlands, a Dialogue of Counsel written later in England, and a Discourse on Utopia written in the Netherlands. This leaves three sections to consider—the Exordium which concludes Book I and introduces the Discourse in Book II (102–108), the Peroration at the close of the Discourse (236–44), and the Conclusion (244–46), both in Book II. The Exordium is continuous with and refers to the Dialogue, which was written in England, so it, too, must have been written in England. And so was the brief Conclusion which ends *Utopia*. In it More remembers Hythlodaeus' previously expressed impatience with people who "thought they might not appear wise enough unless they found some fault to criticize in other men's discoveries." Since Hythlodaeus expressed this impatience in the Dialogue (56/33–58/14), the conclusion must have been written after the Dialogue, that is, after More's return to England from his mission.

[10] For a fuller discussion, see Hermann Oncken's introduction to Gerhard Ritter's German translation of *Utopia* (Berlin, 1922), pp. 11*–12*, and J. H. Hexter, *More's "Utopia,"* pp. 18–21.

About the Peroration it is harder to be completely confident. Its tone, however, as well as its intensity is more in harmony with the Dialogue and the Exordium than with the Discourse. Indeed if we read *only* the somewhat diffuse and rambling, occasionally gay and sportive Discourse we are not wholly prepared for the sharp focus, the consistently intense tone, the steady drive of the Peroration. Only because we have read Book I and thus have already become accustomed to the forcefulness and firmness of Hythlodaeus' social grasp, do we sense no dissonance between the Peroration and the rest of *Utopia.* Moreover, a reading of the Discourse does not itself establish what it was that More thought was most important about Utopia— its way of waging war? its political organization? its philosophy? its religion? Exordium, Conclusion, and Peroration hammer away at the same point: What is most important, what is absolutely crucial, is Utopian communism. And so it seems to make sense to link the Peroration with those parts of *Utopia* with which it runs in marked parallel rather than with the Discourse, and so to assign it to later writing in London rather than earlier in the Netherlands.

Summarizing the above analysis of the structure of *Utopia*, we suggest as probable the following sequence of composition:

Netherlands	Book I	Introduction, pp. 46–58.
	Book II	Discourse on Utopia, pp. 110–236.
London	Book I	Dialogue of Counsel including the Exordium, pp. 58–108.
	Book II	Peroration and Conclusion, pp. 236–46.

From this reconstruction of the composition of *Utopia* another fact about the book, ordinarily assumed, receives further confirmation. It is that within the literary device which More employs in his setting for his book there lie some clues, inevitably obscured by the very fictitiousness of the narrator Hythlodaeus, to the actual circumstances of the writing of the book. Inferences drawn from such evidence are no doubt in varying degrees risky. Despite the risk, it is not improper to draw them, if they are in accord or not in conflict with other available evidence. This is especially so if they help to suggest a plausible account of matters where evidence on which to base such an account is otherwise lacking.

If with this in mind we look at the sections of *Utopia* written in the Netherlands, another point emerges. As they stand, the Introduction and the Discourse on Utopia fit together almost too tidily, the former flows into the latter almost too smoothly. It is hard to believe that, when More made the neat junction between the end of the Introduction and the beginning of the Discourse, he ever intended to break it open. Then what he wrote in London becomes an *unpremeditated* addition to what he wrote in the Netherlands, an afterthought in the strict sense of the word. Two other bits of evidence tend to indicate that the Dialogue may have been an afterthought. Erasmus' statement that it was written *per occasionem* and *ex tempore* suggests lack of premeditation, an element of impromptu, about the Dialogue. And finally in the letter in which More presented *Utopia* to his friend Giles, where he maintains the pretense that Raphael Hythlodaeus is an actual man, there lies a confirmation of the notion that the Dialogue was not a part of More's intention when he wrote the Discourse, or even perhaps when he left the Netherlands for home. More begins his letter, "I am almost ashamed, my dear Peter Giles, to send you this little book about the commonwealth of Utopia after almost a year when I am sure you looked for it within a month and a half." He goes on to say (38) that he was "relieved of all the labor of gathering materials" and had "to give no thought at all to their arrangement," but only "repeat what in your company I heard Raphael relate (*narratem Raphaelem*)."

This applies well enough to the Discourse on Utopia, but it ill fits the Dialogue, which was not merely a relation by Hythlodaeus. If Giles had reason to expect to see More's finished book six weeks after the latter's departure from the Netherlands, he can hardly have expected to see anything beyond the Introduction and Discourse. After all, More had to get back to England, he had to polish the manuscript, have it copied, and return it to the Netherlands. To a man settling back into the yoke of domestic and business cares a month and a half was not an especially generous allowance for the work in hand. More's letter to Giles, Erasmus' letter to Hutten, and the internal evidence of *Utopia* itself all point roughly toward the same conclusion. Giles had a right to expect to see *Utopia* again soon after More's departure from the Netherlands because he thought More was carrying thence a book for all practical purposes completed. He had a right to think so because More thought so too. When he left for home he intended the Introduction and Discourse to be such a book and had so written it. But at some later point More changed his mind. *Ex tempore* and *per occasionem* he inserted the Dialogue of Counsel and rounded off his work with the exordium, the peroration, and the conclusion.

In short, in the Netherlands More wrote a book, the *Utopia* of his first intention. Back in London, he added the portions necessary to make up the work that Erasmus saw through the press at Louvain late in 1516. These additions probably resulted from some alteration in More's circumstances or concerns, from something that he did or that happened to him in the months between his departure from the Netherlands in October 1515 and that of his book for the Netherlands in September 1516. What happened we saw in section 3 above.

APPENDIX B: More's Visit to Antwerp in 1515

Two bits of chronological information in *Utopia* pose a problem closely connected with the composition of the Discourse. At the very beginning of *Utopia*, after describing Prince Charles' delegation for the treaty on trade, More continues:

> When after one or two meetings there were certain points on which we could not agree sufficiently, they bade farewell to us for some days and left for Brussels to seek an official pronouncement from the prince.
> Meanwhile, as my business led me, I made my way to Antwerp. While I stayed there, among my other visitors . . . was Peter Giles (47/30–49/2).

After praising the character of this new-found friend, More adds that his companionship "made me less conscious than before of the separation from my home, wife, and children, to whom I was exceedingly anxious to get back, *for I had been then more than four months away*" (italics mine).

At first sight there seems to be no reason for More to be less than accurate in stating the time of his meeting with Giles, but in fact the two statements he makes on the point appear to conflict. Since he left England about May 12, 1515,[1] the second statement would with considerable probability fix the date of his meeting with Giles between September 12 and October 12. But the adjournment of the meetings with the Prince's commissioners to let those commissioners go to Brussels for instructions took place before July 21. And after that, More "in the meanwhile (*interim*)" visited Antwerp. To stretch that "meanwhile" up to a point at least fifty-four days later in order to fit it to More's other statement is to put a more than considerable strain on it. So we must still decide whether to assign More's visit to Antwerp to a time shortly after July 21 or to sometime after September 12. The latter date does not fit very well with other things we know about More's circumstances at the time. The letter in which the theologian Martin Dorp attacked Erasmus for writing *The Praise of Folly* and for translating the New Testament is dated August 27.[2] More's answer bears the date October 21, and near the end of it he says that as he

---

[1] *LP 1515–16*, 2, nos. 732, 733.
[2] Eras., *Ep.*, 2, 126.

was writing, letters had arrived from his prince recalling him.[3] We have already seen that the literary framework of *Utopia* requires the Introduction and Discourse to have been written in conjunction with each other after More had visited Peter Giles in Antwerp, that we have the credible testimony of Erasmus that they were written while More was at leisure, that by his own account More enjoyed no leisure after his return to England, and that therefore the Introduction and Discourse must have been written in the Netherlands. If we accept the dating after September 12 for More's meeting with Giles, we would allow less than forty days for him to visit Antwerp for an indefinite period, to conceive the details of the Introduction and Discourse, to write some 18,000 words of Latin in which they were composed, and at the same time to do a considerable part of the writing on the long letter to Dorp, besides taking care of whatever business (*res*, 46/29) brought him to Antwerp and winding up any business that his duties as emissary entailed. At this point the question of whether in these conditions More could be said to have written the Discourse at leisure seems to be superseded by the question whether under such circumstances and limitations of time he could have written it at all.

All these difficulties diminish if we date More's "Utopian" visit to Giles somewhere shortly after the departure of the Netherlands commissioners to get new instructions from the Prince's council, that is, about July 21. No date very much earlier will fit the evidence. From shortly after their arrival and settling in at Bruges to shortly before the July 21 recess, the English and Netherlands commissioners had been meeting frequently though fruitlessly. Up to that time all letters from members of the mission had come from Bruges, and More himself signed such a letter on July 21.[4] After July 21 the commission scattered. Richard Sampson, Wolsey's chaplain, had been included in the mission mainly to give him diplomatic immunity while he tried to transfer the revenues of the bishopric of Tournai into his master's grasping hands. So he departed for Tournai to do his duty in executing the intricate and sordid maneuvers that Wolsey was so apt at contriving when his gifts for chicanery and *force majeur* were stimulated by the prospect of power and pelf. There is nothing to show that Sampson left Tournai during the rest of More's sojourn in the Netherlands.[5] Another commissioner, Thomas Spinelly, a Florentine in the English service, did return to Bruges for more than a week in August,[6] but that busy man was buzzing all over the map to show his zeal for his employer—to Brussels or Mechlin, to London, back to Bruges, to

---

[3] *Corresp.*, p. 74.
[4] *LP 1515–16*, nos. 551, 553, 566, 581, 612, 672, 678, 679, 732, 733.
[5] Ibid., nos. 732, 769, 812, 889, 980.
[6] Ibid., nos. 818, 829, 830, 848.

Brussels again, to Antwerp.[7] Tunstal followed the Prince's commissioners to Brussels in early August and appears to have stayed there, except for a journey to Calais, at least until after More's departure.[8] Of the fourth commissioner, John Clifford, we hear nothing; but since he was governor of the English merchants in the Netherlands, he probably went about his ordinary affairs. Of the five commissioners, that leaves only More unaccounted for. From July 21, when the meetings at Bruges broke up, to October 21, when his recall came through, the only evidence about his doings beyond what we find in *Utopia* appears in a letter he wrote Erasmus several months later.[9] It indicates that he as well as the rest of the English commissioners left Bruges at about the time that Prince Charles' commissioners required a recess—that is, late in July. He had gone to Tournai for a while to see if he could wangle for Erasmus the benefice Wolsey had promised him. There is no sign that he accompanied Tunstal to Brussels, where negotiations on the trade treaty seem to have been limping along informally. He signs no surviving letters from there, and no letters from Brussels, Antwerp, Tournai, or Bruges mention him. To all appearances he was left with nothing at all official to do; if ever a man had leisure More had it after July 21. That he used it to go to Antwerp on business and pleasure is what he says in *Utopia*. The probability that he did so shortly after July 21 is enhanced by the fact that while Erasmus and More were both still in London the former had written Giles about his friend's impending mission.[10] Then in June Erasmus had successively seen his two friends within a few days in Bruges and Antwerp on his way through the Netherlands to Basel[11] and thus was offered a second opportunity to urge both to meet each other. Given More's freedom from ambassadorial duties in July and his business in Antwerp, there seems no reason why he should have delayed his visit until sometime between mid-September and mid-October. And, of course, if he made Giles' acquaintance shortly after July 21, he would have had nearly three months instead of one in which to write the Discourse.

If for More's meeting with Giles we provisionally accept the earlier date indicated in *Utopia*, we still need to explain the presence in the text of the later date fixed by More's assertion that he had been away from his family four months when he saw Giles. It is not, in fact, very difficult to propose a plausible explanation, if we consider the purpose or purposes of the prefatory sentences which include *both* dates for

[7] Ibid., nos. 686, 794, 818, 880, 1012.
[8] Ibid., nos. 782, 904, 981, 1047.
[9] Eras., *Ep.*, 2, 194.
[10] Ibid., 2, 68.
[11] Ibid., 2, 90, 113, 151, 194.

the meeting and set the stage for what follows in *Utopia*. One of their purposes is precisely that—to set the stage. The other is to compliment several of the men with whom in one way or another More came into close contact as a consequence of the mission. It was especially his purpose to commemorate his friendship with and warm affection for Peter Giles. It was not at all the purpose of these sentences to provide an exact and accurate historical account of the Netherlands mission; if, in fact, More made more than one visit to Giles in Antwerp, there was no need for him to say so in his prefatory remarks, since the omission would never bother anybody but a scholar, four hundred years later, trying to reconstruct the history of *Utopia*'s composition. As a matter of literary convenience More may simply have telescoped two visits.[12] Even beyond his evident affection for Giles, More may well have had good reasons for wanting to see his friend again in September 1515. Dorp's letter against Erasmus' work was out,[13] and Giles, another intimate of Erasmus, would be a good man with whom to talk over the desirability of answering it. Indeed, if the answer was partly done, he could be shown that part. And if the Discourse on Utopia was partly written he could be shown that too. If he was shown the Discourse almost complete, a self-contained work, Giles had good reason to expect to see *Utopia* ready for publication soon after More got back to England, as More suggests he did in the letter to Giles which goes before *Utopia*. This appears to one scholar the most plausible and probable reconstruction of what actually happened.

---

[12] More was not in any case beset by any consuming passion for chronological accuracy. Already in February 1516, in telling Erasmus about the length of his Netherlands mission, he said it was "more than six months," when in fact it was a little more than five (Eras., *Ep.*, 2, 195–96).

[13] It is dated August 27, 1515 (Eras., *Ep.*, 2, 126).

*C*HAPTER III The Predatory Vision: Niccolò Machiavelli. *Il Principe* and *lo stato**

A scholar who has given much of his life to the study of Machiavelli and Machiavellianism, Prof. Giuseppe Prezzolini, once observed that Machiavelli himself is partly responsible for the weird interpretations of which he has been victim, "because he did not take pains to express himself in a systematic form and with a coherent vocabulary. His way of writing is cited in the history of Italian literature for its perspicuity, simplicity, absence of rhetoric. But it could not be cited for its precision . . . Machiavelli *uses the same word for different concepts and expresses the same concepts with different words*."[1] Prezzolini offers confirmation for his remarks from the corroborative reports of other explorers who wore themselves out slogging through the swamp of Machiavelli's vocabulary. In 1907, for example, Schmidt remarked in his *Niccolò Machiavelli und die Allgemeine Staatslehre der Gegenwart*, "Negligence about terminology attains its peak in Machiavelli."[2] And in 1923 Condorelli noted, "Machiavelli has carried carelessness about the terminology of jurisprudence to such a point that more than once it is difficult or rather impossible for the scholar to penetrate his thought."[3]

The peculiarly inconsistent tales that explorers of Machiavelli's vocabulary have come back with justify Prezzolini's dispiriting account

---

* See "A Note on Citations."
[1] Giuseppe Prezzolini, *Machiavelli Anticristo* (Rome, 1954), p. 3. Italics mine.
[2] Quoted in Prezzolini, p. 4.
[3] Ibid.

of the difficulties and eccentricities of the terrain.[4] For although most reports agree on what the main points of interest *are*—*virtù, fortuna, necessità, libertà, stato*—there is no such consensus as to what those points *are like*. The differences of opinion are indeed so considerable that one is reminded of the trouble the blind men had with the elephant. Yet one is reluctant to accept counsels of despair. For it would seem that if one cannot make sense of the main symbols which Machiavelli or any other man uses to express his thought, then one simply cannot understand what he is talking about, since after all they are the symbols he especially chose to convey what he had in mind. In any case it seems to me that to give the thing up without another try is to throw in the sponge prematurely. In the case of a writer like Machiavelli one has at least no problem of rhetorical verbosity. Rarely indeed does he pile up words out of sheer affection for sound effects. One can feel quite sure almost all the time that when he uses a word, he does so to indicate something he has in mind, and not merely to provide a pleasing tintinnabulation in the reader's inner ear. But if he does indeed have something in mind when he uses words, particularly when he uses the words that provide the ossature of his writing, then with respect to each occurrence of such a word the

---

[4] Several writers have tried to come to grips with Machiavelli's terminology or with certain key words in his vocabulary. There are only two works that attempt to deal comprehensively with his use of language, Fredi Chiappelli, *Studi sul linguagio del Machiavelli* (Florence, 1952), and John di Sciullo, *Il vocabolario politico di Niccolò Machiavelli* (M.A. thesis, Columbia University, 1950). The latter work provides handy examples, drawn from all Machiavelli's works, of the uses of the most important substantives in Machiavelli's political vocabulary. Mr. di Sciullo, however, has been too easily satisfied to pigeonhole those substantives in compartments provided by a modern Italian dictionary, a procedure which obscures the ambiguities in Machiavelli's language and gives an appearance of exactitude and fine distinction to his terminology which it did not always possess. Moreover, by concentrating entirely on substantives and omitting verbs and modifiers, di Sciullo misses the environment, as it were, that determines the complexion of the substantives. Chiappelli alone among those who have written on Machiavelli's use of words has paid some heed to his verbs and modifiers. Other writers have concentrated their attention on a few recurrent and key words in Machiavelli's writings, especially on *virtù, fortuna, necessità*, and *stato*. Among the most important works treating one or several of these words are Friedrich Meinecke, *Die Idee der Staatsräson in der neuren Geschichte* (3d ed., Munich, 1929), pp. 39–56; Francesco Ercole, *La politica di Machiavelli* (Rome, 1926), pp. 20–196; J. H. Whitfield, *Machiavelli* (Oxford, 1947), pp. 92–105; ibid., "On Machiavelli's use of *ordini*," *Italian Studies*, X (1955), 19–39; E. W. Mayer, *Machiavellis Geschichtsauffassung und sein begriff* 'Virtù' (Munich, 1912), *passim*; Grazio Condorelli, "Per la storia del nome 'Stato' (il nome 'stato' in Machiavelli)," *Archivio Giuridico* LXXXIX (1923), 223–35; XC (1923), 77–112. A. L. Burd in his excellent edition of *Il Principe* (Oxford, 1891) has included in his notes comments on several of the key words in that work. Some observations by Felix Gilbert and Loren C. MacKinney on the meaning of *virtù* in Machiavelli will be found in *Renaissance News* IV (1951), 53–55, and V (1952), 21–23.

reader will find himself in one of three positions: (a) by the context in which the word appears he will be able to determine pretty accurately what Machiavelli had in mind; or (b) on the same basis he will be able to determine roughly what Machiavelli had in mind; or (c) he will not be able to determine what Machiavelli had in mind. If the third alternative were found to hold with great regularity in Machiavelli's writings we had as well pack up our kit of erudition and go elsewhere because then it would be quite impossible ever to find out what Machiavelli was talking about. If, however, the other two alternatives are the predominant ones, then it would seem that a thorough and careful analysis of the meanings he assigned to certain key words would provide as good a clue as any to his central preoccupations and to his specific notions. And this is true whether he uses the words consistently or not.

Now one of the most important words in Machiavelli's writings— one of the words he puts down in very crucial places to indicate what he has in mind—is *lo stato*. Because the rise of the modern state is one of the half-dozen central themes in the history of the Western world during the past five centuries, Machiavelli's frequent reliance on *lo stato* as a verbal symbol assumes special significance for historians of civilization. Although the history of the word in its various European forms—*status, lo stato, l'état, der Staat, el estado*, the state—has never been fully explored,[5] it seems fairly clear that at the beginning of the fifteenth century the term was not used in its modern political sense in any Western European language and that by the seventeenth century it was frequently so used in all of them. The emergence of the actual historical phenomenon of the modern state therefore roughly coincides with the emergence of the term universally applied to it. The idea widely entertained that Machiavelli is the first truly modern political thinker has therefore lent particular piquancy to his obvious enamorment with the word *lo stato*. The question naturally raised by Machiavelli's frequent recourse to the word is this: when Machiavelli uses the term *lo stato*, does he have in mind the modern state?[6]

Most of the discussions with respect to the use of the term *lo stato* in Machiavelli's writings have in fact focused on this problem. Yet, although the question is a natural one, it is also a bad one. For, looked at one way, the answer is so obviously "no" that the question need hardly have been asked. A fully and precisely elaborated juridical conception of the state was hammered out by lawyers and publicists in

[5] There are some indications on the use of the term before Machiavelli's time in Mayer, pp. 108–109, Ercole, pp. 67–72, and Condorelli, pp. 77–112.

[6] This is essentially the question recently posed and answered in the affirmative by Fredi Chiappelli, a careful student of Machiavelli's traits of style and expression. For analysis of the consequences of starting with this *question mal posée*, see Appendix A.

the years *after* Machiavelli's death. Their conception was sharpened and defined by controveries that Machiavelli knew nothing of, especially the controversy about the extent of the authority of Europe's secular governing bodies over the religious practices of their respective subjects. Machiavelli stands at or even before the beginning of this juridical process of definition.[7]

Yet this "no" answer is surely unsatisfactory. For if Machiavelli did not have the modern juridical conception of the state in mind because he could not, most people who talk about the state today do not have the modern juridical conception of the state in mind either, although they could. In fact it is doubtful if the term is very often used today with a full sense of its juridical complexity except by international and constitutional lawyers. And yet the term is on everyone's lips in every country in the Western world. And however varied the shades of significance today casually ascribed to the "state" in its political sense, they have at least this *negative* trait in common: they rarely if ever have *any* of the political meanings that *status* and its Romance and Germanic derivatives usually had for men before the fifteenth century. So we might better pose the question, "Did Machiavelli use *lo stato* in any or many of the various senses in which we use 'the state'?" But there is perhaps a better way still. Instead of trying to hook Machiavelli's language to our own, let us permit him to speak to us in his own language; let us simply ask, "In what senses, and with what significations, does Machiavelli in fact use the term *lo stato*?"

To the question so posed a method of finding the answer immediately suggests itself. We can go through Machiavelli's works and try to decipher from the context in which we find *lo stato* the various senses in which Machiavelli used the word. Yet this happily innocent approach has a serious drawback. For if we work this way, then every signification of the word will appear to have the same importance as every other. Yet it is surely obvious that if Machiavelli uses *lo stato* in one sense once and in another a hundred times, then for him the latter sense is considerably more important than the former. A far more desirable alternative would be to collect all the uses of *lo stato* in *Tutte le opere* and find which ones Machiavelli leaned toward most heavily. But here, alas, the life expectancy, the intellectual interests, and the capacity for sustaining boredom of the author of this study combine to interpose an insuperable barrier. It would take too long, I have other things to do, and the process would bore me to death. There remains a third compromise alternative—that of a study at

[7] For the hammering out of a juridical conception of the state in the sixteenth century, besides general treatises on political theory, see J. W. Allen, *A History of Political Thought in the Sixteenth Century* (London, 1960), and W. F. Church, *Constitutional Thought in Sixteenth-Century France* (Cambridge, Mass., 1941).

once exhaustive and limited. This involves studying Machiavelli's use of *lo stato* only in a single important work, but examining *every* use in that work. It is this kind of exhaustive and limited study that I have undertaken. For this purpose I have chosen *Il Principe*, partly because it is one of the two most important political writings of Machiavelli and partly because it is a great deal shorter than the other, the *Discorsi*.

A fairly painstaking working over of *Il Principe* has dredged up 115 occurrences of *lo stato* (or its plural form). In a work scarcely 15,000 words long and full of concrete narrative *exempla*, this is a quite heavy frequency for a term at least quasi-technical in character. These 115 uses of *lo stato* are widely though somewhat unevenly distributed throughout *Il Principe* in the dedication and 21 of the 26 chapters.[8]

It is instructive to compare Machiavelli's use of *lo stato* with the various meanings of that term and its equivalents current in the Middle Ages.[9] During the medieval centuries *status* and its derivatives in the vulgar tongues tended to cling fairly close to a matrix that emphasized the notion of being established, fixed, permanent. Most generally it bore the implication of a fixed or definite *condition*, a meaning that survives in our phrase "man's estate," and, in view of the contemporary *mores* somewhat anomalously, in the phrase "the state of matrimony." When put to social use in the Middle Ages *status* ordinarily signified *social* condition, place in the social order, rank. A man was of *haut, moyen*, or *bas état*, of high, middle, or low rank, depending on his wealth and prestige and the social acceptability of his way of living. In a society in which a passion for legal prescription and definition paralleled, if it did not seriously temper, a native proclivity toward violence and in which custom quickly became transformed into law, the social condition or *status* or estate of individuals and especially of groups could more or less accurately be described by the cluster of legal duties to which they were subject and of legal privileges which they enjoyed.

---

[8] Both the number of editions of *Il Principe* in general use and the monstrous elaboration of apparatus that full documentation of this study would demand have led me to limit my *general* indications on the occurrences of *lo stato* to the list in Appendix B, where the number of occurrences in each chapter and in each column in the Mazzoni and Casella edition of *Tutte le opere . . . di Niccolò Machiavelli* (Florence, 1929) is given in tabular form. Each quotation is identified in a footnote which gives *first* the chapter of *Il Principe* and *second* the page and column in Mazzoni and Casella, e.g., 1: 5a. See also "A Note on Citations."

[9] The following three paragraphs on the use of *lo stato* and its equivalents in the Middle Ages are based on the studies of Condorelli and Ercole cited in n. 4, on the dictionaries of Tommaseo, La Curne de Ste. Palaye, and Godefroy, on du Cange, on the *Oxford English Dictionary*, and on such impressions as the present writer has picked up from his reading.

This led *status* toward the first of its medieval political meanings. The duties and privileges of princes were sufficiently different from those of other men to require separate legal definition. So the law came to speak of the estate, *l'état*, *lo stato* of the prince—king, duke, or other. Now the legal duties and privileges of the various conditions or orders or estates of men were theoretically at least concomitants of their social function; they provided the defined sphere of obligations and rights allotted to the various orders of men so that they might perform the tasks, necessary to the welfare of the social whole, to which God had called them. Like all callings, the calling of the princes came from God, but it was by virtue of the very function of the prince a call to authority, to rule. So the legal definition of the prince's *status* took the form of a bundle of rights and duties with respect to ruling, what the English were fond of calling the royal prerogative. This bundle defined what the prince *did* as a ruler; put into practice it described—in a sense, was—the government of his principality. So the *status, lo stato*, the estate of the prince came close to identification with the political governing of his principality.

Status, however, acquired a second political meaning during the Middle Ages. Just as the prince had an estate, or *status*, the principality itself was always in a certain condition or *status*, a signification of the word still preserved in America in the regular presidential report to Congress on "the state of the union." As early as 1258 a ruler speaks of taking the lead in rectifying the *status regni nostri per concilium fidelium*. About a century thereafter the use of the term in connection with a body politic had come at times to refer to its *fundamental condition*, its constant ordering, its constitution, and Giovanni Villani speaks of one who aimed to *tradire il popolo e sovertire lo stato della città*. So by the fifteenth century *status* and its vulgar derivatives had acquired two strictly political senses, one of which focused on the ruler and the acts of ruling, the other on the order, political structure, way of life of the ruled.

The first significant fact about Machiavelli's use of the word *stato* in *Il Principe* is that he very rarely indeed employed it in the broad inclusive sense, very frequent in the Middle Ages, of conditions in general—the notion we have in mind when we say, "Here's a pretty state of things." The second significant fact is that Machiavelli used *lo stato* just as infrequently in the extended medieval social meaning of rank or degree within the social hierarchy of privileges, duty, honor, and prestige. With but few exceptions where Machiavelli talked about *lo stato* in *Il Principe* it was in a narrowly political sense. The subject of his discourse lay in the general orbit of the ruler and the ruled in a principality or a republic. In fact, of the 115 occurrences of *lo stato* in *Il Principe* only five at most, an insignificant fraction of the whole,

clearly fall outside that narrow ambit. However hard it may be to
specify *exactly* what Machiavelli had in mind each of the other 110
times he spoke of *lo stato*, he had in mind something that lay in the
sphere of either the *status regis* or the *status regni*, in the senses that
those two phrases had acquired in the later Middle Ages.

If we approach these remaining 110 occurrences of *lo stato* without
preconceived notions or a tidy rationally elaborated scheme, if we
simply collect and scan these occurrences in their contexts, we can
save ourselves a good bit of time and trouble. For if we do so, the
one thing that almost violently thrusts itself on our attention is a
thing that no previously elaborated plan would be likely to take into
account. It is the remarkable frequency with which *lo stato* occurs in
association with five verbs—*acquistare, tenere, mantenere, togliere,
perdere*: to acquire, to hold, to maintain, to take away, to lose. In fact
it appears in conjunction with one or another of these verbs no less
than thirty-five times. Or putting it another way, over thirty per cent
of the times that Machiavelli used the term *lo stato* in *Il Principe*, he
used it with *acquistare, tenere, mantenere, togliere, perdere*. Nor is this
all. Today we might frequently speak of a state *acquiring* territory,
holding prisoners, *maintaining* a legal position, *taking away* property,
losing a possession. Now the curious thing is that not even once in
Il Principe does Machiavelli speak of *lo stato* doing any of these
things. *Lo stato* does not acquire, or hold, or maintain, or take away,
or lose anything or any one. With those verbs it is *never* the active
subject, it is *always* passive or the object: someone *always* acquires
it, holds it, maintains it, takes it away, loses it.

In the five-word cluster we have been examining, one at first sight
seems a bit of a maverick. *Acquistare, tenere, togliere, perdere* somehow have a common feel. Without going into detail on a matter that
must be reserved for later discussion we may say that by and large
they suggest acts that a man does primarily on his own account, for
himself. Thus in ordinary discourse if someone tells us that he has
acquired something, holds it, has taken it away, or has lost it, we
assume, unless it is clearly specified otherwise, that he has done these
things for himself, not for the sake of someone else, certainly not for
the sake of the thing acquired, held, or taken. Roughly we might describe these verbs as words with an exploitative tonality. To "maintain"
or "support," however, rather suggests something that one does not
only *to* someone or something else but *for* someone or something else.
But in this instance appearances are deceptive. In fact, as used by
Machiavelli in *Il Principe* and commonly at the time by other writers,
the verb *mantenere* does not connote an act of giving. It stands well
away from the present-day meaning of *maintain*: to uphold, to sup-

port. This is unmistakably clear in three of the instances in which *lo stato* is coupled with *mantenere*.

"In hereditary *stati*," says Machiavelli, ". . . there is considerably less difficulty in maintaining them than in new ones . . . so that if a prince has ordinary industry he will always *maintain himself in his* stato."[10] And again: "If the prince wants to maintain *lo stato* he is often forced not to be good, because when that faction . . . which you judge that you need *in order to maintain yourself* is corrupt, you had better adapt yourself to its humor in order to satisfy it."[11] Machiavelli's line of thought here is easy enough to follow. He does not distinguish at all between the prince maintaining *lo stato* and the prince maintaining himself in *lo stato* or simply maintaining himself. *Mantenere* retains its etymological significance: to hold in hand. Hereafter if we have reason to translate the phrase *mantenere lo stato* we shall render it, for the sake of accuracy, "keep *lo stato* in hand," or "keep a grip on *lo stato*," for, as it occurs in *Il Principe*, *mantenere* is clearly just as exploitative as *acquistare, tenere, togliere*, and *perdere*.

Once we have entered this line of investigation by way of our five-word group, we are bound to continue beyond it, for they are merely the more prosperous senior members of a large family; those five verbs are not the only ones by means of which it is possible to express what we have called an exploitative relation vis-à-vis *lo stato*. If we look in *Il Principe* for other members of that family conjoined with *lo stato*, we have no trouble finding them. We find *aggiungere* (twice), *assaltare, disarmare, guadagnare, nuocere, occupare* (twice), *possedere, concedere, pigliare, prendere, riperdere, recuperare, rendersi sicuro in, rimanere sicuro*. Each of these verbs appears with *lo stato*, and, as in all cases with our initial five-word group so in each case here, *lo stato* is passive or the object; never is it the acting subject. Besides acquiring, holding, keeping in hand, taking away, and losing *lo stato*, a man may add to it, assault it, disarm it, win it, injure it, occupy it, possess it, concede it, seize it, take it, reluse it, regain it, render himself secure in it, remain secure in it. These are all things that men can do to *lo stato*. There is nothing to suggest that *lo stato* does or for that matter can do any of these things to anyone or to anything. So we add sixteen exploitative uses of *lo stato* to our previous thirty-five. The end is not yet.

All of the verb forms just examined seem obviously to belong to the exploitative *acquistare-tenere-mantenere-togliere-perdere* clan: they wear the tartan conspicuously enough. There are others that do not flaunt their connection; yet the relationship is not hard to discern if

[10] 2; 5b. Italics mine.
[11] 19; 38a–b. Italics mine.

one examines the words with some care. To *save* the *state*, for example, surely sounds like an unexploitative act; but is it unexploitative to *salvare lo stato*? Machiavelli says that a prince must not mind incurring "infamy for the vices without which he could only with difficulty *salvare lo stato*."[12] This seems to have an air of heroism; it seems to say that the true patriot will sacrifice his very good fame for the salvation of his state or country. *Dulce et decorum est pro patria peccare.* But is that what Machiavelli really means? Let us read what he is saying about "saving" *lo stato* in context. "A prince must not mind incurring the infamy of vices without which he could only with difficulty *salvare lo stato*, for a certain thing may appear to be a virtue, and following it would ruin *him*, and some other may appear to be a vice, and following it he achieves *his own* security and well-being."[13] It is evident that as in the case of *mantenere* so in that of *salvare* we were taken in not by what Machiavelli said but by our own predisposition to inject our sense of "the state" into Machiavelli's *lo stato*. In *Il Principe* in conjunction with *lo stato*, *salvare* does not mean to save or rescue it; it means just what *mantenere* and *tenere* mean—to keep one's grasp on it. One saves *lo stato* not for *itself*, but for *oneself*.

The only complication about *avere*, to have, is its simplicity; it is such a common, inconspicuous little verb that one pays little attention to it. When we do notice it, however, its ordinary affiliation is apparent, as the following examples demonstrate:

"Barons like these *have stati* and subjects of their own."[14]
The question is "whether a prince *has* enough *stato* so that if necessary he can defend himself by himself."[15]
The Venetians "in the beginning of their expansion on land did not have much to fear from their captains because they did not *have* much *stato* there, and they had a big reputation."[16]
Philip of Macedon "did not *have* much *stato* compared to the greatness of the Romans and Greeks attacking him."[17]

To *avere lo stato* is simply to *tenere lo stato*, just as in the marriage service to have and to hold one's spouse are one and the same thing.

Now before going on with our exploration we had better pause to see how far we have got. The answer is that we have got past the middle. We eliminated five occurrences of *lo stato*, and of the 110

[12] 15; 31a.
[13] Ibid. Italics mine.
[14] 4; 10b. Italics mine.
[15] 10; 22a. Italics mine.
[16] 12; 26b. Italics mine.
[17] 24; 47b. Italics mine.

remaining occurrences we have now investigated 57—and we still have not got beyond the shadow of the word group we started with: *acquistare-tenere-mantenere-togliere-perdere*. And the uniformity we noticed at the beginning has persisted down to this point where we have exhausted over half of the occurrences of the word in *Il Principe*: more than half the time in *Il Principe lo stato* does nothing whatever; it is passive; it is the object of action, never the active subject. Finally the action of which *lo stato* is the object is almost always the kind we have called exploitative; it manipulates and manages *lo stato* for the benefit of him who is in control or wants to be in control.

Having gone this far in checking the verb-company *lo stato* keeps in *Il Principe*, we may as well run out the string. Well, *lo stato* appears in close company with other verbs only about twenty-six more times in *Il Principe*. On the fairly rare occasions when it is not being exploited by someone it is likely to be being bossed by someone (*insignorare, reggere, governare, ordinare*); or created or increased by someone (*creare, accrescere, ampliare*); or defended and conserved by someone (*defendere, conservare*). Except for a few odds and ends that is the sum of what is done to *lo stato* in *Il Principe*. And while all these things are being done to it, what is *lo stato* doing? Really very little. *Lo stato* shows up as the active subject of a verb just about seven or eight times in the whole of *Il Principe*, and then its activity does not come to much. It seems symbolic of its passivity even in the active voice that on the only occasion when Machiavelli uses *lo stato* as subject of a good violent verb *ribellarsi* it is to tell us about a *stato* that did *not* rebel.[18] So *lo stato* deploys its anemic activity in about one-twelfth of the instances in which it occurs in *Il Principe* conjoined with a verb. In the remaining eleven-twelfths someone is doing something to *lo stato*, and in three-quarters of those instances what the someone is doing is rather exploitative.

The figures adduced above may seem reasonably impressive. Actually they do only partial justice to the situation. That situation is obscured in part by a grammatical fog. Frequently the verb to which *lo stato* is immediately conjoined is not clearly exploitative, and yet the general sense of the argument is concerned with *lo stato* from a strictly exploitative point of view. Consider, for example, the following passage:

When those *stati* that are acquired . . . are accustomed to live according to their own laws and in liberty there are three methods available to him who wishes to hold (*tenere*) them; . . . the third . . . [is] creating among them *uno stato di pochi*. For the *stato*, created by a prince, knows that

[18] 4; 10a.

it cannot survive without his friendship . . . and a city accustomed to live freely *si tiene* more easily by means of its citizens. . . . The Spartans *tennono* Athens and Thebes by creating a *stato di pochi* of them.[19]

Now the verbs that *lo stato* grammatically belongs to in the last three cases are *creare, sapere,* and *creare.* Grammatically *lo stato* does not go with *tenere* at all; but *tenere* remains the heart of the matter; each sentence in the selection is wholly devoted to ways of *holding* a *stato* accustomed to living by its own laws.

This situation suggests a reclassification of Machiavelli's use of *lo stato* in *Il Principe* that will circumvent the artificiality of a strict grammatical approach. Let us ask how often *lo stato* occurs *in the same sentence* with an exploitative verb, in such a way that, as in the example given above, *lo stato* is *in fact,* even if not in grammar, the object of that verb. The verbs to be considered exploitative are those that we have already so classified. If there are two such verbs in the same sentence we will give preference to the one in the *acquistare-man-tenere-tenere-togliere-perdere* group.

When we examine the 110 occurrences of *lo stato* in a political sense, employing the set of ground rules just proposed, the results are rather startling. More than *seven out of every ten times* that *lo stato* so occurs in *Il Principe* one of the exploitative verbs controls it. It appears under such control *more than twice, almost two and a half times, as often as it appears in all other ways.* In over one-half of all its occurrences in a political sense, 61 out of 110, it is controlled by *acquistare, man-tenere, tenere, perdere,* and *togliere.* It is primarily involved in being acquired, kept in hand, held, lost, or taken away, *almost twice as often* as the total number of times that it occurs without an exploitative verb. Thus before we have even had to ask precisely what *lo stato* denotes for Machiavelli we have discovered something of fundamental significance about its function in *Il Principe.* Whatever *lo stato* denotes (whether indeed it has a precise unambiguous denotation or not), it functions in *Il Principe* primarily as the object of political exploitation.

Now at the outset of this chapter we indicated that some scholars found that Machiavelli was not at all consistent in his use of his key words. And we had to acknowledge that in a sense this was true. But our investigation of *lo stato* suggests that perhaps in this case those scholars have been looking for the *wrong kind* of consistency. Postulating at the very outset that Machiavelli was *not* technically a political philosopher and *not* a professor of jurisprudence, they have then proceeded to look for the kind of consistency with respect to the

[19] 5; 12a.

word *lo stato* that one might hope for in the works of a political philosopher or a professor of jurisprudence. Under the circumstances their surprise at not finding that kind of consistency seems almost disingenuous, a little like the surprise of the card sharps who come up with four aces. After all, they are dealing from a cold deck.

By a method about as empirical and inductive as a method can get and still have any coherence at all, we have stumbled upon a very distinct consistency in Machiavelli's use of the key word *lo stato* in *Il Principe*. But it is not the consistency of a political philosopher or a professor of jurisprudence; it does not hinge on a finicking care to have *lo stato* always and clearly denote a single unambiguous thing or at the worst two or three things that in context could never possibly be confused with one another by Machiavelli or anyone else. In fact, if one tries to make sense of *lo stato* in *Il Principe* in terms of its denotations one jeopardizes one's sanity. Sometimes it seems to mean the people: *lo stato* is governed. Sometimes it seems to mean the land: in France some baron can always be counted upon to open the road to *lo stato* to an enemy.[20] Sometimes it seems to mean the land and the people: the Venetians wanted to win half *lo stato* of Lombardy.[21] Sometimes it seems to mean resources in general: it is important to know if the prince has enough *stato* to defend himself.[22] Sometimes it means the ruling class: the Spartans created *uno stato di pochi* in Thebes.[23] Sometimes it seems to mean the government apart from the people: the people need *lo stato*, and *lo stato* needs the people.[24] Sometimes it seems to mean people, land, and government taken together: Italy is divided into *più stati*.[25] Just once *lo stato* "has command"; ordinarily it is ruled. And so on. But clearly this way madness lies; the awful truth is that for most of the occurrences of *lo stato* in *Il Principe* it is quite impossible to tell whether it has none, or one, or several, or all of these possible denotative meanings. For most of the time *lo stato* simply lies about indecently passive and quite nude, bare of the slightest vestige of modest descriptive or denotative covering, being acquired, or held, or kept, or had, or taken away, or lost by somebody.

And that, of course, is the consistency that really matters as against the inconsistency that did not matter in the least to Machiavelli and should not matter to anyone else. The consistency rests not in a clearly specified and continuously adhered-to denotation for *lo stato*, but in

[20] 4; 11a.
[21] 3; 8b.
[22] 10; 22a.
[23] 5; 12a.
[24] 9; 22a.
[25] 12; 26b.

an extraordinarily consistent attitude toward it; and that attitude is exploitative.

Machiavelli said emphatically that what he wanted to do was to go right straight to the *verità effettuale della cosa*.[26] We of a slightly less self-confident era may at once admire and smile at Machiavelli's bold certitude that effective truth is so easy to come by and that the road to it is straight away. But we may be quite sure that if he had noticed what he was doing, he would not have felt it mattered a fig as far as the effective truth of the matter was concerned that he sometimes talked as if *lo stato* were the people, sometimes the government, sometimes both, or something else. The effectual truth, the truth that counts, the only truth that matters to Machiavelli in *Il Principe*, the only truth that should matter to the prince himself, is whether the prince wins out, keeps what he has, holds *lo stato*, or loses out, loses what he had, loses *lo stato*.

In fact it is not very hard to understand why Machiavelli slips so insouciantly from one ostensible meaning of *lo stato* to another. One of the rare instances in *Il Principe* in which *lo stato* is not object but subject clears up the difficulty. It is the very first sentence in the treatise.

> Tutti gli stati tutti e' dominii che hanno avuto e hanno imperio sopra gli uomini, sono stati e sono o republiche o principati.[27]
>
> (All *stati*, all dominations that have had and have political command over men have been and are either republics or principalities.)

So what a prince has is a principality, and a principality is a *stato*; and what a *stato* has, that without which it ceases to be a *stato*, is political command, *imperio*, over men. If the people do not obey, the prince has no real command, and in effective truth he does not hold *lo stato*. If the people obey, but the real command is that of another, the prince in effective truth does not hold *lo stato* either.

It is because of his concern with what he regards as the effective truth of the matter that in *Il Principe* Machiavelli uses *lo stato* in one way that must seem alien and unintelligible to anyone who reads it with any presently current uses of the word "state" in mind. For with such uses in mind what can we make of Machiavelli's problem of whether a prince has enough *stato*, much *stato*.[28] For us a state is a state is a state. But to Machiavelli the notion of enough *stato* makes perfectly good sense. When the prince has *lo stato*, he has what *lo stato*

---

[26] 15; 30b.
[27] 1; 5a.
[28] E.g., 10; 22a and 24; 47b.

confers: command over men. If he does not have command over
enough men or if his command is not effective enough, he stands in
constant danger of losing whatever command over men he has, of
having *lo stato* taken away from him. And if he loses all of his command over men that is the best possible evidence that he did not
have enough command, or enough men, enough *stato* in the first place.

Again before advancing further we had better follow the sound
military principle of consolidating our present gains. It seems to me
they are substantial and that they are unlikely to be reversed in the
sequel. For what we have discovered is what Machiavelli persistently
and dominantly had in mind when he set down the word *stato* in *Il
Principe*; we have discovered, as it were, the angle of view from which
he regarded and considered that word. Persistently and dominantly
he had in mind political command over men, and his angle of vision
was that of the prince concerned to do what was necessary to acquire
and hold *lo stato*, to avoid losing it or having it taken away from him.
We have now to inquire whether Machiavelli ever had anything else
in mind when he spoke of *lo stato* in *Il Principe*, whether he ever
shifted his angle of vision. But before we do so, we ourselves need to
keep two points in mind. Whatever we find cannot cancel out what
we have already found: that the predominance and persistence of
the pattern we have just described suffuses the whole of *Il Principe*.
If by any chance once in a while Machiavelli did have something
else in mind when he wrote down the word *lo stato*, he did not have
it in mind very often or very long. In the second place it seems to me
we have established for ourselves a right to a prejudice, or, to put it
more respectably, established a presumption in favor of one signification for *lo stato* as against any and all others. This means that if
we run into a doubtful or ambiguous case or two we may hesitate to
resolve them in favor of the dominant signification, but we should
doubly hesitate to resolve them some other way, for which, in the
nature of the case, the presumption is bound to be a great deal weaker.

If in any instances in *Il Principe* Machiavelli regarded *lo stato* un-
exploitatively it must be among those thirty-two occurrences of the
term in which an exploitative verb does not control it. Now in a few
of these uses the exploitative element is unmistakable even though
the environing sentence does not happen to include an exploitative
verb. Such, for instance, is the sentence in which Machiavelli recommends that among newly conquered people the prince settle colonists
to act as "fetters to the *stato*."[29] Mostly the context is so indeterminate
(Italy was divided into *più stati*[30]) or so ambiguous (the prince controls,

[29] 3; 7a.
[30] 12; 26b.

defends, establishes, or preserves his *stato*) that it is impossible to make out how Machiavelli was conceiving *lo stato* in the particular instance.

In a few cases the context is somewhat clearer. The beginning, the *principio* of a prince's *stato*, is not the time when a body politic ruled by a prince receives its constitutive organization; it is the moment when and the means by which the prince acquires effective command over his subjects. And when in reply to the remark of the Cardinal d'Amboise that Italians do not understand *della guerra*, Machiavelli replies that the French do not understand *dello stato*,[31] he means nothing more esoteric than that the French do not know how to keep a grip on a newly acquired *stato* once they have seized it, a point he has just spent a long chapter proving.

All that remains now requiring close attention is a cluster of eight uses of the word *lo stato* in *Il Principe*. Here are six of them:

1. Ferdinand of Aragon "in the beginning of his reign attacked Granada, and that enterprise was the foundation *dello stato suo*."[32]
2. In Egypt where the Mameluke Sultan rules not by inheritance but by election, "although the prince is new, *gli ordini di quello stato* are old and are arranged to accept him as if he were their hereditary lord."[33]
3. With respect to the danger of an incurable disease developing in *lo stato*, "It happens in this matter as they say it does in medicine in the case of hectic fever, which is easy to cure but hard to diagnose or treat at the outset, but with the passing of time it becomes easy to diagnose and hard to cure. So it happens *nelle cose di stato*."[34]
4. "Like all other natural things that are born and grow fast, *gli stati* that come suddenly cannot have roots . . . so that the first spell of bad weather destroys them."[35]
5. "The few do not dare oppose the many who have *la maestà dello stato* to protect them."[36]
6. "The principal foundations of *tutti li stati*, new or old or mixed, are good laws and good arms."[37]

So here we have *lo stato* with institutions, with foundations, a living thing with roots, a living body with sickness and health, a thing possessed of majesty. To this cluster of instances the first and natural reaction might well be, "Well, here we are at last. This is more like it." This *stato* that has institutions, foundations, roots, ills, and majesty

[31] 3; 10a.
[32] 21; 43b.
[33] 19; 40b.
[34] 3; 8a.
[35] 7; 14b.
[36] 18; 35a–b.
[37] 12; 24b.

is a bit nearer to the "state" one would expect than what we have seen hitherto—that odd-looking contraption that the princely puppeteer competently or incompetently dangles from his strings.

But what do we see when we move in closer? The Granadan war was the foundation of Ferdinand's *stato* in the sense that, while it was on, "the barons of Castile . . . did not think of rebelling" and by the time it was done Ferdinand had "gained . . . *imperio* over them without their realizing it." With the money he had been able to gouge out of the Church and the people for that war he was also put in a position to establish his army.[38] So the foundations of Ferdinand's *stato* through the Granadan war were the arrangements he made by means of it for getting and holding command over the Castilians. We have here simply an echo of the first sentence of *Il Principe*.

The institutions or *ordini* of the *stato* of the Mamelukes were, as far as Machiavelli was concerned, merely the rules of succession that insured the undisturbed accession of one sultan after another to political command over the Egyptians, in brief to the *stato* in the only sense that we have so far seen Machiavelli giving that word.

Machiavelli's two lapses into organic analogies carry us no further. For though there is talk of roots and of disease—talk that will ring very familiarly to anyone who has had doings with the endless resort to such analogies by medieval and Renaissance writers on the organic, hierarchical structure of society—the roots in *Il Principe* are not roots of the body politic and the disease is not a disease of the body politic. The disease that Machiavelli is concerned about is rebellion from within or attack from without against a newly acquired princely possession; the victim of the disease is not the body politic but the ruler; and the remedies involved—planting military colonies in the newly acquired possession, dispossessing part of its population and exterminating the hostile, razing the towns and scattering their inhabitants[39]—may do wonders in saving the prince from the fatal disease of losing his *stato*, but they really cannot be regarded, and of course they were not intended, as specifics for the ills of a body politic. As with the disease so with the roots. They are not roots *of* the body politic by means of which *it* lives and grows; they are the roots that the *stato* of a new prince needs to push down among those over whom *lo stato* has *imperio*, the powers of political command that the prince needs if he is to get a grip on his new possessions.[40] And the *maestà dello stato* seems not much more than the capacity of the prince's power of command to inspire awe in the loutish masses.[41]

[38] 21; 43b.
[39] 5; 11b–12b.
[40] 7; 15a.
[41] 18; 35b.

We have saved the most interesting case for the last. Along with *salvare lo stato* it provides one of the best examples of the proclivity of the human mind to take words in hand and provide them with the sense most in conformity to its own deepest habits and patterns. In Chapter 12 Machiavelli says: "The principal foundations of *tutti li stati*, new or old or mixed, are good laws and good arms."[42] We see *buone legge* and *stati* together in a sentence; something clicks in our head; and our eye takes a picture of laws good for the state, for the body politic. Yet what we have taken a picture of is something inside our heads, not something out there in *Il Principe*. For we have seen that the new, old, mixed, hereditary, and civil *stati* of the preceding eleven chapters were not bodies politic but new, old, and mixed tenancies of command over men. And we have *not* seen that what Machiavelli deems good in *Il Principe* is necessarily good for the body politic. Yet clearly the likelihood of any inference we make as to whom or what the laws should be good for depends on whom or what in *Il Principe* "good" things are ordinarily good for. Now if we examine *Il Principe* to find out whom the good is good for and the bad ill for, we discover that for the six times that *buono, bene, malo,* and *male* refer to the welfare or illfare of the subjects or people, they refer to the advantage or disadvantage of the prince forty-one times. So in the sentence under consideration there are about seven chances that *buone legge* are laws to the advantage of the prince to one that they are laws for the welfare of the body politic. That they are in this particular case under consideration good for the prince rather than for the body politic is quite clear in the context provided by the preceding sentence: "It is necessary for a *prince* to have his foundations good else it follows of necessity that *he* will fall to ruin."[43] So the good laws and goods arms that are the good foundations for *lo stato* are good in the sense that they will keep the prince from falling into ruin, that is, from losing *lo stato*.

And now two last and curious instances of the use of *lo stato*:

"Nabis . . . sustained the onslaught of all Greece and a Roman army victoriously, and against them defended *la patria sua e il suo stato*."[44]

The new prince "ought to . . . think of everything of every sort to *ampliare la sua città e il suo stato*."[45]

What makes these instances curious is a trait of Machiavelli's style in *Il Principe*. He is relentlessly spare; he is never redundant. Pairings

[42] 12; 24b.
[43] Ibid.
[44] 9; 21b.
[45] 21; 45a.

like "brave and bold," "man of honesty and integrity," "magnificence and splendor" do not occur in *Il Principe*; two conjoined terms invariably signify two different things. The quotations above therefore imply a clear distinction in Machiavelli's mind between *patria* and *stato*, *città* and *stato*, in which neither can include nor yet be subsumed under the other. The difference is such that the defense of the *patria*, the improvement of the *città* cannot be taken necessarily to involve or be involved in the defense and improvement of *lo stato*. What is the substance of the difference? It seems to me that for Machiavelli the *patria* and the *città* are entities to which men belong but which do not belong to any man. The prince does not acquire, or hold, or lose a *patria* or a *città*; he does acquire, hold, lose *lo stato*. And while he has it, *lo stato* belongs to him.

And so our detailed investigation ends. We have gone through all occurrences of *lo stato* in *Il Principe*. The outcome suggests some small modification of the customary verdict on Machiavelli's consistency, at least as far as his use of *lo stato* in *Il Principe* is concerned. He used the term there 110 times in some political sense, and in not a single instance out of 110 does he use it in a way clearly to preclude the connotation established by the way he unambiguously used it at least four-fifths of the time. In no instance is it demonstrable that he conceives *lo stato* in a fashion that is other than manipulative and exploitative or in conjunction with anything but power of command over men.

As we searched in vain for some meaning of *lo stato* that carried the implication that it was *not* merely an instrument for the manipulation and exploitation of people at the hand of the prince, we must have become aware that *lo stato* was not at all "the state" as we ordinarily conceive it today. This is not because today we never conceive of the state as the object of the manipulations and schemes of those who would exploit its powers of political command. We do indeed conceive of it that way to some extent. But we conceive of it in other ways too, and this makes a real difference. Now what distinguishes Machiavelli's *stato* from the state as we ordinarily think of it is not that he thinks of *lo stato* in an exploitative way, but that in *Il Principe* he does not think of it in any other way. We have already stumbled on a phrase to express the difference. For us the state is among other things a body politic. In *Il Principe lo stato* is never a body politic. But if *lo stato* is not a body politic we have run head on into a difficult problem. One of the most important intellectual achievements ascribed to Machiavelli is the conception, however embryonic, of the idea of reason of state. But if *lo stato* is not the state in *Il Principe*, then how can there be any reason of state in *Il Principe*? After all, it is hard to see how one can have reason of state unless there is a state for there to be reason of.

The English phrase "reason of state" and the German phrase *Staats-raison* are unfortunate, or at least inadequate, translations of the Italian *ragione di stato* and the French *raison d'état*. They are unfortunate because they obscure the fact, clear in both Italian and French, that reason of state is in some measure concerned with the right of the state. As the modern state expanded its authority and increased the range of its activity, it more and more frequently required men, and particularly statesmen, to act in ways that did not square with current codes of private conduct. Now the theory of reason of state does not merely allege that rulers and their officials sometimes act badly, nor does it merely allege that the state *can* make its subjects behave badly. It may note these facts, but only in order to assert that rulers and statesmen under certain circumstances *ought* to act badly from the point of view of private morality, that under certain conditions subjects ought to act and to be made to act in ways contrary to the dictates of their conscience and the ordinary rules of ethics. Reason of state is not merely a statement of fact about the way the rulers of states act; it is also a theory of right; it is concerned ultimately not only with what is but with what ought to be. In fact, Rousseau came very close to stating the problem of reason of state in the first chapter of *The Social Contract*. Putting it in Rousseau's language, statesmen everywhere do what is contrary to the ordinary rules of human conduct; what makes it legitimate? The theorists of reason of state had to do more than assert that in the pursuit of their calling rulers and statesmen *ought* to be exempt from the laws of morality to which other men are bound. They had to say why rulers should be exempt. They said with Burke that it was so because the state transcended each and all of the individuals who at any moment composed it, because the state possessed "the mode of existence decreed to a permanent body composed of transitory parts, wherein by the disposition of a stupendous wisdom moulding together the great mysterious incorporation of the human race, the whole, at one time, is never old, or middle-aged, or young, but, in a condition of unchangeable consistency, moves on through the varied tenor of perpetual decay, fall, renovation and progression." Or they said it was so, with Hobbes, because all subjects had surrendered to the ruler of the state their absolute right to do whatever they thought would conduce to their own self-preservation. Because, somewhat more briefly, the state is a body politic, because indeed it is, par excellence, *the* body politic. Since it has a life beyond the life of the individual, be he statesman or private person, since on its health, well-being, and survival the welfare of all its citizens now living and of their children yet unborn, and of their children's children, depends, for these reasons those who serve it must set aside the qualms of private conscience when its welfare is engaged, must do whatever needs be done to defend it from its enemies, without and within; for in so transcendent a cause the end justifies the means.

This is the kernel of the theory of reason of state. There is no doubt that Machiavelli had caught the spirit of the doctrine, however limited, crude, and inadequate his formulation of it may be. The formulation will be found in Chapter 9 of Book I of the *Discorsi*. There, confronted with the traditional account of the most important single event in the history of Rome—the founding of the city—Machiavelli was confronted also with an acute issue raising the fundamental problem of reason of state. For by that account Romulus founded Rome on the blood of his brother Remus, whom he slew. Was Romulus right to kill Remus? This is the problem that Machiavelli wrestles with in Chapter 9 of Book I of the *Discorsi*:

> Many men perchance may judge it a bad example that a founder of a civil polity [*vivere civile*], as Romulus was, should have killed his brother . . . judging that on this account with the authority of their prince's example, citizens out of the ambition and desire to command might take action against whoever opposed their authority.

The argument condemning Romulus

> would be true [he continues] if one did not consider the purpose that induced him to perpetrate this homicide. But this ought to be accepted as a general rule: that it never or rarely happens that any republic or realm may be ordered rightly at the outset or reformed wholly anew beyond the scope of its ancient institutions unless the work of establishing it is performed by one man . . . But the prudent founder of a republic who is of a mind *to wish to advance not himself but the common good, not his own succession but the common fatherland* ought to extend himself to have sole authority, nor will a wise person reprehend any one for any extraordinary action he takes to order a realm or found a republic. It is appropriate that, the act accusing him, the purpose should excuse him, and *when the latter is good,* as that of Romulus was, it will always excuse him; for it is he who is violent in order to destroy, not he who is violent to reconstruct who ought to be condemned . . . but . . . Romulus . . . in killing his brother . . . deserves pardon; *what he did, he did for the common good.*[46]

Surely this passage—in which by the way the word *lo stato* does not once appear—entitles Machiavelli to whatever accolade is due

[46] *Discorsi* I, 9; Mazzoni and Casella, pp. 72b–73a. Italics mine.

to a man who on the margin between the Middle Ages and the modern era discerns the wave of the future through the mists of the past. At the edges no doubt his argument is rough and inconclusive: the intellectual innovator never can produce the neat and lapidary demonstrations possible to successors who have the advantage of his pioneering work to go by. But the center of the argument—the main points—is already well formed.

1. The *vivere civile*, the civil polity, the body politic, the state is itself a transcendent good; it stands over the goods of private intercourse and private morality.
2. To establish a state or to save it in time of danger any extraordinary act is permissible and excusable.
3. He who perpetrates such acts is pardonable because of the good for which he perpetrates them; *accusandolo il fatto, lo effetto lo scusi*, though the act accuses him the effect excuses him; the end justifies the means.

We need not ask whether the ideas so expressed precisely conform to the lineaments of the doctrine of reason of state in its full development. The child does not have the complete form of the adult but he carries the life and the potentiality for attaining to that form. So it is, as regards the idea of reason of state, with Chapter 9 of Book I of the *Discorsi*.

But that really is not the question after all. The question concerns *Il Principe*. In *Il Principe* what justifies those *azioni estraordinarie* that are justified by reason of state in the *Discorsi*? Is it reason of state in *Il Principe* too?

We must repeat, before we can find reason of state in *Il Principe*, we have to find a state, a body politic, there. For there is a body politic in the *Discorsi*. Sometimes it is called *il vivere libero, il vivere civile, il vivere politico, il bene commune*, and so on.[47] When we look in *Il Principe* for the words that Machiavelli used in the *Discorsi* to signify the state, we do not find them. *Vivere libero, vivere civile, bene commune*—none of them are to be found.[48] There remains *lo stato*, but we already know about that. One thing that *lo stato* never means in *Il Principe* is the state conceived as a political body transcending the individuals who compose it.

Now the theory of reason of state is an ethical doctrine. It may be a very bad ethical doctrine, or a very good one, or like most ethical

[47] E.g., *Discorsi* I, 2, 3, 5, 6, 7, 9; Mazzoni and Casella, pp. 62a, 62b, 64b, 68a, 69b, 72a.
[48] *Vivere* appears with *libero* several times in *Il Principe*, but not as a substantive, only with the meaning, "to live in freedom."

doctrines it may be just middling. It is an ethical doctrine because it is concerned with the good and the right. It neither rejects nor seeks to destroy established rules, nor does it regard them as items of indifference to statesmen. In the best tradition of Western thought it tries, however inadequately, to bring a modicum of order into an emergent area of human activity with which the established rules are patently and hopelessly incompetent to deal. To make such adjustments inevitably involves modification of the previous arrangement of the web of values. It may be argued that the modifications implicit in the conception of reason of state were ultimately subversive of the web of values into which that concept was projected. This indeed may be true by logical implication. It might be somewhat harder to demonstrate as a matter of historical fact. And here below we live amid the temporal contingencies of history, not amid the eternal necessities of logic. Whatever the ultimate consequences of the idea of reason of state, that idea neither describes nor justifies the relation between the prince and *lo stato* as that relation is consistently conceived of in *Il Principe*. To that conception it is in some measure an alternative, however unsatisfactory.

In *Il Principe* there is no justification for the relation of the prince to *lo stato*. There can be none because *lo stato* is not a matrix of values, a body politic; it is an instrument of exploitation, the mechanism the prince uses to get what he wants. So instead of reason of state we get the *verità effettuale della cosa*. The effective truth of the matter is that if the prince exploits *lo stato* with astuteness he will keep his grip on *lo stato* and even tighten it, and will be glorified as a man of honor and praised by everyone, for, as Machiavelli says in the climactic sentences of *Il Principe*, the mob is always gulled by appearances and by the way things work out, and the mob is all there is in the world. So *si guarda al fine*, take heed of the result.[49] The result is political success or failure. It is not right to succeed, it is not wrong to fail. It is merely success to succeed, and failure to fail. Right is not might, might is not right; might is might, and that is what *Il Principe* is about. As to right—any kind of right of the individual or of the state—that is not really what *Il Principe* is about.

We said before that *lo stato* as conceived by Machiavelli in *Il Principe* is radically at variance with the modern conception of the state. That is only partly true. One nineteenth-century writer, who in succeeding years gained a considerable following, did conceive of the state precisely as Machiavelli conceived *lo stato*. To him states were simply the instruments by means of which the rulers exploited the ruled for their own ends, employing every device of force and fraud

[49] 18; 35b.

that Machiavelli deemed indispensable if rulers were to *mantenere loro stati*. And they were nothing else whatever. For Karl Marx, however, the rulers were not individuals but social classes. And for him in the end the state, *lo stato*, the ultimate instrument of ruling-class exploitation, itself would wither away. This illusion Machiavelli—a man with a considerable capacity for illusions—never entertained.

APPENDIX A: Professor Chiappelli on *Stato*

After I had completed the foregoing exhaustive study of the term *lo stato* in *Il Principe*, Prof. Felix Gilbert called to my attention the section in Fredi Chiappelli, *Studi sul linguagio del Machiavelli* (*Bibliotechina del saggiatore*, Florence, 1952), pp. 59–73, in which the author embarks on a similar undertaking. Chiappelli's conclusions are widely at variance with mine, and as a student of linguistics working with his native tongue he performs with a technical skill which I, as an amateur autodidact in Italian, do not command. Therefore, in order to show that my intransigeance is not merely the consequence of pique or obtuseness, it becomes necessary for me to indicate why after reading his work I did not alter a line of my own study.

Chiappelli's general thesis is that in contrast to Machiavelli's other works *Il Principe* is a technical or scientific treatise. One piece of evidence that this is so, according to Chiappelli, lies in the especially scientific way in which Machiavelli uses the term *stato* in *Il Principe*. In *Il Principe* in 75% of its occurrences "the word *stato* has the signification of 'the state' in complete maturity: the fundamental implications (political, national, territorial) coexist in the individual passages, whether the state is treated syntactically as 'object' or as 'subject'" (p. 68). In all those occurrences "the term *stato* has unequivocally political-national territorial signification of the strictly technical sort, the subjective and objective senses being fused" (p. 61). It is to Chiappelli's specific analysis of the use of *stato* in *Il Principe*, not to his more general arguments, that we here address ourselves.

Chiappelli's procedure then is "to examine in their totality" (ibid.) *all* the instances of the use of *stato* in *Il Principe*, and to set down in their context the instances in which it is used "unequivocally" in "the political-national territorial signification" of "the state." We leave aside for the moment the question of whether the instances Chiappelli cites actually have the signification he ascribes to them. He actually cites 55 passages in which *stato* occurs 64 times (pp. 61–68) and asserts that these passages "comprise 75% of the total material." They do not, in fact, do so. If they did, *stato* would occur only 85 times in *Il Principe*. It actually occurs at least 115 times, introducing an error of 25% into Chiappelli's figures. The supposed instances cited of the use of *stato* to mean "state" are thus reduced from 75% to 56%. From the fictitious 75% (actually 56%), Chiappelli distinguishes a fictitious 10% in which *stato* is taken to mean rank, condition, or status because it appears with the verbs *mantenere, perdere,* and *togliere* while when it appears with *acquistare* and *tenere* he takes it to mean "the state." The grounds for this distinction are in the first place wholly obscure.

In *Il Principe perdere* and *togliere* are frequently contraposed to *acquistare* and *tenere* in reference to the *stato* or to a particular kind of *stato*, the *principato* (e.g., "*acquisto lo stato con la fortuna del padre e con quella lo perde*"), so it is difficult to see how *stato* could denote "the state" in connection with the former and "rank" in the latter.[1] In the same way *mantenere* is used in conjunction with *acquistare* in reference to *lo stato*.[2] In the second place, Chiappelli's distinction runs against the facts. There are instances of the use of *mantenere*, *perdere*, and *togliere* where the reference clearly *cannot* be to rank or status in the ordinary sense, e.g., Louis XII *ha perduto* Lombardy.[3] Finally the distinction is artificial. Whatever jurists may have had to say in the matter, Machiavelli made no fine discriminations between a prince's status or condition and his *stato*, his possession of rule over men. To lose the latter was in fact to lose the former; there is not a single instance in *Il Principe* in which losing *lo stato* or having it taken away does not signify loss of actual possession of command.

We need not consider the remaining "15%" of the occurrences of *lo stato* that Chiappelli deals with. We need only note that even if the 56% of the occurrences to which he ascribes the signification "the state" were actually intended by Machiavelli to mean just that, and to have a strict technical value, then Machiavelli made things inordinately hard for his readers 44% of the time by throwing *lo stato* in with some non-technical meaning.

The truth of the matter is that in the 64 occurrences of *lo stato* that Chiappelli actually cites as meaning "the state" in the technical sense, that national-political territorial entity is often quite patently in the eyes of the beholder rather than in the text of *Il Principe*. Consider only a few examples.

> The arms with which a prince defends *il suo stato* are his own or are mercenary.[4]
> Hannibal having died, and no one remaining who could *reggere lo stato*. . . .[5]
> To hold *lo stato* securely some princes have disarmed their subjects.[6]

Now it is quite evident that in each of these instances *lo stato could* mean "the state" as defined by Chiappelli, *if* "the state" was in fact what Machiavelli had in mind; what is lacking is any grounds for believing that in any of the three cases *lo stato* does *indeed* mean "the

[1] 7; 14b–15a; see also 3; 7b and 5; 12a.
[2] 11; 22a; see also 6; 14a and 7; 15b.
[3] 3; 10a.
[4] 12; 24b.
[5] 19; 36a.
[6] 20; 41a.

state," that "the state" *was* what Machiavelli had in mind. Chiappelli's analysis falls into the very trap that I pointed out and tried to avoid in the present essay, the trap of committing oneself in advance to some exact denotative definition of *lo stato* and then looking for it in *Il Principe*. This is a trap because, given the nature of the data, it leads inevitably to a pre-cooking of the results. It does so because the contexts in which *lo stato* appear are often so indeterminate as to make *possible* any of three or four denotations of *lo stato*. This assertion is easy to test. Take (1) "territory," (2) "the governed," (3) "ruling power," (4) "status, position, or rank," (5) "national-political territorial entity," and try substituting *each* of them wherever *lo stato* appears in *Il Principe*. It is rare indeed that two of the meanings will not fit. It is surprising how often three, four, or occasionally even all five of the meanings will fit.

By avoiding the quest for some denotation of *lo stato* prescribed by the investigator rather than by Machiavelli, the method we adopted prevented us from accidentally pulling out of our investigation results that we ourselves put into it. Whatever Machiavelli meant to denote by *lo stato* (and we have seen that when the denotations are clearly determinate, they are also quite varied), he, and no one else, coupled *lo stato* as object or passive subject with verbs of exploitative tonality in *Il Principe*,[7] and he did so with remarkable frequency. This is the result not of our preconceptions about the meanings of words but of Machiavelli's use of language. That when *lo stato* is not used passively with exploitative verbs it still *does* practically nothing is also evident from the rarity with which Machiavelli ascribes any action to it, the frequency with which it continues to appear as passive in fact, or at best as neutral and indeterminate. So while freely confessing Chiappelli's superior erudition in the area of our common concern, I am sticking to my story because I think it represents the common-sense view of the matter.

[7] I have inserted "in *Il Principe*," which was not in the original article. Its absence was responsible for a misconstruction of my meaning by Prof. Gilbert. (Felix Gilbert, *Machiavelli and Guicciardini: Politics and History in Sixteenth-Century Florence* [Princeton, 1965], p. 329.) He understood me to suggest that nobody else in Machiavelli's time ever used the term *stato* as Machiavelli consistently used it in *Il Principe*. Such was not my intention. Gilbert also suggests that "the 'exploitative' meaning of *stato* plays a greater role in *The Prince* because in *The Prince* Machiavelli considers politics from the point of view of the ruler." Yet few of Machiavelli's contemporaries would have suggested that the ruler's relation to politics was primarily exploitative. In *La Monarchie de France,* also written "from the point of view of the ruler," in 1515 Claude de Seyssel uses the *estat* in a political sense but does not ordinarily conceive of *estats* as passive objects of exploitation. Indeed I suspect that the vision of politics as exploitative comes more readily to the mind of the ruled than to the rulers.

APPENDIX D: Occurrences of *lo stato* in *Il Principe*

1	2	3	4	1	2	3	4	1	2	3	4	1	2	3	4
3a	dedi-	0		15b	VII	0		27b	XIII	0		39b	XIX	0	
3b	cation	1	1	16a	cont.	0		27a	cont.	0		40a	cont.	0	
4a	blank	0		16b		0		28b		0		40b		2	
4b	blank	0		17a		1		29a		0	0	41a		2	10
5a	I	2	2	17b		0		29a	XIV	1		41a	XX	3	
5a	II	0		18a		0	8	29b		0		41b		4	
5b		2	2	18a	VIII	0		30a		0		42a		3	
6a	III	0		18b		0		30b		0	1	42b		5	
6b		3		19a		0		30b	XV	0		43a		3	18
7a		4		19b		1		31a		2	2	43b	XXI	1	
7b		3		20a		2	3	31a	XVI	0		44a		0	
8a		3		20a	IX	0		31b		0		44b		0	
8b		2		20b		0		32a		0		45a		2	3
9a		0		21a		0		32b		0	0	45a	XXII	0	
9b		1		21b		1		32b	XVII	0		45b		1	
10a		1	17	22a		3	5	33a		0		46a		0	1
10a	IV	2		22a	X	1		33b		0		46a	XXIII	1	
10b		6		22b		0		34a		0	1	46b		0	
11a		2		23a		0	1	34a	XVIII	0		47a		1	2
11b		4	13	23a	XI	0		34b		0		47a	XXIV	2	
11b	V	1		23b		4		35a		1		47b		2	4
12a		3		24a		0		35b		3	4	48a	XXV	0	
12b		0	4	24b		0	4	35b	XIX	0		48b		0	
12b	VI	1		24b	XII	2		36a		0		49a		0	
13a		1		25a		1		36b		2		49b		0	0
13b		1		25b		0		37a		1		49b	XXVI	0	
14a		0	3	26a		1		37b		0		50a		0	
14a	VII	0		26b		1		38a		1		50b		0	
14b		3		27a		1	6	38b		0		51a		0	
15a		4		27a	XIII	0		39a		2		51b		0	0

Legend
Column 1: Page and column in *Tutte le opere . . . di Niccolò Machiavelli,* ed. Mazzoni and Casella.
Column 2: Chapter in *Il Principe.*
Column 3: Number of occurrences of some form of the noun *stato.*
Column 4: Total number of occurrences of *stato* by chapters.

APPENDIX E: Occurrences of *stato* and *stati* in *Il Principe* by chapter, page, and line: Bertelli-Feltrinelli edition

Page	Line	Page	Line	Page	Line	Page	Line
Dedication		V		XII		XX	
14	4	28	19	53	16	85	4
			24		22		8
I			25		24		11
		29	6	56	11	86	4
15	4			57	5		6
	10	VI			22		10 (2)
II							30
		30	5	XIII		87	17
16	3		27				19
	8	31	30	XIV			32
						88	3
III		VII		62	11		8
							12
18	10	33	21	XV			18
	11	34	8				21
	27		24	66	2		30
19	2		28		6	89	5
	11	35	7				
	14		8	XVI		XXI	
	19		17				
20	4	39	4	XVII		89	25
	6					92	24
	26	VIII		69	10	93	7
21	13						
	16	44	6	XVIII		XXII	
	28		16				
22	13		18	73	32	94	17
	16			74	13		
24	14	IX			16	XXIII	
25	10				25		
		47	11			95	15
IV		48	2	XIX		96	23
			10			97	5
25	23		12	76	26		
	26		17	77	10	XXIV	
26	9				19		
	11	X		80	5	97	19
	22			81	8		25
	25	48	23		23		28
	26			84	7		
27	19	XI			16	XXV	
	25				32		
	31	50	26		34	XXVI	
	34		28				
28	2		29				
	12	51	19				

APPENDIX F: Conflation of initial pages of chapters in Mazzoni and Casella and Bertelli-Feltrinelli edition of *Il Principe*

Chapter	Page Numbers*		Chapter	Page Numbers*	
	M & C	B		M & C	B
D	3a	13	14	29a	62
1	5a	15	15	30b	64
2	5a	15	16	31a	66
3	6a	16	17	32b	68
4	10a	25	18	34a	72
5	11b	28	19	35b	75
6	12b	30	20	41a	85
7	14b	33	21	43b	89
8	18a	40	22	45a	93
9	20a	45	23	46a	95
10	22a	48	24	47a	97
11	23a	50	25	48a	98
12	24b	53	26	49b	101
13	27a	58			

* M & C—Niccolò Machiavelli, *Tutte le opere*, ed. Mazzoni and Casella (Florence, 1929)

B—Niccolò Machiavelli, *Opere*, I, *Il principe e Discorsi*, ed. S. Bertelli (Milan, 1960)

CHAPTER IV The Predatory and the Utopian Vision: Machiavelli and More. The Loom of Language and the Fabric of Imperatives: The Case of *Il Principe* and *Utopia**

T HIS essay concerns the way two men, Niccolò Machiavelli and Thomas More, in two books, *Il Principe* and *Utopia,* used a few words. It argues in effect that the peculiar ways in which these men worked at the loom of language indicates that they stood in a peculiar relation to the fabric of imperatives of their own time.

The loom of language provides men with the words and word patterns by means of which they communicate with one another. By processes so complex as to require a separate branch of the science of linguistics for their explication, words and patterns of words undergo a great variety of changes under a wide variety of circumstances with the passage of time. By glacially slow modifications of an ancient tongue whole new language families evolve. Words come to point to things they did not formerly designate, or cease to point to things

* See "A Note on Citations."

they did designate. New words are created to designate new-found things, or old ones are put to new uses in the process of discovery. And, massively, words and word sequences drop out of use and become archaic or obsolete, which is to say unintelligible or nearly so. The changes even in a language relatively as stable as English during the past four hundred years have been such that in teaching Shakespeare or expounding Scripture from the King James Version, the expositor finds himself becoming more and more the translator in the technical sense—the person engaged in finding equivalents of the words of his text that will be intelligible to his audience.

This essay proposes to deal with a small sample of a particular kind of change in language, and that kind itself amounts to only a tiny fraction of the changes that language constantly undergoes. The few changes to be investigated here, however, may have a particular interest for historians, especially for historians of ideas, of moral sentiments, of political institutions, and of social structures, which means for a great many historians today. They may have this interest because of the peculiar circumstances in which they took place. For one thing they did not emerge anonymously from the folk; they were the work of readily identifiable individuals—More and Machiavelli—each of whom made a strong and indelible mark on the history of his times. In the second place the changes were not casual word coinages. The words that will concern us concerned More and Machiavelli; in effect they are not words merely *dropped* by their authors but words *placed* (or in one instance not placed) by them. Finally when Machiavelli and More tampered with the sense of the words that will concern us, they cared not at all or not solely for the aesthetic impact or the logical efficiency of what they were doing. They were concerned with the relation of those words and their meanings to the men and communities of men that they knew best. They were in effect concerned with the product of the loom of language in the area where it weaves the fabric of imperatives.

In contrast to the region of "I want," the fabric of imperatives occupies the whole region of "Thou shalt," of "You ought," of "I ought."[1]

---

[1] To pile yet one more metaphorical phrase on an area already blanketed by "patterns of culture" and "webs of values" may seem a contribution only to a confusion of tongues already quite sufficient. But although what the phrase "fabric of imperatives" refers to in this essay certainly lies in the blanketed area, the part it covers, while overlapping the parts covered by the other phrases, is not identical with either of them. "Patterns of culture" refers to the things the people of a culture normally do. Thus in the adolescent male American subculture of my day, boasting—sometimes quite remarkable in its inaccuracy—about one's amorous achievements was a standard pattern. It was not, however, part of the fabric of imperatives; there was no explicit rule to the effect that wholesome American boys ought to lie like Ananias about their priapic exploits. The notion of "web of values" will not do because the term "value" appears to have become highly

Between these two regions there is for each of us a greater or lesser measure of congruence, but whatever the correspondence may be, the regions are functionally distinct. The one concerns the satisfaction of human desires, the other the rules of human conduct. The function of any fabric of imperatives is so to regulate the satisfaction of human desires as to make the living together of men at least possible, and at most to make it good. The fabric of imperatives regulates the satisfaction of human desires by sanctions ranging from the overtly coercive ones of law enforced by public power, through the pressure of community opinion working by means of gossip and social acceptance or rejection, to the still small voice within.

Because the fabric of imperatives determines the ordinary day-to-day expectations of men with respect to the actions of their fellows, it is resistant to drastic and sudden change. It is also of varying density at a given time and over spans of time. Thus in the Middle Ages it lay relatively thick with respect to matters of male attire and relatively thin with respect to acts of physical violence, whereas today it lies thin with respect to the former and thick with respect to the latter. And this is as much as to say that despite its resistance to alteration, the fabric has in fact undergone alteration. Thirdly, it is subject to stress from a variety of sources: changes in technology, in the range and depth of human understanding, in the direction of human aspirations and desires, in the forms of social and political institutions, in the relative power and the demands of interest groups, in the character of men's faith and hope. Finally, to cope with the tensions generated by such changes, and to prevent them from fatally rending the fabric of imperatives, all but very primitive societies support a specialized maintenance force to keep it in repair. In most societies we find among these specialists the doom deemers or law givers, the judges, the priests or holy men, and the pedagogues. Moreover, in particular ages and particular cultures the maintenance work is undertaken by different kinds of men—in ancient Greece, for example, successively by epic poets, lyric poets, dramatists, and philosophers; in the West by theologians, humanists, *philosophes*, and today by sociologists, psychoanalysts, novelists, and editorial writers. What these men have in

---

ambiguous, and in the process of aggravated bifurcation it has left uncovered an important area lying between its two segments. In one sense it seems to mean the highest goals that individuals and communities set for themselves; in the other sense it means whatever men and groups of men want, as revealed by their actual choices and stated preferences. It has long been used in approximately this sense in economics and is occasionally so used in sociology, e.g., in Bernard Berelson, *Content Analysis in Communication Research* (Glencoe, Ill., 1952). The notion of a "fabric of imperatives" covers but also extends far beyond the web of values in the first sense, and it occupies a different cultural region altogether from the web of values in the second sense.

common is an expertise at the loom of language that enables them to produce the material they deem necessary to reinforce or patch or rebuild or modify the fabric of imperatives in accord with their often varying estimate of the need.

Most specialists at the loom of language are satisfied most of the time to work to preserve the fabric of imperatives pretty much as they find it. This is why what they produce is often insufferably monotonous and repetitive. But all the specialists are not always satisfied. Most of the subversive initial and direct onslaughts on the fabric of imperatives have been delivered by men who came out of the milieux of the maintenance specialists. Their divine or daemonic discontent is not a rarity to wonder at; it is a common and repeated fact of history.

Since the work of registering or initiating the transformation of imperatives falls to maintenance specialists who are word weavers, in the course of drastic changes, attempted or achieved, in the fabric of imperatives, something odd usually happens at the loom of language. This fact may provide us with a useful tactical resource for the investigation of the history of ideas at a point where, to borrow the title of a very poor book, "ideas have consequences." A careful study of activity at the loom of language may render possible the close identification of points of stress in the fabric of imperatives at a particular moment.

The stress or breakdown in the fabric of imperatives does not always register in the sort of change at the loom of language that so sharply calls attention to itself when one word wholly replaces another in an area of human discourse. Sometimes the change is not a change *of* words but a change *in* words, an alteration of meaning that leaves the verbal shell intact. When such a change takes place in words widely current prior to the change and still widely current today, he who attempts to understand the fabric of imperatives by studying the loom of language needs to proceed with considerable caution. In the first place it is easy to miss such a change altogether. Having described the change, however, the investigator may unwarily assume that the word has shifted all the way from its previous sense to its present range of connotation. This is by no means always the case.

The above monition about changes in words is necessary because the examination of several such changes will be our concern in what follows. The changes occur in two works on politics written in the years just prior to the Reformation: Machiavelli's *Il Principe* (1513) and More's *Utopia* (1515–16). From the time they reached the public to the present those two slim books have exercised a powerful and continuous fascination over men's minds, a fascination more powerful than that of any works contemporary with them. Yet, is it useful to attempt to understand what More and Machiavelli were doing to the fabric of imperatives by an investigation of the language of *Utopia* and *Il Principe* only? To do so raises serious and difficult questions. Is the More of *Utopia* the *real* More? Did More *really* believe what he wrote in *Utopia*? Did Machiavelli *really* believe what he wrote in *Il Principe*? Is the Machiavelli of *Il Principe*, that hasty chance tract, the *real* Machiavelli? Is not the real Machiavelli rather the author of the *Discorsi*, the work that represents the meditation of a lifetime?[2]

If by the real Machiavelli one means that aspect of the man which expressed itself in his most durable concerns, convictions, habits of thought, and patterns of action, then probably the *Discorsi* better than *Il Principe* reflects the real Machiavelli. But this identification of the real Machiavelli is a dangerous game; it has led to the dubious inference that only those elements in *Il Principe* duplicated in or reconcilable with the *Discorsi* represent the real Machiavelli, and that what is left over is to be disregarded or explained away. Yet so to treat *Il Principe* is to miss perhaps the most important point about it. What gives *Il Principe* its remarkable power and its perennial liveliness is that in it Machiavelli's imagination takes wings and his vision soars above his ordinary perceptions and conceptions to a new height.

And so it is with Thomas More in *Utopia*. If the Machiavelli of the *Discorsi* rather than of *Il Principe* is the real Machiavelli, the More of the letter to Martin Dorp in defense of Erasmus and Christian humanism,[3] the More of the *Dialogue Concerning Heresies* supporting Christian unity against its enemies,[4] rather than the author of *Utopia*, is the real More. The unique heights they attain above their own times put *Il Principe* and *Utopia* beyond the ordinary reach of the contemporaries of Machiavelli and More—beyond the reach of *all* their contemporaries, and therefore beyond the reach of More and Machiavelli, too. For it is not necessary to believe that almost two decades or even two years later Machiavelli and More saw all things precisely as they saw them in the moments of acute perception that possessed them when they wrote *Il Principe* and *Utopia*. Sustained imaginative vision is indeed like being possessed; it is not necessarily progressive or cumulative or even readily preserved intact. It is a dizzy height that a very few men scale once or twice in a lifetime and fewer still attain more often. When such vision is turned on the ways men live together,

---

[2] This issue is frequently raised with respect to both these books and a considerable number of other great books, Plato's *Republic*, for example. It was raised, in fact, by one of the readers to whom the editor of the *American Historical Review* sent this study. The following section, first written to meet the issue with respect to *Utopia* alone as part of the introduction to *Utopia* (reprinted above, pp. 25–26), is repeated here in slight paraphrase.

[3] *Corresp.*, no. 15.

[4] *Works*, pp. 105–288.

it may bring some facets of human affairs into focus with a fierce brilliance, but in so doing it is almost bound to throw whole spans of men's experience, the visionary's as well as others', into the shadow. The greatness of a book that does this lies not in its harmony but in its intensity. And after he has attained this height the writer of such a book may seem not to advance from it but to recede from it. In regaining his balance he loses some of his impetus. This happened to Machiavelli after he wrote *Il Principe*; it happened to More after he wrote *Utopia*. In both cases the convictions the books express are not so much repudiated as drawn back into the setting from which something like poetic inspiration had momentarily freed them. They are not consciously rejected but integrated with their writer's previous habit of thought and thereby transmuted and toned down.

Although in *Utopia* and *Il Principe* More and Machiavelli rise above their milieux, it is their own milieux they rise above and therefore have in view as they write. This much relation at least each man's book bears to his own time and place, and although the times of More and Machiavelli were closely contemporaneous, their places were different in ways most significant for what they wrote in their great little books.

The place of Machiavelli was Italy; the rest of Europe and the rest of the world he saw only with fragmented, unfocused, peripheral vision.[5] To him as to his contemporary fellow Florentine and fellow student of the past, Francesco Guicciardini, the Italy of his day was the scene of massive and utterly appalling political disarray, of *calamità*, following with catastrophic suddenness an era of order, prosperity, and peace.[6] This view is at odds with that of a number of historians who have seen and see the entire age of the Renaissance in Italy as one of political confusion, violence, and decay. It is nevertheless confirmed by a reasonable consideration of the evidence. From the death of Giangalleazzo Visconti in 1403 to the incursion of Charles VIII of France in 1494 Italy enjoyed a level of tranquillity among its centers of political power and even within its political units that to contemporary Frenchmen, Englishmen, Spaniards, and Germans could only have seemed Elysian. If everything was not well— and of course during those ninety years everything was not always

[5] This is evident enough even in Machiavelli's descriptions of France and Germany written after he had been engaged in legations to both those lands. (Niccolò Machiavelli, "Ritratto di cose di Francia," in Machiavelli, *Opere, 2, Arte della guerra e Scritti politici minori*, ed. S. Bertelli (Milan, 1960), 164–182; "Ritratto dellet cose della Magna," *ibid.*, 209–215.

[6] Francesco Guicciardini, *Opere*, ed. Vittorio de Caprariis (La Letteratura Italiana, Storia e Testi, XXX [Milan, n.d.], 373).

well anywhere in Italy and was about as bad as ever in Naples—still it was better than the hideous turmoil that plagued the transmontane monarchies for decades on end.[7]

Machiavelli had lived out his youth in the last golden days of a near century of political stability. In that happy autumn of illusion the brutal interventions of barbarians from across the mountains were but a memory of dark days past. In his young manhood Machiavelli saw the bitter end of Italy's autumnal dream. The barbarians came again. In 1494 the French host of Charles VIII swept, irresistible as a winter storm, from the Alps to Naples. That storm of armed force left the old political lines of order among the Italian powers and of rule within them in blasted disarray. And this was but the beginning of a series of political disasters for the Italians that reached a climax but did not end in Machiavelli's lifetime. He not only lived in the midst of these disasters; in his most active years he wholly gave himself to an attempt to stave them off or temper their effects in his native Florence.[8] In this he failed wretchedly and utterly, and his failure captured him. He spent the rest of his life in an almost obsessed contemplation of the apparatus—the levers and gears—of political power.

With the passion of the failure who seeks his own justification, Machiavelli tried to find in political action some sort of meaning not canceled by each random gesture of that fickle bitch Fortuna. Never was Machiavelli more fully obsessed by politics than in 1513, the year when with a rude hand Chance swept away at once his means of livelihood and his way of life. With the Medici in tow, a Spanish force had thrust aside as if it were not there the Florentine militia on which Machiavelli had lavished his pains, effortlessly turning into a nightmare joke the fifteen years he had given to the work of maintaining the political viability of the republic. The restored Medici deprived Machiavelli of his office, tortured him on suspicion of complicity in a plot against them, and exiled him from the city.[9] The fate of Italy and his own fate had become inextricably intermeshed, and he needed above all to know how it had come about that in his day Italy was "overrun by Charles, sacked by Louis, outraged by Ferdinand, and disgraced by the Swiss,"[10] while he had to spin out his life on a wretched farm in the hills of Tuscany. And so in 1513 he channeled but scarcely

[7] Mattingly, *Renaissance Diplomacy*, 83–100, has pointed out how precarious and imperfect the order of Italy was from 1403 to 1494. The contrast between Italy and the great transmontane realms remains nonetheless remarkable.

[8] Roberto Ridolfi, *Vita di Niccolò Machiavelli* (Rome, 1954), 22–197; John Hale, *Machiavelli and Renaissance Italy* (London, 1961), 31–131.

[9] Ridolfi, *Vita di Machiavelli*, 197–214; Hale, *Machiavelli and Renaissance Italy*, 131–41.

[10] Niccolò Machiavelli, *Il Principe*, Chap. 12.

controlled his passion for politics, pouring his frustrated urge for deeds
into a spate of words, somehow compounded of ice and fire, which
became *Il Principe*.

Others might talk sensibly about silks and woolens, about profit and
loss, but, he wrote, "for me it is fitting to talk sensibly about *lo stato*,
and I must do so or take the vow of silence."[11] Machiavelli took no
such vow. Whether sensibly or not, during the next few months in
Il Principe he talked much about *stato*,[12] and readers of that work
have long recognized that Machiavelli had done something to *stato* that
wrenched it out of its medieval matrix of connotation.[13] The men who
made this discovery were themselves heavily committed to political
nationalism. The consequence was almost inevitable: they took Machiavelli's *stato* and decked it out in all the finery of the modern national
state, passionately and romantically conceived as the politically unitary
expression of the will of the nation's people.[14] For a number of reasons
this view of the matter just will not do. The most obvious difficulty
is that in Chapter XXVI of *Il Principe*, where somewhat belatedly
Machiavelli holds to the stance of an Italian patriot (belatedly since
Chapter XXVI is also the last), the word *stato* does not appear at all,
although it occurs in all but three preceding chapters;[15] in effect where
Machiavelli starts talking about Italian patriotism is where he stops
talking about *lo stato*.

The problem then comes to this: in *Il Principe* Machiavelli imparts
a peculiar twist to the term *stato* which might indicate that when
he wrote the book he was doing something odd to the current fabric
of imperatives. But what is the peculiar twist? And precisely what, if
anything, does it do to the fabric of imperatives? In the first place
stato appears in *Il Principe* only rarely in the senses in which it appeared very frequently in medieval political writing and in the writing
of such a contemporary of Machiavelli's as Claude Seyssel. Machiavelli scarcely ever used it to mean "condition in general" as in "solid
state," "state of war," "state of mind." Nor did he use *stato* much more
often in the sense of "social condition" or "order of society," as the
"estate of the nobility" or "estates of the realm." The word occurs 115
times in *Il Principe*. In 110 occurrences it does not have either of the
common medieval denotations just described. All those 110 times it
denotes something that we would call political, not something we
would call either social or general.

[11] Ibid., *Opere*, 8 vols., VI, *Lettere*, ed. F. Isaeta (Milan, 1961), pp. 239–40.
The letter is dated April 1513.
[12] His letter to Francesco Vettori of December 10, 1513, indicates that he had
nearly finished *Il Principe*. (Ibid., II, 304–305.)
[13] For a full elaboration of most of what follows about *stato*, see above, Chap. III.
[14] See, e.g., Ercole, *La Politica di Machiavelli*, 65–196.
[15] All except Machiavelli, *Il Principe*, Chaps. 13, 16, 25.

But what exactly does it denote those 110 times? To this question the embarrassing answer is, "We cannot say," or more justly, "*Il Principe* does not tell." One Italian student of linguistics, Fredi Chiappelli, thought it did tell,[16] and proceeded to classify the denotations of *stato* he believed he had found in the book. He came up with 75 per cent of the occurrences denoting "state in its full maturity with its fundamental political, territorial, and national implications."[17] Unfortunately Chiappelli's method vitiated his own argument. He started by substituting "state in its full maturity" wherever *stato* occurred. Where it happened to fit, he accepted it as the denotation Machiavelli intended; he did not try any of his other denotations of *stato* to see if they fit. Then he divided the *stati* he had left over, the ones that "state in its full maturity" did not fit, among those other denotations. The trouble is that in almost every case where "state in its full maturity" fits in the immediate context, one or more of the other untried denotations of *stato* also fit quite as well, because the context is just not full enough to provide an univocal denotation.[18]

The failure of an examination of denotation of *stato* in *Il Principe* to reveal what Machiavelli was doing to the word suggests that we next search syntax for a clue. In effect there are about seven occurrences of *stato* as the subject of an active verb in *Il Principe*. Eleven times as often as this—about 70 per cent of all its appearances in a political context—it is either the object of an active verb or the subject of a passive one. Syntactically, therefore, *stato* is not up to much in *Il Principe*. If *lo stato* is not doing much, what is being done to it? It is not being worked for, or helped, or served, or revered, or admired, or feared, or loved, as Chiappelli's *stato* "in its full maturity" would be worked for, helped, served, revered, admired, feared, and loved in the twentieth century—not once, not ever. Time after time it is being added to, assaulted, disarmed, won, injured, occupied, possessed, conceded, seized, taken, regained, had, and most often of all acquired, held, kept, lost, and taken away. Indeed, *lo stato* never acquires, holds, keeps, loses, or takes anything from anyone, but on a reasonable rather than a strictly grammatical construction of its situation, in about half its occurrences someone is acquiring, holding, keeping, and losing *lo stato* or having it taken away from him. If we go further and examine the occurrences of *stato* where it is in less immediate syntactical relation to a verb, nothing happens to alter the impression left by the peculiar verbs with which it ordinarily keeps company and the peculiar way in which that company is kept. Whatever Machiavelli meant to

[16] Chiappelli, *Studi*. For a fuller discussion of Chiappelli's method, see Chapter III, Appendix C.
[17] Chiappelli, *Studi*, 59–73, esp. 68.
[18] See examples above, pp. 173–75.

denote by *stato* (on this point the evidence is most ambiguous), in *Il Principe, lo stato* is what is politically up for grabs. And it is nothing more than what is up for grabs. It therefore lacks at least one important dimension of what Chiappelli calls "the state in its full maturity with its fundamental political, territorial, and national implications." *Lo stato* is no body politic; it is not the people politically organized, the political expression of their nature and character and aspirations, their virtues and their defects. Rather it is an inert lump, and whatever vicarious vitality it displays is infused into it not by the people, but by the prince who gets it, holds it, keeps it, and aims not to lose it or have it taken away. Our investigation has led us to a curious conclusion. In *Il Principe* Machiavelli has not stretched *stato*; he has shrunk it. He has drained away most of its medieval social meanings and has not given it its modern political amplitude.

What implications this devitalization of *stato* has for the fabric of imperatives we will try to discern shortly. At the moment we want to explore another linguistic corridor: what might be called motif-word magnetism. Common sense suggests that when a sense shift like the one in *stato* occurs it ought to pull the sense of other words with it. In the case of *Il Principe* the word that immediately recommends itself for a test of *lo stato*'s magnetism is *virtù*. Machiavelli's use of the term *virtù* exercised a kind of fascination for a considerable number of persons in the twentieth century interested in politics as idea or act. Before the First World War a number of Germans wrote extentively about Machiavelli's concept *virtù*,[19] and between the wars Italians whose stomachs or whose eyes to the main chance were stronger than their political prescience saw the modern embodiment of Machiavelli's *virtù* in the posturing lantern-jawed bully and charlatan who unfortunately for them ended dangling head down from the end of a rope in Milan.[20]

Nevertheless *virtù* is not what *Il Principe* is mainly about. As the alternative titles, *Il Principe* and *De Principatibus, De Principati* or *De Principe*,[21] that he gave his little book indicate, Machiavelli thought it was about princes and *principati*. And a *principato* is a species of *stato*; about *stato* we already know something. On a gross count *virtù* occurs about two-thirds as often as *stato* in *Il Principe*.[22] And while

---

[19] Friedrich Meinecke, *Machiavellism*, tr. Douglas Scott (New Haven, Conn., 1957), 31–44; E. W. Mayer, *Machiavellis Geschichtsauffassung und sein Begriff "Virtù"* (Munich, 1912).

[20] Ercole, *La Politica*, 5–64.

[21] Machiavelli, *Discorsi sopra la prima deca di Tito Livio*, Bk. 2, Chap. 1: reference to *nostro trattato de principati*; Bk. 2, Chap. 42: reference to *nostro trattato de Principe*.

[22] *Stato* appears 115 times, *virtù* and its adjectival form 70. The discrepancy is the more marked since, for Machiavelli, *stato* had no adjectival form and there are besides 51 occurrences of *principato*.

stato or *principato* fail to show up in only one chapter of *Il Principe*,[23] on the other hand *virtù* is missing from over a quarter of the chapters.[24] More than this, *virtù* is not always necessary to a prince for getting or even keeping a *stato*, while qualities intentionally distinguished from *virtù*—*industria, prudenzia, astuzia, scelleratezza*; industry, prudence, craft, even orneriness[25]—also come in handy. And when one subjects the denotations of *virtù* and its derivatives in *Il Principe* to the dreary rigors of linguistic analysis, they turn out to be as perplexing as the denotations of *stato*, but in a different way. In most cases they are not particularly ambiguous or hard to ascertain. But they are rich in variety and very poor in novelty. Machiavelli does not use the term with any signification different from those of *virtus* in classical Latin. More than this, in the half century before Machiavelli wrote *Il Principe* the English used their cognate term "virtue," and the French used theirs, *vertu*, with every denotation *virtù* has in *Il Principe*.[26] This does not mean that there is nothing especially worthy of note about the way Machiavelli used the term. It does mean that once again the mere listing of denotation is a dead end.

The first useful thing to note about *virtù* in *Il Principe* is that it tends to occur in thick clots: of its seventy occurrences, forty-five (a little short of two-thirds) appear in less than one-fourth of the chapters of the book. Moreover, the chapters in which *virtù* shows up with high frequency themselves form a couple of clusters: Chapters 6–8, Chapters 12 and 13, and off alone at the very end, Chapter 26. We start with that last chapter and its famous appeal for union among Italians to end the barbarian domination, which "stinks in the nostrils of every man." In that chapter half the time *virtù* is not the *virtù* of the prince but that of the Italian soldiers. It refers unmistakably to their fighting quality, their valor. The whole point of the chapter is that all Italy needs is a military leader as valiant—with as much *virtù*—as its soldiery, and that the time is propitious for such a leader to come forward. The next cluster to consider is the ten occurrences in Chapters 12 and 13. But those chapters deal with military problems specifically and exclusively. Probably in all ten occurrences, certainly in nine out of ten, *virtù* refers to soldierly qualities, sometimes of kinds of soldiers (auxiliaries), sometimes of peoples (the Venetians, the Romans, the Goths), and sometimes of military commanders.

[23] Machiavelli, *Il Principe*, Chap. 25.

[24] Ibid., Chaps. 2, 5, 10, 18, 20, 22, 23. For an index to occurrence of *virtù* and *virtuoso*, see Chapter IV, Appendix G.

[25] Ibid., Chaps. 2, 3 (*industria*), Chap. 3 (*prudenzia*), Chap. 9 (*austuzia*), Chap. 8 (*scelleratezza*).

[26] For Latin, see Forcellini's *Lexicon* and du Cange's *Glossarium*; for English, the *Oxford English Dictionary*; for French, the dictionaries of Godefroy and La Curne de St. Palaye.

And now as to the largest cluster of all: nearly two-fifths of the *virtùs* in *Il Principe* show up in Chapters 6–8,[27] that is, in about one-eighth of the chapters and one-sixth of the book. It is this section above all that has provided the material for the more elaborate fantasies that have enveloped *Il Principe*. To put these chapters in perspective, they treat of new principalities, one of the five types into which Machiavelli divides *principati*: hereditary, mixed, new, ecclesiastical, civil. To get hold of *lo stato*, of what was politically up for grabs in a country, a new prince had to have an army of his own or someone else's, or craft, or villainy, or luck (*fortuna*), or *virtù*, or some combination of these. But once having acquired a *stato* the only secure way to keep it was with an army of one's own and with *virtù*, that is the capacities and qualities, the valor or prowess, needed to keep the *stato* and command the army. If a prince had "lucked" into rule or got there by using someone else's army, then he had particular need of *virtù* to hack through the difficulties of holding onto a *stato* so acquired. Thus with Savonarola in mind, who had the *stato* of Florence in hand but for lack of prowess and an army lost it, Machiavelli says contemptuously *"profeti disarmati ruinorno"* (prophets without arms go down in ruin).[28] This seems to be about the residue of the *mystique* of *virtù* so dear to the heart of Machiavelli worshipers of a later day. *Virtù* usually refers to that cluster of qualities which makes a military commander successful, whether on the offensive—taking—or on the defensive—keeping. This is not, however, quite all that needs to be said about *virtù* in *Il Principe*.

Whatever else it may be, *Il Principe* is a book written early in the sixteenth century about ruling. In that age men who wrote such books always instructed the ruler on the *virtus* or *virtutes*, or the *vertu* or *vertus*, or the virtue or virtues, or the *virtù* he ought to have. In these treatises there is no disharmony between the significances of *virtù*. In a military or political context *virtù* is still suffused with the aura of moral qualities or goodness, and it recurs again and again in a clearly moral sense in the wearisome lists of virtues that the prince is admonished to possess himself of. In *Il Principe*, however, *virtù* appears unmistakably and unambiguously in the sense of the moral qualities and personal goodness of the ruler only thrice,[29] that is, once out of every twenty-three times that Machiavelli uses the term. The disjunction of *virtù* in the sense of moral qualities from *virtù* in its other senses is sharp and decisive; there is no continuity or overlay between the former sense and the others. The way in which Machiavelli marks the disjunction is especially significant. In effect, when he talks of the

---

[27] Twenty-seven occurrences equaling 38 per cent.
[28] Machiavelli, *Il Principe*, Chap. 7.
[29] Once ibid., Chap. 15, twice ibid., Chap. 16.

virtù that a prince needs if he is to hold onto a *stato*, or get more of it, or not lose it, he is never talking about moral virtues or goodness. And this is evident from the fact that on each of *virtù*'s rare appearances in this very common sense of moral qualities, it is accompanied by an admonition to the prince that for his own good he had better avoid it or by the observation that only a lucky prince can get away with it, while without *virtù* in the other sense a prince cannot hold a new *stato*, no matter how he acquires it. In thus driving a wedge between the *virtù* the prince could not get along without and the *virtù* he could not get along with, Machiavelli did more than strain the contemporary fabric of political imperatives; he contemptuously swept much of it aside as useless for the guidance of political action.

And now we can answer our question about the magnetic pull of *lo stato*. In *Il Principe*, Machiavelli's preoccupation with how to acquire *lo stato*, how to keep it, hold it, and avoid losing it has violently modified the accustomed orbit of *virtù* in the political universe. Not only has half that orbit disappeared, but it is the half that then lay and still lies in the realm of universal ethical imperatives. The impulsions to which *virtù* respond in *Il Principe* emanate from *lo stato* and the military and political means necessary to its appropriation and exploitation.

Of all value-bearing modifiers the most general and all-encompassing are the family, good-well, bad-ill, or in Italian, *buono-bene, malo-male*. One would expect the sort of magnetic force that *stato* exercised on *virtù* also to affect this wide-span group of words in *Il Principe*. Again a mere listing of denotation proves useless. The whole gamut of denotations is there from the neutral emphatic function of denoting "really" or "indeed"[30] to the notion of a universal good, *bene alla università delle uomini*.[31] It is when we try to find out who the good in *Il Principe* is good for and who the ill is ill for that we note a replication of that somewhat terrifying shift in the object of words of ethical specification which we have already found in *virtù*. The good refers to the common good or general welfare twice and to what we might call civic goodness or merit five times. In contrast forty-three times what is good or bad is simply good or bad for the prince, to his advantage or to his disadvantage. What was to his advantage and therefore good was to be able to acquire a *stato*, or more *stato* (*più stato*), to build it, to keep it, to defend it, to occupy it, possess it, seize it, take it. What was disadvantageous, and therefore bad, was to lose *stato*, have it taken away. In these instances to ask whether what the prince did was good or bad for anyone else—the people, say, or even the state in its present-day sense—is a mere irrelevance. When Machiavelli

[30] Ibid., Chap. 16.
[31] Ibid., Chap. 26.

capitulated to his own need to *ragionare dello stato* in *Il Principe*, he was not concerned to "talk sensibly" about what was good or bad for anyone but the prince.

Buono-bene-malo-male also appear in the sense of "morally right" or "morally wrong" in *Il Principe*. And here their verbal orbit is precisely symmetrical with that of *virtù*. In almost every instance in which they appear in this sense Machiavelli is taking pains to point out that to get *stato* and keep or increase it a prince must look as good as he can and be as bad as he needs. By its magnetic force *stato* has here altered the orbit of the most ordinary of all words used for discriminating between right and wrong.

In the study preceding this one, I limited my attention to Machiavelli's use of one term, *lo stato*, in *Il Principe*. I concluded: "In *Il Principe* there is no justification for the relation of the prince to *lo stato*. There can be none because *lo stato* is not a matrix of values, a body politic; it is an instrument of exploitation, the mechanism the prince uses to get what he wants. . . . If the prince exploits *lo stato* with astuteness he will keep his grip on *lo stato* and even tighten it, and will be glorified as a man of honor and praised by everyone, for, as Machiavelli says in the climactic sentences of *Il Principe*, the mob is always gulled by appearances and by the way things work out, and the mob is all there is in the world. So *si guarda al fino*, take heed of the result. The result is political success or failure. It is not right to succeed, it is not wrong to fail. It is merely success to succeed, and failure to fail. Right is not might, might is not right; might is might, and that is what *Il Principe* is about. As to right—any kind of right of the individual or of the state—that is not really what *Il Principe* is about."[32] Now that we have examined in detail some of the further operations Machiavelli performed on the loom of language in *Il Principe*, the examination seems to confirm our earlier conclusion.

The relation of *Il Principe* to the fabric of political imperatives of Machiavelli's own day should be evident enough: it makes a shambles of it.

In England, shortly after Machiavelli wrote *Il Principe*, another worker at the loom of language, Thomas More, dealt in a very peculiar way with the fabric of imperatives of his day in his greatest book, *Utopia*. His native land, which stood at the focus of More's vision and experience when he wrote *Utopia*, was one of those *stati hereditari*[33] that did not evoke Machiavelli's interest because by a rapid but inaccurate reading of the past in the light of the present he had concluded that they were easy to hold. Since in about 1514 he was getting

---

[32] See above, p. 171.
[33] Machiavelli, *Il Principe*, Chap. 2.

ready to write his history of the reign of Richard III,[34] and since like
most of his contemporaries in his native land he saw his own times
against the background of the bloody chronicle of English kings in
the fifteenth century, More knew better than that. Nevertheless, he
wrote *Utopia* with his mind fixed on his own land in his own time,
and in the second decade of the sixteenth century England was not
disturbed by the sort of political upheaval that was the milieu of *Il
Principe* and that confirmed and strengthened Machiavelli's obsession
with *lo stato*. What concerned More was not *lo stato* but, as the full
title of *Utopia* indicated, the *status reipublicae*.[35] Between Machiavelli's
stato and More's *status* the connection is solely etymological. More
was impelled to write *Utopia* by "the state of the nation," as we might
say, or perhaps better, by the "condition of the commonweal" of England and Christendom. When he wrote of the traits that in the minds
of ordinary men constituted the true worth of commonweals, he produced curious effects on the loom of language. He did so again by
his way of using some of the terms ordinarily used to designate the
masters of the commonwealth of England and of Christendom. Indeed
because of an oddity of language, which reflects an oddity of contemporary thought, those latter terms are not, as we shall see, readily
separable from the then current common notion of true worth.

It requires an intensive microscopic investigation of his language in
Il Principe to make out precisely the impact of that work on the fabric
of imperatives. To trace through the words of *Utopia* its relation to the
fabric of imperatives in More's milieu when he wrote his work is
easier. In his way of using *lo stato* Machiavelli cut away a large part
of the range that a motif word had in his own day but did not extend
that word to the range which it has today. More did something equally
drastic but more simple and conspicuous. He took a cluster of words
that gave a particular character to an important sector of the fabric
of imperatives in his day and reversed the signs on them. From pluses
he turned them into minuses; from honorific terms he transformed
them into pejorative ones. Thus, there is no more honorable (*magis
honorificum*) source of profit to the king, according to More, than
penalties for disobeying laws long unenforced and forgotten, since
they have the outward mask of justice.[36] When it is offended, the
brightest manifestation of earthly power, majesty (*majestas*), even the
majesty of the highest temporal dignitary, the Holy Roman Emperor,
can be salved with gold.[37] Elegance and splendor are disgraceful,

[34] *The History of King Richard III* (New Haven, Conn., 1963), Volume II of
The Complete Works of St. Thomas More, ed. Sylvester, lxiii–lxv.

[35] More, *Utopia,* opposite p. cxciv, *De optimo reipublicae statu deque nova insula
Utopia libellus vere aureus . . .*

[36] Ibid., 93/9–10.

[37] Ibid., 88/5.

the vain show a set of foolish popinjays.[38] *Gloria* is *ostentatio*, ostentation.[39] At worst, when it is the satisfaction a ruler derives from acquiring and holding a land other than his own, it is *gloriola*,[40] petty self-satisfaction. In the common language of More's times, majesty, splendor, and glory are attributes of God; honor is what men owe Him. They are also attributes ascribed to the alleged chosen viceregents of God on earth, the princes, and what they claim as their due. But in *Utopia* they are what men with power and riches seek and demand for themselves merely as their due for possessing power and riches. They are the things of God that a host of petty Caesars claim and force men to render unto them. And in demanding such things the rulers of the earth subvert their meaning, making them literally preposterous.

More striking than the foregoing is the treatment *nobilis* and *generosus* received in *Utopia*. These two words were tightly keyed into the whole image of the cosmos by means of which for centuries most men who thought about such matters at all arrayed and ordered vast tracts of their experience and provided them with ostensibly rational meaning. That image had two dimensions. The first dimension was the "great chain of being," the conception that in His outflow of creative love God left uncreated no kind of thing from the insensate gross earth at the bottom to the highest rational spirits, the angels, at the top.[41] The cosmos then was scaled from top to bottom, from highest to lowest, from best to least good; it was shot through with a conception of graded worth. The other dimension was the conception of correspondences.[42] The best-known correspondences perhaps are those among the human body, the body of the family, the body politic, and the body, so to speak, of the cosmos itself, with the head, the father, the king, and the sun paramount in each. Parallels ran horizontally between corresponding levels of each genus of entities. The effect, it would seem, of this mode of perception would be to diminish precision and clarity of specific observation, at once to enrich and becloud the imagination, and to impart to certain words a massiveness of connotation and of implication of worth or merit that we can only with difficulty grasp.

Nobilis, generosus, and their equivalents in the various languages of Europe were words possessing this massive quality in a pre-eminent degree. They were indicators of high status in a world where status was a fundamental assumption rather than a recent discovery of sociologists. They were also symbols of merit, and through the process

[38] Ibid., 154/7, 8, 22; 166/32.
[39] Ibid., 138/7.
[40] Ibid., 90/3.
[41] Arthur Lovejoy, *The Great Chain of Being* (Cambridge, Mass., 1936), esp. 45–51, 67–80.
[42] E. M. W. Tillyard, *The Elizabethan World Picture* (London, 1952), 77–93.

of correspondences the notion of merit was firmly fixed to the notion of status. There were noble men and base men as there were noble metals and base metals. Scarcely a half year before Thomas More began to write *Utopia*, a French contemporary gave perfect and naïve expression to this cultural stereotype, expression the more notable because the author was not otherwise a particularly naïve man. In *La Monarchie de France* Claude Seyssel discusses the favor the crown owed to the noblesse over the other orders of society. Other things being equal or perhaps just a trifle less than equal, Seyssel justifies that favor because the nobility is more *digne*, more worthy than the well-to-do or the common people and because *"ils sont de meilleur étoffe* [they are made of better stuff].*"[43] This, he says, is as reason would have it. Obviously he identifies reason with the whole climate of opinion or spiritual syndrome created by the juncture of the great chain of being with the parallel ladders of correspondence. Under such circumstances to change the signs on *generosus* and *nobilis* implies more than a downgrading of a segment of the social hierarchy; it means the displacement of a whole sector of the fabric of imperatives.

Men who were charged with or had assumed responsibility for the care of the fabric of imperatives in the late Middle Ages and the Renaissance made much of the noble and the gentle in their word spinning. The older tradition excoriated the lives lived by nobles and gentlemen in the degenerate days of the current excoriator. This denunciation was a prelude to an appeal to the noble and gentle to return to the ancient or original or natural virtues of their order, forgotten or abandoned in the present degenerate age. The more recent literary ploy, a favorite of the humanist, was to raise the question of what constituted true nobility. With a degree of consensus unusual among them the humanists tended to agree that being noble was not a matter of long lineage, wealth, or great ancestry; it was rather a matter of being a man of true excellence. On examination it turns out, not too surprisingly, that the humanists' man of true excellence bears a marked likeness to the humanist ego ideal. If More had used *nobilis* or *generosus* in either of these ways in *Utopia*, he would have fallen into one of two well-known literary stereotypes: that of the "defections of the estates,"[44] standard in medieval social polemics, or that of the "debate on true nobility,"[45] standard in the self-serving effusions of humanists.

In fact he did neither. In the first place *generosus* and *nobilis* never

---

[43] Seyssel, *Monarchie de France*, 122–23.
[44] Mohl, *The Three Estates in Medieval and Renaissance Literature*, 341–66.
[45] Sir Thomas Elyot, *The Boke named the Governour*, ed. H. H. S. Crofts (2 vols., London, 1880), II, 26–38, and references in footnotes there.

appear in a favorable context when More is referring to the cosmopolitan military élite, the aristocracy of his own day. They occur seventeen times with pejorative overtones, thrice with doubtful connotation, and just once with honorific implications.[46] And that once, *generosus* is used to describe the stouteartedness of the citizen militia of Utopia in language that would have given joy to Machiavelli.[47]

What More was up to is clear from his speech; it is yet clearer from his silence, especially his silence in the second part of *Utopia* where he describes the best ordering of a commonweal or civil society. For in that society there are no "true" nobles or "true" gentlemen; there are no *nobiles* or *generosi* at all; there are only citizens. This is curious enough, most eccentric indeed with respect to that large sector of the current fabric of imperatives which assimilated excellence to status by blanketing both with the terms *nobilis* and *generosus*. Yet the language of Part II of *Utopia* is even more revealing and more curious if one looks at it from the vantage point provided by the English translation of the book that Ralph Robinson made in the 1550's.

Robinson lightly sprinkled Part II of that translation with the adjectives "gentle" and its cognates used in an honorific sense comportable with the contemporary fabric of imperatives. When one looks at the identical places in More's Latin original for the equivalent word *generosus* and its cognates, however, one does not find them. More had used entirely different words to designate the qualities he was praising. Thus Robinson says that King Utopus brought his new subjects to "humanity and civil gentleness," where More had written *cultus humanitatisque perduxit*.[48] He described clemency as "the gentlest affection of our nature," but More had called it *humanissimum naturae nostrae affectum*.[49] Where Robinson translates, "Nature biddeth thee to be good and gentle to other[s but] she commandeth thee not to be cruel and ungentle to thyself," we find *bonus* and *inclementem* in

---

[46] More, *Utopia*.

	Nobilis	Generosus
Honorific		210/15
Doubtful	74/30; 154/10; 156/15	56/9; 94/8
Pejorative	62/3; 66/3; 68/25; 88/9, 16; 130/4; 168/6, 9, 10; 204/28; 238/22	62/15, 22; 64/18, 23; 66/3; 68/23; 130/4; 240/7
Neutral		238/17

[47] Ibid., 210.
[48] Thomas More, *Utopia*, ed. J. H. Lupton (Oxford, 1895), 118; ibid. (Yale), 112/4–5.
[49] Ibid. (Lupton), 158; ibid. (Yale), 138/17.

More's Latin, but we find no equivalent at all for "gentle" and "un-gentle."[50] A little later Robinson simply put "gently" where More put *clementer*,[51] and then wrote "gently and favorably" where More only had *indulgenter*.[52] Again where More writes of a *humanitatis ac benig-nitatis officium*, Robinson translates "a point of humanity and gentle-ness."[53] Thus one way or another Robinson equated gentility with humanity, goodness, clemency, kindliness, and benignity. More, how-ever, had done nothing of the sort. There were abundant humanity, goodness, clemency, kindliness, and benignity in the Utopian common-wealth, but More never linked any of these traits with gentility or nobility, with gentlemen or noblemen. The ascription of these qualities to ordinary men who worked with their hands in town and country ran counter to one of the most persistent of all linguistic phenomena of the English language, the movement of terms from the point where they simply designated low status or mere youth to the point where they designated some sort of moral depravity or viciousness. The *ceorl*, or "ordinary guy," became a churl, while unpleasant conduct became "churlish"; the knave, started as a young boy (a *knabe*), became a servant, and thence a rascal; the boor began as a farmer and became a gross lout; the villain came to a worse ending still, just because he stayed down on the farm working for the owner of the villa.

In one place Robinson took action the reverse of that which we have caught him in above. More had charged *nobilis*, *aurifex*, and *foenerator*, who did nothing or did ill to the commonwealth, with the injustice of living idly while the true supporters of society—laborers, carters, carpenters, and farmers—worked like beasts of burden. Rob-inson carries the charge home to the "rich goldsmith" and the "usurer," but he leaves the nobleman out.[54] The asynchronous silence of More's Latin and Robinson's English in these instances is perhaps even more significant than the tone of contempt with which the words *nobilis* and *generosus* so often ring when they do appear in the Latin original. A view of the world that rejected the assimilation of the good to the noble and the gentle was alien to Robinson, as it was to most articulate men in the sixteenth century. He translated Part II of *Utopia*, but the idea behind it did not fully penetrate his consciousness. In his translation, quite unconsciously one suspects, Robinson sets the loom

[50] Ibid. (Lupton), 192; ibid. (Yale), 164/9–10.
[51] Ibid. (Lupton), 222; ibid. (Yale), 184/28.
[52] Ibid. (Lupton), 232; ibid. (Yale), 192/12.
[53] Ibid. (Lupton), 193; ibid. (Yale), 164/27–8. For further examples, see ibid. (Lupton), 168, 212, 220; ibid. (Yale), 146/8, 178/30–31, 184/4–8.
[54] Ibid. (Lupton) 301. There is another possible instance of the same thing, only involving *generosus*, ibid., 47.

of language to work to repair the holes More had torn into the current fabric of imperatives. What was the import of that rending?

> When I consider . . . the condition of all commonwealths flourishing any-
> where in the world today so help me God, I can see nothing but a kind
> of conspiracy of the rich aiming at their own interests under the name of
> the commonwealth. They devise every available way first to keep without
> fear whatever they have amassed . . . and second to buy as cheap as
> possible and exploit the labor of the poor. These become law just as soon
> as the rich have decreed their observance in the name of the public—
> that is in the name of the poor, too![55]

In the eyes of Thomas More, who had envisaged, he believed, the conditions for the right ordering of a commonwealth the very structure of the princely commonwealths of Europe is an enormous fraud perpetrated by the rich and powerful on the poor and weak. In saying this in *Utopia*, More was impelled to set on some quite common words values opposite to those they bore among most of his contemporaries.

The immediate implication of our examination of the loom of language as it appeared in Machiavelli's *Il Principe* and More's *Utopia* is that in the years just before the Reformation Machiavelli in *Il Principe* and More in *Utopia* did indeed wreak strange havoc on the fabric of imperatives. Moreover, although they were men whose temperaments and convictions stood far apart, they wrought a similar sort of havoc in overlapping though not identical areas of the fabric. In effect they treated the language of politics each in a different way, yet each in such a way as to make clear their view that the current imperatives of politics were an exploitative swindle by means of which the possessors of power grabbed chunks of it from one another and withheld it and its advantages from those who did not possess it. No more for the English writer than for the Italian was the existing order of the human community a true *vinculum juris*, a bond of rightful law, and as long as that order remained what it was, talk about political obligation, which has been described as the central problem of politics,[56] could have very little meaning.

Our detailed inquiry into the way Machiavelli and More used a few words in *Il Principe* and *Utopia* may permit the following tentative and general conclusions about the possibilities latent in this kind of investigation.

A careful examination of the loom of language can provide solid

[55] Ibid. (Yale), 241/24–35 (slightly reworded by me).
[56] Alessandro Passerin d'Entrèves, *Medieval Contributions to Political Thought* (Oxford, 1939), 3.

evidence about shifts in the fabric of imperatives at least in the minds of particular writers at certain points in their lives.

The changes in words that provide this evidence vary in kind. They may be grossly conspicuous word substitutions. They may be curtailments in the current senses of a word or reversals in its value. Or they may show themselves in a word's syntactical posture and in the company it keeps with other words.

This is a monitory point, and one only hinted at in the preceding chapter. The kind of probing here illustrated should not lead to indulgence in precipitate statements about changes in the entire climate of opinion of a society, statements made in haste to be repented at leisure. The relation between the sort of language shifts we have described and changes in the climate of opinion are the appropriate subject not for assumption but for painstaking investigation.[57]

Most historians tend to be impatient, perhaps too quickly impatient, with discussions of the general implications and possibilities of a mode of historical investigation. They prefer to hear in detail what follows in a particular case. What follows in the particular case of the foregoing study of the language of *Il Principe* and *Utopia*? In relation to the fabric of imperatives both Machiavelli and More were of the group of men we have described as maintenance specialists. The effect of their books, however, was not to reinforce, to mend, or to adjust that part of the fabric which was their immediate concern; it was to destroy it. In very different ways the language of *Il Principe* and that of *Utopia* express a common sense of the condition of things and a common

[57] How these very tentative remarks will strike investigators working in relevant and related areas of the linguistic sciences and how this investigation relates to those conducted in those sciences, I do not know. I was warned by the reader of an early draft of this chapter that it would appear naïve if it made no reference to parallel studies by students of historical linguistics. Because, however, I had read no such works, nor indeed any work at all on linguistics, when I wrote the paper, the warning has not been heeded. Since then, I have studied the subject a bit, but a little knowledge is a dangerous thing, especially dangerous to him who is rash enough to display it before those who possess a great deal of it; thus my recently acquired dim light will remain judiciously hidden under a bushel. One particular point about method, however, may appropriately be made. The metaphor of the loom of language and the fabric of imperatives is strictly *ad hoc*, for the particular task to which this chapter addresses itself, and it is not fully elaborated. It may or may not be worth such elaboration, and it may overlap or even duplicate kinds of concepts or imagery already used in linguistics. In the various areas of human inquiry there are times for conceptual rigor and times for a certain imaginative looseness, times when premature precision may reduce a whole area to sterility. My little reading has persuaded me that the area of linguistics on which this chapter touches is of the latter kind. An undue zeal for scientific rigor in hypothesizing in that area at this point might seriously hamper investigation, as the attempt to subject them to the rigor of Galilean mechanics hampered the life sciences in the seventeenth century. This of course in no way should license any but the most meticulous accuracy in the testing and use of *historical* data.

spiritual malaise. They express alienation. This alienation is, of course, in some measure personal to Machiavelli and More, but in their view their personal alienation was but an image of alienation, cleavage, disjunction in the world they lived in. For Machiavelli that disjunction lay between the fabric of political imperatives and the conditions of effective political action. For fools who took them seriously such imperatives lit the way to death or defeat. For the shrewd and bold, who used them to gull the mob, they were means to get, hold, or increase *stato*—whatever happened to be up for grabs in the region of politics.[58] They certainly did not provide a viable set of rules to give legitimate order to and guide men in their doings in that region. In sum they were a swindle; the language of *Il Principe* makes it clear enough that Machiavelli considered them a swindle. In the same way the language of *Utopia* makes it clear that More regarded the imperatives supposed to legitimate the position of those who dominated the social order in his world a swindle. It might be argued with some plausibility that the language of More and Machiavelli betrays an alienation from the areas of the contemporary fabric of imperatives to which it relates more radical than that of Luther to the religious imperatives of the same age.

A year after the publication of *Utopia*, however, Luther's alienation set in train the events that shortly wrought a violent, long, and shattering upheaval—a great revolution—in the Western world. What did the alienations of Machiavelli and More wreak? What followed directly from their onslaughts on the fabric of imperatives? Nothing or almost nothing. And for this there was good reason. To believe *Il Principe*, men must believe that the repository of the ultimate earthly power to which they are subject is merely the passive prize of a game in which they may take part or not as they will. They must also believe that unless they are willing to carry a frightful handicap they can only play the game by cutting clear away from the fabric of imperatives. Such a view was too radical, the alienation it embodied too absolute to be acceptable to Machiavelli's contemporaries; indeed, as is evident in certain chapters of the *Discorsi*, it was too radical for Machiavelli himself.[59] More's alienation as expressed and discussed in *Utopia* was even larger in its scope than Machiavelli's, involving a greater area of the fabric of imperatives, encompassing the whole *status reipublicae*, or, as we would say, the entire political, economic, and social order. Nor was More ready to let it go at that, and, like Machiavelli, simply to investigate the qualities and stratagems useful for the exploitation of the chances for aggrandizement which that order and its fraudulent fabric of imperatives made available. Instead, More presented an alter-

[58] Machiavelli, *Il Principe*, Chap. 18.
[59] Especially, *Discorsi*, Bk. I, Caps. 9, 10.

native fabric of imperatives, an *optimus status reipublicae*, in which the means of alienation in his own society—money, private property, inequality, and the fabric of imperatives that support them and that they support—would not exist. In such a commonweal his own alienation—he calls it a prison[60]—would end, and so would the alienation— he calls it "the lot of slaves"[61]—of almost all humankind. But how are men to pass from this world of alienation and bondage to that world of reconciliation and freedom? To this question More gives no answer, but only tells a tale of Utopus, a king who never was, who seventeen hundred years ago brought this blessed consummation to Utopia, a land that never was. *Utopia* is literally nowhere.[62]

For more than three hundred years *Il Principe* and *Utopia*, two of the most radical repudiations and two of the most drastic onslaughts on the fabric of imperatives of Western men, two of the most powerful images of the alienation which that fabric engendered, stood isolated and separated at the threshold of the modern age. Separated because no imagination emerged powerful enough to bind together and reduce to a mutual coherence the nightmare of the Florentine official and the daydream of the English humanist.

Only in the 1830's and 1840's did some Europeans, new prophets of a new age, grasp the possibilities latent in the visions of Machiavelli and More. Property was theft; the state was the supreme instrument of exploitation. Together they brought about that alienation of man from his true nature which was the sum of human history. But if the state was merely a means of exploitation, a weapon in the warfare forever waged by those who had against those who had not, then it was for the exploited and alienated to seize the weapon and destroy it or use it to destroy the means of their alienation: private ownership and the system of buying and selling for money which maintained it. By means appropriate to that totally alienated man, Machiavelli's prince, the totally alienated class, the exploited and dispossessed, were to grasp *lo stato*, and through the exploitation of the exploiter, uproot alienation itself, thereby clearing the way for the restoration of men to the family of man, the classless society, utopia. The link between the Machiavellian actuality and the Utopian dream was not a mythical King Utopus; it was class war, seizure of power, revolution.[63] But in

[60] Eras., *Ep.* 2, 414.

[61] *Utopia* (Yale), 127/28.

[62] "Nowhere" (Lat. *Nusquama*) is, of course, the meaning of the Greek name for the island—Utopia.

[63] This potpourri of conceptions, intentionally not sorted out or made precise here, was concocted in the milieu of Paris between 1840, the publication date of Pierre Proudhon's *What Is Property?* and 1848, that of the *Communist Manifesto* of Karl Marx and Friedrich Engels. For brief but excellent accounts, see Isaiah Berlin, *Karl Marx* (London, 1939), 80–120, and Robert Tucker, *Philosophy and Myth in Karl Marx* (Cambridge, Eng., 1961), 95–161.

the second decade of the sixteenth century, the secular *kairos,* the ripeness of time, which was to bring into the arena of action the alienation for which Machiavelli and More in their divergent ways found words, was hundreds of years off. In the meantime *Il Principe* and *Utopia* retained a high level of intellectual visibility; people did not forget them. But men have ways of dealing with inconvenient, wide-eyed, small boys who shout in the street, "The Emperor is wearing no clothes!" They called *Il Principe* wicked and *Utopia* a mere fantasy. And this may have been as sensible a way of dealing with them as any. At least, since men a hundred-odd years ago discovered means of fusing the visions these little books contained, nothing has happened that demands that we believe otherwise.

APPENDIX G: Occurrences of *virtù* and *virtuoso* in *Il Principe*

Page	Line
Dedication	
I	
15	14
II	
III	
22	5
IV	
28	14
V	
VI	
30	9
	12
	15
	21
	23
	28
31	12
	13
	22
	24
	26
32	29
33	6
VII	
34	5
	13
	18
	21
	27
	31
	39 (2)
VIII	
40	25
41	10
	29
42	4
	7
	15

Page	Line
43	34
IX	
45	7
X	
50	23
XI	
XII	
53	3
54	22
55	21
56	8
	9
	15
57	18
XIII	
59	19
60	20
61	17
	20
XIV	
62	6
XV	
66	7
XVI	
66	15
67	1
XVII	
71	2
	4
	7
XVIII	

Page	Line
XIX	
78	13
79	29
80	22
	24
84	28
XX	
XXI	
92	31
XXII	
XXIII	
XXIV	
97	7
98	18
XXV	
99	16
	21
XXVI	
101	32
102	5
	9
	28
103	18
	25
104	2
	16
105	13

*C*HAPTER V The Predatory, the Utopian, and the Constitutional Vision: Machiavelli, More, and Claude de Seyssel. *La Monarchie de France* and Normal Politics on the Eve of the Reformation[*]

O NLY two writers of the Age of the Renaissance produced books directly concerned with politics that are nowadays widely read. Indeed they produced the only two books on the subject written in that era that have been persistently and widely read ever since they wrote them. The books were written within three years of each other, and both were written, so to speak, by accident. That is to say, they came into being in the midst of and in relation to odd conjunctures of circumstances in the lives of their authors, and there was little in the previous careers of those authors to suggest that, had it not been for those conjunctures, they would have produced such works. They had both been too busy, and neither had foreseen the interruption to his busyness that turned him to a sustained literary effort. Both had had time for occasional bits of literary scribbling; both had literary and even poetic pretensions. They had been too busy, however, for that steady concentrated contemplation of their fragmentary insights that enables a man to sense the general pattern into which his insights are falling, to bring out sharply the details of that pattern, and to press to their conclusion the implications the pattern suggests.

Suddenly and accidentally, through no intentions of their own, both of these busy men found themselves with time, and nothing but time, on their hands. The circumstances of their involuntary idleness led one of them certainly, the other possibly, to turn their very sharp vision most intently on the problem of the general structure of politics in their own day.

The certain case is that of Niccolò Machiavelli, age forty-six, for fifteen years an official of the Republic of Florence, unemployed as of November 7, 1512. Others than he lost positions of authority or teetered precariously in them when, with a Spanish army running interference, the Medici returned to Florence after a long exile. Many, however, were able quickly to arrange for themselves a peace, or at least a truce, with the new order. After all, with the great Florentine houses which had served the Republic during their exile it was well for the Medici to avoid trouble. But what trouble could that shabby-genteel family, the Machiavelli, make? By serving as general factotum to Piero Soderini, Gonfaloniere of Justice, leader of the late anti-Medici regime, its scion Niccolò had achieved a political position rather above what his condition in life warranted.[1] He never would be missed.

More overwhelming to Machiavelli perhaps than the troubled state of his outward fortune—arrest on suspicion of complicity in a plot against Medici, imprisonment and torture, forced retirement to his modest house in the country—was the utter disarray in which the torrent of events had left his notions about politics.[2] For Machiavelli was not a political hack who cared for nothing but a safe city job. Throughout his career he had been an ideologist at heart. Although he had never put them together in an orderly way, he had a number of rooted notions about politics. His recent experiences had been such as to shake his faith in all his deepest convictions, and as with good ideologists his need to restore order among his notions was as urgent as, perhaps more urgent than, his need to get his political career back on its tracks. Since his political career never did get back on the

---

[1] For details on Machiavelli's activities and circumstances during the crisis that preceded, accompanied, and followed the return of the Medici to Florence, see Ridolfi, *Vita di Niccolò Machiavelli*, pp. 183–232.

[2] Letter to Soderini, in Niccolò Machiavelli, *Opere*, VI *Lettere*, pp. 228–31.

tracks, he ended up with plenty of time to think things over. Machiavelli was not to know that, however, when in 1513 he made his first essay at restoring some order to his badly shaken political cosmology. That essay—*Il Principe*—was written at considerable speed with the stench of failure, a falsified faith, and hopes burnt-out still reeking in his nostrils and a hunger for the political life still gnawing at his vitals. The auspices for a detached impersonal effort were poor; and indeed *Il Principe*, whatever the appearances, is not such an effort. It is a book extraordinary and extravagant.[3]

So is the other book, finished three years later by another man, that was to take its place alongside Machiavelli's exercise in catharsis among the classics of political literature. The circumstances of its composition, however, were not so devastating. Thomas More had larger literary pretensions than Machiavelli and, at the age of thirty-eight, not much to show for them. He, too, had lacked time. Some of it, as with most Londoners of his eminence, had gone to that unpaid or ill-paid public service that the Crown and the City extorted from men who were capable, conscientious, and well-to-do, service not in the great world of diplomacy where Machiavelli had lived, but in the intimate one of local government. Most of More's time, however, seems to have gone to making enough money to support a considerable family plus a certain number of peripheral and occasional spongers in a style which without being lavish or luxurious managed to be very expensive indeed.[4]

From the rush of legal business More was suddenly becalmed in the most undemanding of human pursuits, that of the emissary abroad without a mission. Negotiations in Bruges with the agents of Prince Charles, ruler of the Netherlands, having been suspended for talks at a higher level, More had abundant time for contemplation.

What he seems to have contemplated was the contrast of the biblical Christian way of life that the humanists in his circle of friends held forth as the standard for man's imitation with the actual ways of life he had seen about him—from the low life that as deputy sheriff he had observed weekly for several years in the London sheriff's court all the way to the very high life that he occasionally encountered because of his friendships with men in the inner circle of the court of Henry VIII. The confrontation of a going society with biblical Christianity always has latent explosive possibilities, and in More's case these were realized when it led him to ask himself what the temporal conditions for a true Christian commonwealth actually were. Before he had quite

---

[3] For a somewhat fuller attempt to come to grips with Machiavelli's state of mind when he composed *Il Principe*, see above, pp. 185–7.

[4] For a convenient general account of More's life up to his thirty-eighth year, see R. W. Chambers, *Thomas More* (London, 1935), pp. 48–144.

finished writing what he intended to write about what a Christian commonwealth ought to be, he was offered a high position at the English court on terms both honorable and financially attractive. The comparison thus abruptly forced on his attention between the conditions necessary for a true Christian commonwealth and the conditions which actually prevailed in the putatively Christian commonwealth ruled by his native prince, Henry VIII, magnified the explosive force of his confrontation of the world as it was with the world as scripture said it should be. The result was a book, *Utopia*, that was both extraordinary and extravagant.[5]

I have emphasized the extravagance, the abnormality, of both *Il Principe* and *Utopia* because, as a result of their incorporation into the body of great literature on politics, we are prone to forget how completely they prescind from the normal view of politics in the early sixteenth century. Their authors, however, were well enough aware of what they were doing; they were indeed quite explicit about it. Machiavelli made his intention clear very early, in Chapter 2 of *Il Principe*.

> In hereditary states . . . the difficulties of maintaining power are considerably less than in new principalities. . . . If their prince possesses an ordinary amount of energy he will always maintain himself in power.[6]

So much, in *Il Principe*, for hereditary rulers and what concerns the governance of the lands they rule. So much, in effect, for the normal politics of all the great monarchical states of Europe and for the problems of ruling that faced every viable political society in the Western world of Machiavelli's day except Venice and the Swiss cantons. So much for any place, indeed, where politics was something more than the smash-and-grab game that it had become from the Po Valley to the Kingdom of Naples since Machiavelli entered on his political novitiate at the turn of the century.

In the climactic chapter of *Il Principe*, Chapter 18, he points to his intention in a more telling way; but one must read closely to understand just what he has done. He begins this chapter, "How Princes Should Observe Good Faith,"

> Everyone understands well enough how praiseworthy it is in a prince to keep his word, to live with integrity and not by guile. Nevertheless, the experience of our times teaches us that those princes have achieved great

---

[5] For successive attempts to relate *Utopia* to More's immediate circumstances when he wrote the book, see J. H. Hexter, More's *"Utopia,"* Torchbook Edition, pp. 11–30, 90–110, a correction of these views, pp. 161–65, and above, pp. 26–40, 138–149.

[6] Machiavelli, *Il Principe*, 2. All subsequent references to this work are by chapter.

things who have looked upon the keeping of one's word as a matter of little moment and have understood how, by their guile, to twist men's minds; and in the end have surpassed those who have rested their power upon faithfulness.

You ought to understand therefore that there are two ways of fighting, the one by the laws, the other with force. The first is proper to men, the second to beasts; but since in many instances the first is not enough, it is necessary to have recourse to the second. A prince, consequently, must understand how to use the manner proper to the beast as well as that proper to man. . . .

Since, then, a prince must of necessity know how to use the bestial nature, he should take as his models from among beasts the fox and the lion; for the lion does not defend himself from traps, and the fox does not defend himself from wolves. One must therefore be a fox to scent out the traps and a lion to ward off the wolves. Those who simply act the lion do not understand the implications of their own actions.[7]

It is all done so smoothly that even a careful reader may associate "laws," which are "proper to men" and therefore implicitly preferable to the "force . . . proper to beasts," with the prince who lives with integrity, keeps his word, rests his power on faithfulness. Not at all: *Le leggi* like *la forza* are a *generazione de combattere*, a way of fighting, a mode of conflict. The line of Machiavelli's argument comes clear when we compare it with the passages which it echoes.

Those passages from Cicero are as follows:

. . . since there are two ways of settling a dispute: first, by discussion; second, by physical force; and since the former is characteristic of man, the latter of the brute, we must resort to force only in case we may not avail ourselves of discussion. . . .[8]

While wrong may be done, then, in either of two ways, that is, by force or by fraud, both are bestial: fraud seems to belong to the cunning fox, force to the lion; both are wholly unworthy of man, but fraud is the more contemptible.[9]

Machiavelli's paraphrase must be one of the most efficient perversions of a writer's intention in the long history of literary hocus-pocus. He has slightly altered the passages paraphrased, he has conflated two passages separated in Cicero's *De Officiis* by several pages and dealing with two different topics, and he has removed both passages from contexts inconvenient to his line of argument. In the Florence of Machiavelli's day the striking language of his paraphrases must have wakened

[7] Ibid., *18*. The wording of the legend of Chiron inserted between the two passages quoted above confirms the interpretation just offered.
[8] Cicero, *De Officiis*, i. 11. 34.
[9] Ibid., i. 13. 41.

in many minds memory echoes of their Ciceronian origin. Thus by his three-way bit of verbal legerdemain he makes it appear that his view has the support of the highest classical authority on the right conduct of politics.

To make it seem that he stood shoulder to shoulder with the man who in the eyes of the Renaissance was the wisest Roman of them all was quite a feat. The first passage from Cicero has as its context the relations of a state with its potential enemies. It is preceded by this sentence: "Then, too, in the case of a state in its external relations, the rights of war must be strictly observed."[10] It is followed by the sentence, "The only excuse, therefore, for going to war is that we may live in peace unharmed."[11] Thus Cicero is concerned with the conditions of rightful and humane warfare with *enemies*, while the over-all context of Machiavelli's observations is "the way a prince ought behave to *his subjects and allies*."[12] It is against them he must act both as a lion and a fox, preying on them lest he be preyed on by some of them. In the second passage, while Cicero's attention is focused on the relative position of two vices on the moral scale, Machiavelli, in an attitude of moral neutrality, is simply weighing up the expediences for a prince of using force or fraud as the occasion demands. And finally, while both passages from Cicero are part of his general discussion of justice, "the crowning glory of the virtues on the basis of which men are called 'good men,'"[13] in *Il Principe* Machiavelli's paraphrase has nothing whatever to do with justice but only with what "it is necessary for a prince wanting to maintain himself" to do.[14]

According to Machiavelli then law and force are separate species, but for the prince they are of the same genus; they are the two types of weapon that he needs to acquire and hold power, to avoid losing it or having it taken from him.[15] The distinction that Machiavelli is making between the use of laws proper to the human and of force proper to the bestial in men has recently found a succinct statement in the Beggar's Song from *Three-Penny Opera*:

When the shark bites with his teeth, dear,
Crimson billows start to spread;
Fancy gloves, though, wears McHeath, dear;
They don't show a trace of red.

[10] Ibid., i. 11. 34.
[11] Ibid., i. 11. 35.
[12] *Il Principe*, 15.
[13] Cicero, *De Officiis* i. 7. 20.
[14] *Il Principe*, 15.
[15] For the remarkable role of the verbs *acquistare, mantenere, tenere, perdere,* and *togliere* in the rhetoric of *Il Principe*, see above, pp. 156–57.

The prince must know the arts of using both natures of man, the bestial and the human; but the difference between the practice of the two arts is not that between Richard III and St. Louis, between Alcibiades and Pericles; it is the difference between the shark and Mac the Knife.

Thought is bound to have its impact on vocabulary and syntax. The extravagance of Machiavelli's thought in *Il Principe* leaves a sharp impress on certain key words he uses and their relation to each other. From the time of Aristotle and especially from that of Cicero for fifteen hundred years, several such words had provided the hard currency by means of which men exchanged political ideas at all levels of abstraction higher than that of positive substantive law. Among such words were *nature, experience, law, right, good, custom, justice, reason, virtue,* and *order.* The considerable stability of the value of those words in relation to one another, and the intricate symbiosis by which all sustained each, had for centuries effectively guaranteed the general intelligibility of serious political discourse, although they did nothing to assure its practicality or immediate relevance. In *Il Principe* Machiavelli radically altered the values of several of these words, well-nigh abandoned one or two, and thus thoroughly snarled up the structure of values (both exchange and moral) that they had hitherto supported.

The operation Machiavelli performed on the common sense of the language of politics of his day was quite drastic. It involved the dislocation of virtue and reason and nature from their customary relations with each other, and the literal abandonment of justice. Without alteration medieval writers had taken over from antiquity the assumption and conviction that justice was a virtue discernible to man by means of that right reason with which Nature and "Nature's God" had endowed him. This capsule statement of twenty centuries of "the conventional wisdom" becomes utterly meaningless if one assigns to its single terms only such meaning as Machiavelli assigned them in *Il Principe.* Yet he assigned to *reason, nature,* and *virtue* meanings quite common in his own time. *Natura* is linked with *qualità, naturale* with *ordinaria.* The *natura* of things is the way they actually are, the *natura* of men what they actually think or do or want; it is just the spectrum of their observed traits, so that no observed trait of men can be described as unnatural. Thus it is natural, not unnatural, for men longer to resent the loss of their property than the slaughter of their fathers.

The *ragionavole,* the reasonable, is merely "what figures," what is explicable; it is also paired with *ordinaria.* To *ragionare* is "to figure," to discuss or discourse, to explain. And there is no *ragione,* no Reason, in *Il Principe,* only the *ragioni,* the reasons, or explanations, or the *ragione,* the reason or explanation, the yield as it were, of figuring.

Thus Machiavelli's *ragione* is instrumental, concerned wholly with means; in the language of Weber it is not *wertrazional*, concerned with the orderly arraying of ultimate goals. And since his *natura* has nothing to do with ultimate ends either, but with what men happen to want, to *ragionare* can help men, be auxiliary to their *natura*, but no more than force and fraud can. By making *ragione* and *natura*, again in Weber's terms, *wertfrei*, practically divesting them of normative value, Machiavelli has effectively separated them from *virtù*, from virtue or the virtues, in a common classical sense and the most common Christian sense. But he further ensures his subversion of the common sense of his day by only rarely and most equivocally using *virtù* in any such sense. Except in those rare and equivocal instances he keeps *virtù* pretty strictly within the connotational ambit of *prowess* or *valor*, or, to offer a, perhaps closer, recent slang equivalent, "moxie." Amid the *Götterdämmerung* of so many semantic values, *giustizia* for all practical use disappears until the last hortatory chapter of *Il Principe*. There it crops up when Machiavelli describes the aim of ridding Italy of the barbarous as an act of justice, somewhat beclouding the issue, however, by equating the just with the necessary. In *Il Principe* justice does not amount to much.

The heart of the matter (or pehaps one might say the trick) then is that Machiavelli frequently uses most of the key words of the normal thought about politics of his day and for fifteen centuries before, and he uses them in quite common senses readily intelligible to his readers. But he almost never uses them in the particular senses that they had been shaped to in order to fit with each other in normal political discourse. The one term that was resistant to the trick was *giustizia*, since from Plato's day justice was what political discourse had mainly been about. Its effective banishment from the consideration of politics in *Il Principe* is a dead giveaway.[16] Scant wonder then that generations of scholars seeking a central core of normal politics in *Il Principe* have got hopelessly lost without ever finding what they seek. They are men wandering through a labyrinth in quest of a center that is not there.

What they look for in vain in *Il Principe* appears clearly and perspicuously in *Utopia*. There most of the key relations sanctified by centuries of common use are packed into two pages: man's highest good, happiness, is attainable only through the practice of virtue; virtue is living according to nature; to this end men were created by God; to follow the guidance of nature is to obey the dictates of reason; right reason directs men into the course suitable to their God-given

---

[16] The preceding remarks are based on a reasonably careful search for all occurrences in *Il Principe* of the terms analyzed and a consideration of the meaning of each *in context*.

natures, the distinguishing virtue of which is humanity; to foster these relations, laws were instituted among men, deriving their just powers from their promulgation by a just ruler or from the "consent of the people, neither oppressed by tyranny nor deceived by fraud"; in a society where justice rules, the laws promote human happiness, and the public good becomes the concern of reasonable men.[17]

Thus More deploys the traditional vocabulary and syntax of politics rapidly·and with practiced ease in *Utopia*, the book. But according to that book the relations explicated by that vocabulary and syntax are actually to be found only in Utopia, the place. That is, they are to be found no place, since Utopia is literally no place. Utopia is not merely not-Europe; it is anti-Europe, the society More knew and lived in turned upside down and backward. Reason, nature, virtue, and justice stood in right relation to one another in the land of Utopia because the law made the necessary provisions for maintaining that relation. The necessary provisions were the equality of goods, the abolition of private property, and the banning of the use of money. In the so-called commonwealths of Europe the law, based on and concerned to maintain private property, was imposed on the people, oppressed by tyranny and deceived by fraud, through a conspiracy of rich and powerful men parading themselves as the commonwealth. These men managed to dress out the self-serving decrees by which they robbed and bled the poor with the false appearance of popular approval, the specious approval of the very people the decrees themselves were designed to exploit.[18] In such commonwealths virtue does not receive its due, and instead of naturally imbuing men with public concern, reason naturally drives them to a ruthless pressing of private advantage.[19] The result is not the best-ordered and most just society, enjoying universal happiness, but a fierce and worse than bestial scramble for power, wealth, and worship culminating in universal wretchedness and misery. And the lives of most men are poor, nasty, brutish, and short.

In the sixteenth century the terms *custom* and *experience* ordinarily carried a high value charge. Often they were conjoined with virtue, reason, nature, and so on. In the language pattern of *Utopia* they are left out or oddly treated. This is not an accident. In the common view custom and experience were the links between the ultimate values of men and their day-to-day practices. It was through custom that those values found their expression in actual law, and law was itself a re-

[17] This pastiche of assertions occurs mainly in *Utopia*, 162–66, supplemented from *Utopia*, 104 and 194.

[18] Ibid., 240/14–28.

[19] Ibid., 238/1–6.

flection and embodiment of collective experience. In *Utopia*, however, appeal to the custom and experience of More's day and of his
land is either irrelevant or provides only negative instances, since the
experience was of evil and the custom was corrupt. The only relevant
experience and custom was that of Utopia, which is to say that it was
wholly the product of More's imagination.

Utopia and *Il Principe* are books very different from each other in
structure, in tone, in outlook, and in impact. But in one respect they
are remarkably alike. Following widely divergent paths, their authors,
one in 1513, the other three years later, arrived at the same pinnacle,
a point from which they saw in the same lurid light the society in which
they lived. For a society without justice is a mere den of robbers. One
must recognize it for what it is, since only thus can one rationally
make up one's mind about one's relation to it, whether, like the princes,
one seeks to get hold of and keep hold of as large a share of the loot
as possible or whether, like the Christian-humanist philosopher Hythlodaeus in *Utopia*, one decides to opt out.

Because in their extraordinary books Machiavelli and More saw the
world in which they lived in much the same way, they could not or
would not try to bring it into any useful connection with the traditional set of relations that was the indispensable frame of reference
for normal thinking about day-to-day political actualities in their time.
To do this, a man had to be willing to accept the greyness of ordinary
political life, the mixture of human motives, the ambivalent tensions
between group interest and public concern, the existing structures
of power, wealth, and status. Having accepted them, one had to
squeeze them somehow into the traditional frame of reference. The
job could never have that neat and surgical precision which Machiavelli displayed in cutting day-to-day politics free from the frame; but
anyone who attempted it might hope to gain something in relevance
for what he lost in effective force; political prefrontal lobotomies are
desperate measures even with very sick bodies politic.

Fortunately, one trying to get at least an inkling of the normal look
of politics in the age of Machiavelli can find some reflection of it in
the eyes of a man far less remarkable than Machiavelli or More. In
the space of three years which separated the former's loss of high
office and the offer of an important official post to the latter, another
thoughtful man came to a point of change in his political career; but
that change had almost nothing of a crisis character. A young prince
had succeeded to the throne of the old king Louis XII, whom Claude
de Seyssel had served more than fifteen years, but even before Francis I became ruler of France, Seyssel, well stricken in years, had announced his intent to turn his attention from the service of his earthly

to that of his heavenly king. It was about time. Priest and pluralist since 1503, in 1515 he had already been for five years Bishop of Marseille, a diocese into which it seems he had not yet set foot. Indeed, his communication with his flock had been so exiguous that once the cathedral chapter inadvertently elected another man bishop under the erroneous impression that Seyssel was dead.[20]

The most serious crisis of Seyssel's career occurred some nine months before his birth about 1450, since he was conceived on the wrong side of the blanket. For an offspring of the upper aristocracy, a Seyssel of Savoy, however, even the bar sinister was not a disastrous impediment to advancement, but it may have led Claude to seek that advancement with a rather wider and deeper education than a more conventional entry into the world would have required of him. With some of the humanist's embellishment that then accompanied such an education, he was well trained in law; for several years he lectured on both the Digest and the law of fiefs at Turin; and he finally left his academic post to shuttle for several years between the service of his native duke and that of Charles VIII of France. In 1498 he settled into a career of office-holding in the service of Louis XII, in which he remained throughout the reign. An early member of the newly constituted Grand Conseil, counsellor in the Parliament of Toulouse, then that of Paris, man of all works and some wisdom during the French administration of Milan, he also undertook a number of diplomatic missions, notably to England, the Emperor, and the Swiss cantons. He also found leisure to translate from Latin into French a number of classical histories—Xenophon, Appian, Justin, Diodorus, Siculus, Plutarch, Thucydides—not merely as a pastime but with the conscious intention of enriching French, as Latin had been enriched before it, by transfusing into its vocabulary some of the riches of the Greek lexicon.

In Louis XII's last years Seyssel had had the hard job of restoring peace and amity in Franco-Papal relations, badly upset by the King's ill-advised and wholly unsuccessful effort to drive the Pope into line with French policy in Italy by summoning a Church Council to threaten his ecclesiastical authority. Apparently Seyssel did his work with considerable skill, for he remained in Rome as a member of the Lateran Council, which the Pope had gathered to counter Louis XII's move. He returned to France for the coronation of Louis's successor,

[20] For the details of Seyssel's biography, see Alberto Caviglia, *Claudio di Seyssel (1450–1520): La vita nella storia di suoi tempi* ("Miscellanea di Storia Italiana," Vol. LIV; Turin, 1928). For a brief account, see the modern edition of Claude de Seyssel, *La Monarchie de France*, ed. Jacques Poujol (Paris, 1961), pp. 11–19.

Francis I, but as he explained, "I wish to withdraw to the service of God and my church as my present situation and age require." He felt it his duty at the end of his career to set down for Francis to consider at leisure what he had learned from the affairs he had dealt with during his long period of service.[21] What he set down he entitled *La Monarchie de France*. His equipment for producing a great work on politics was excellent. Seyssel had in abundance that "long experience of modern affairs and continued reading about those of antiquity"[22] on which Machiavelli claimed he based *Il Principe*. Perhaps, however, he lacked the monocular intensity of vision that his sudden catastrophic uprooting gave to Machiavelli, that the peculiar circumstances of his rapid transfer from busyness to idleness and back to busyness again gave to More. Or, as seems more likely, Seyssel's extensive education and experience were not an altogether adequate substitute for being terribly bright in the way Machiavelli and More were terribly bright. In any case *La Monarchie* has neither the force nor the fascination of *Il Principe* and *Utopia*.

It is nevertheless an interesting little treatise. At the crucial point where *Il Principe* and *Utopia* are extravagant and heterodox, *La Monarchie* is orthodox. The old statesman constructs his book of advice to young Francis I on the rooted traditional values of the relations among reason and nature and experience and virtue and justice and custom and law. He does not so alter several of them that they no longer can function in the traditional exchange system, which is what Machiavelli did with *ragione* and *natura* and *virtù*, or omit one altogether, which is what Machiavelli did with *giustizia*. Nor does he preserve the values intact only to maintain that their relevance is confined to Never-Never Land or Utopia. Their relations are what they had long been, and they are relevant to the rule of the kingdoms of this world, and therefore to the rule of France.

To say only this of *La Monarchie*, however, is to say of it nothing that is not equally true of scores of dreary, cliché-ridden books of advice to princes and reworkings of the Pseudo-Aristotelian *Secreta Secretorum*, written during the preceding three centuries for rulers who, if they read them, must have had an egregious tolerance for sustained ennui.[23] Seyssel, who was no fool, was inclined to suspect that they had not read them. In any case he resolved not to produce an-

---

[21] *La Monarchie*, 95–98.

[22] *Il Principe*, dedicatory epistle.

[23] For full information about this literature, see Allan H. Gilbert, *Machiavelli's "Prince" and Its Forerunners* (Durham, N.C., 1948); Desiderius Erasmus, *The Education of a Christian Prince*, ed. and trans. Lester K. Born (New York, 1936), pp. 94–130.

other highly dispensable increment to the already massive literature of banal moral exhortation to rulers. *La Monarchie* is not such a book.

It is not such a book because of traits which, transcending their differences, it shares with *Il Principe* and *Utopia*, traits which distinguish all three books from medieval writings that concern themselves with ruling in the city of this world. We sometimes speak of men who do not see the forest for the trees, and we might equally well speak of men who do not see the trees for the forest. Medieval writers on civil rule seem to fall into one or the other of these categories, and it is at least probable that in this matter medieval categories of writing fairly represent the topography of medieval thinking. Much of what we now classify as medieval political theory was given over to general discussion of the nature, the origin, the substance, and the rightful extent of political authority on the one hand and of political obligation on the other, and to the related consideration of the nature, the source, and the ultimate sanction of law. From such discussion were directly deduced the unconditional divinely sanctioned rights and duties of subjects and rulers. Such writings stand so far off from the day-to-day bread-and-butter activities of officials, ecclesiastic and temporal, that only rarely and then with some difficulty, as in the investiture controversy, can we see how on occasion they were brought to bear on those activities.

On the other side were the officials carrying out the rule-bound work of their offices—receivers of petitions, counselors, stewards of estates, administrators of the receipts and expenditures of princes, judges of many varieties. Within their limited spheres they knew what their offices required of them, what their duties were, and what dereliction of duty was. All this, however, was a long way off from the abstract value patterns of the medieval philosophers and moralists, and if the men who handled the affairs of society were aware of and understood what the men who handled its ideology were talking about, they might well have wondered what in reason they could be expected to do about it. They could no more see the forest for the trees than the theorists could see the trees for the forest. For centuries that middle distance where one could see both trees and forest and contemplate them together seems to have been virtually a no man's land. In effect the area of thinking about politics that devotes itself systematically to considering the problems created by the relations or lack of them between ultimate principles and actual practice was waste.

It is hard to say where, when, or why this situation began to change; and given the wide circulation in the late Middle Ages of Aristotle's *Politics*, standing solidly in the designated area, the more interesting question might be why it had not changed at least two centuries earlier.[24] What medieval men seem to have been deficient in was a living awareness that any set of normative political goals could only be achieved or approximated through adequate institutional means. Therefore they did not feel impelled to analyze the means or resources necessary to achieve those goals, which they simply prescribed as categorically imperative. Even less did they feel impelled to examine the means actually available for the attainment of such goals. And so they had no coherent way of formulating a policy either for providing the necessary means or for adjusting the goals to bring them within shooting distance of the existing means.[25] "The means actually available," "the existing means," are the institutions of government, the laws, the material resources, the social clusters and interest groups, the religious convictions, the habits of thought and modes of living of the people to whom the policy is to be applied. On such matters medieval writers on politics have little to say.

Before the end of the fifteenth century Sir John Fortescue in his *Governance of England* and his *De laudibus legum anglie* and Philippe de Commines in his *Mémoires* seem occasionally to have glimpsed the importance of relating the general rules of conduct for princes to the brute local facts of life. What is somewhat tentative in Fortescue and Commines has become a steady disposition of the mind with Machiavelli and More and Seyssel. Supporting its seemingly sudden appearance in three separate places and three men of markedly divergent temperament and character within the brief span of three years was no doubt a great deal of previous political talk, still sporadically audible in surviving fragments—in the minutes of the *Pratiche* in Florence and in Masselin's journal of the French Estates General of 1484.[26] It seems as if the articulate citizen of those days, whose Eng-

[24] What appears in the text as the silence of the Middle Ages may in fact be merely an indication of the ignorance of the author. It is based only on such acquaintance with the secondary literature on medieval political thought as he has acquired over the years, and that affords but a fairly superficial and shaky foundation. If it is indeed the case that for two or three centuries a knowledge of Aristotle's *Politics* with its elaborate comparisons of the constitutions of ancient states did not generate imitation in which contemporary constitutions were so considered and compared, that fact would be important to keep in memory during any attempt to inventory the content and character of "the medieval mind."

[25] This may help to explain why so much of medieval law was "secreted into the interstices of procedure," while so much medieval legislation was *vox et praeterea nihil*. Law got inserted into the interstices of procedure because officials who had to get on with the business of governing had to make the kinds of rules adapted to the situations that faced them; so the rules stuck. Much medieval legislation (and a good bit of modern legislation, if one comes down to it) embodies the higher aspirations of the rulers, their putative commitment to be good rulers, without much reference to the availability of institutional structures adequate to transform that commitment into political actuality.

[26] Felix Gilbert, *Machiavelli and Guicciardini: Politics and History in Sixteenth Century Florence* (Princeton, 1965), pp. 28–78; Jehan Masselin, *Journal des États Généraux . . . en 1484 . . .*, ed. and trans. A. Bernier (Paris, 1835).

lish epiphany Arthur Ferguson has recently investigated,[27] was articulating some interesting views, few of which found their way into the surviving historical record.

Be that as it may, Machiavelli and More and Seyssel are more precise and more perceptive in tracing the interrelations of the political and social facts of their day and in exposing the connections of those facts with the theoretical and actual imperatives of ruling, "the way things actually are and the way they ought to be," as Machiavelli puts it,[28] than any writers on politics during the preceding fifteen hundred years. I hardly need to dwell here on Machiavelli's exercise in describing the modulations a new prince must make in his policy to suit both the varying circumstances under which he acquires power and the condition of those over whom he acquires it. Scarcely less well known is More's brilliant feat of tracing the failure of criminal justice in England to a legally maintained set of social and economic arrangements which by locking men into their poverty drove the poor to steal out of despair, and then, by establishing the death penalty for theft, made it only prudent for the thief to murder his victim.[29]

It was the same sort of clear-eyed awareness of what went on in the world that enabled Seyssel to make sense of a social situation of which, for at least half a millennium before and sporadically for several hundred years after, almost all European social critics made nonsense. The movement of men out of the place in the social hierarchy into which they were born, whether that movement was up or down, was for centuries a standard subject for professional and amateur viewers-with-alarm, the pet bogeyman through the display of which they elicited the appropriate shudders from the ruling elite. Thus Piers Plowman:

> Bondsmen and bastards · and beggars' children,
> Thus belongeth to labor · and lord's kin to serve
> Both God and good men · as their degree asketh; . . .
> But since bondsmen's bairns · have been made bishops,
> And bastard children · have been archdeacons,
> And soap-sellers and their sons · for silver have been knights,
> And lord's sons their laborers. . . .
> Holyness of life and love · have been long hence,
> And will, till it be worn out · or otherwise changed.[30]

[27] Arthur B. Ferguson, *The Articulate Citizen and the English Renaissance* (Durham, N.C., 1965).
[28] *Il Principe*, 15.
[29] *Utopia*, 61–75.
[30] Quoted in Ferguson, *Articulate Citizen*, p. 60.

Such was the time-hallowed response of centuries of European social moralists to the facts of what sociologists today call social mobility: it was a Bad Thing to be exorcised by assuming a posture of appropriate horror.

To this response Seyssel pays no attention. Society, in his day, he knows, is indeed hierarchical, but in his very analysis of its structure he rejects the pat and standard procedure. For him the effective divisions in society are not the traditional ones of medieval literature or even of medieval law: the clergy who pray, the warrior aristocrats who fight, and the rest who work for those who pray and fight. He does not regard the clergy as an estate at all. The actual estates are the nobility, the well-to-do, and the common people. Having thus revised the customary medieval social taxonomy, he makes a far more radical and realistic observation:

> Everyone in this last estate can attain to the second by virtue and by diligence without any assistance of grace or privilege. This is not so in going from the second to the first, for to attain to the estate of nobility one must secure grace and privilege from the prince, who renders it readily enough when he who asks it has done or is about to do some great service to the commonwealth. Indeed, in order to maintain the estate of nobility the prince must do this whenever there is legitimate reason. This estate is always being depleted because in the wars in which it engages great numbers are often killed and because some nobles become so impoverished that they cannot maintain their station in life. He must also do it to give those of the middling estate the hope of arriving at the estate of nobility and the will to do so by doing virtuous deeds, and to those of the innumerable popular estate the hope of attaining to the middling, and through the middling of then mounting to the first. This hope makes every man satisfied with his estate and gives him no occasion to conspire against the other estates, knowing that by good and rightful means he himself can attain to them and that it would be dangerous for him to seek to make his way by any other route. If, on the other hand, there were no hope of mounting from one to the other or if it were too difficult, overbold men could induce others of the same estate to conspire against the other two. Here, however, it is so easy that daily we see men of the popular estate ascend by degrees, some to nobility and innumerable to the middling estate. The Romans always maintained this same order, for from the common people one rose to that of the knights and from that of the knights to that of senators and patricians.
>
> In France the church offers another means, common to all the estates, for attaining to a high and worthy station. In this matter the practice in France is and has always been that by virtue and knowledge those of the two lesser estates may attain to great ecclesiastical dignities as often or more often than those of the first, even to the rank of cardinal and

sometimes to the Papacy. This is another great means to satisfy all the estates and to incite them to train themselves in virtue and learning.[31]

Surely this combination of the lessons of antiquity with the quick and accurate reading of the economic and demographic facts of life as they affected the aristocracy, this perception of the church as a useful by-route for a social mobility which was itself a means of releasing and diffusing social pressures, surely all this in face of the contemporary habit of thought which almost automatically triggered a spasm of horror at the mere notion of such mobility, entitles Seyssel to join More and Machiavelli among the select group of pioneers who by confronting contemporary political credos with contemporary political facts strengthened their own political vision and therefore ours. It was this habit of confrontation shared by all three that enabled them to see through and beyond the stale hortatory moralism which had hitherto spared those who wrote for rulers about ruling the inconvenience and discomfort of examining and exploring or even being aware of any serious political problems connected with what they were writing about. In the very first sentences of his preface to *La Monarchie*, Seyssel renounces the serene delights of this sort of intellectual lotus-eating.

> Several philosophers, theologians and other wise men . . . have disputed, written, and dogmatized on what the government of the commonwealth in general ought to be, and among the several forms of government which is the best . . . and on these matters have been made many treatises and great volumes hard to read and to understand. It would be harder still, however, to put them into practice, for, in writing, men set down what is desirable and what reason and natural sense quite readily teach; but human weakness is so great that no men are so wise, virtuous, and prudent as those the learned described, nor is there any city or republic, great or small, ruled entirely by moral and political reason, and few are without more imperfections than perfections. Therefore, to recite the arguments, reasons and opinions of the authors treating these matters would be repetitious, prolix, and . . . very difficult, and would make a book the mere size of which would frighten off anyone who wanted to read it, unless he had a great deal of leisure. Even if he were willing to take the pains, after he had read it, he would remain confused. . . .[32]

---

[31] *La Monarchie*, 125–26. Seyssel's taxonomy of the social orders, heterodox in his day north of the Alps, probably reflects his education in Italy, long accustomed to distinguish between the *popolo grosso* and the *popolo minuto* (Seyssel: *peuple gras, peuple menu*).

[32] *La Monarchie*, 95.

The renunciation is somewhat less caustic but no less decisive than the more notorious one of Machiavelli:

> It remains now to consider the manner in which a prince should conduct himself toward his subjects and his friends. I know that many writers have treated this topic, so that I am somewhat hesitant in taking it up in my turn lest I appear presumptuous, especially because in what I shall have to say, I shall depart from rules which other writers have laid down. Since it is my intention to write something which may be of real utility to anyone who can comprehend it, it has appeared to me more urgent to penetrate to the effective reality of these matters than to rest content with mere constructions of the imagination. For many writers have constructed imaginary republics and principalities which have never been seen nor known actually to exist. But so wide is the separation between the way men actually live and the way that they ought to live, that anyone who turns his attention from what is actually done to what ought to be done, studies his own ruin rather than his preservation.[33]

Such firm and unflinching confrontation with actuality and such an end of idyllic innocence are likely to have an explosive impact on the mind of the man who achieves them, especially if he is among the first in centuries to do so. Seyssel, More, and Machiavelli did so, and, as we have seen, their achievement blew the thinking of the latter two right out of the normal orbit of political speculation as it was practiced by their contemporaries. The relation between moral political imperatives and actual political conduct was so hard to discern and the human habitudes and institutional structures through which any linkage between the two had to be traced were so dense and tangled that, having coped successfully with the first problem, they turned their backs on the second and thus freed themselves to write their brilliant and extravagant tracts *Il Principe* and *Utopia*.

Seyssel did not have the will to do what his two great contemporaries did, or he did not have the imagination, or, most likely, he did not have either. His only option then was to try to bring that new sense of political actualities which he shared with them into some fruitful relation to the traditional view that in the city of this world virtue and nature and experience and reason and justice and custom and law ought somehow to be conjoined to provide the framework of rules by which men live together in civil societies. We have already witnessed the first decisive move Seyssel made; it was to jettison the abstract and vacuous moralism which permeated most books on governance by medieval philosophers and poets and Renaissance humanists, and to do this in the interest of what Machiavelli would have

[33] *Il Principe*, 15.

called *la verita effetuale de la cosa.*[34] "Human weakness is so great
that no men are so wise, virtuous, and prudent as those the learned
describe, nor similarly is there any . . . commonwealth . . . ruled entirely by moral and political reason, and few are without more imperfections than perfections."[35] The consequence of this sharp deflation
of expectations was to render Seyssel's enterprise possible, for by
means of it he could avoid the despair that a comparison of inflated
expectations and dreary reality engendered in More and Machiavelli.

The next thing Seyssel did was to give an entirely new orientation
to two common species of political treatise—the treatise *de optimo
reipublicae statu* and the treatise *de regimine principum.* (Note that
Utopia was a wild mutant of the former, *Il Principe* of the latter
species.) As a number of his predecessors had done, Seyssel combined
the two species in *La Monarchie.* But in dealing with the question of
the best form of government, Seyssel does not limit himself to an
abstract rehashing of abstract arguments derived from Aristotle's
Politics about the relative merits of democracy, aristocracy, and monarchy. He runs fast through that argument in the first chapter of
La Monarchie, brings it to an inconclusive end,[36] and promptly turns
to an examination of the merits and defects of the democratic regime
of the ancient Romans and the aristocratic regime of the contemporary Venetians.[37] Having shown to his own satisfaction that these
two regimes, each the best of its kind, have dangerous defects, Seyssel
states that reason both divine and human, natural and political, shows
that one head is better than many in dealing with difficulties and
dangers, while experience demonstrates that both in ancient times and
his own day monarchical regimes are more stable and peaceable than
the others. Among monarchical regimes experience and reason also
show that hereditary monarchies will prosper better than elective
ones.[38] Thus having whipped in jig time through the customarily
pavane-like motions of this ancient abstract argument for monarchy,
he turns to tell why among hereditary monarchies that of France is
best.[39] For the rest of the first part of his treatise Seyssel examines
those elements of the French political and social order which in his
view indicate and are responsible for the superiority of the French
monarchy. The proportions of this first part are striking. Less than an
eighth of it is given over to theoretical discussion of the best political

[34] Ibid., 15.
[35] *La Monarchie*, 95.
[36] Ibid., 103–4.
[37] Ibid., 104–10. The chapter on the Venetians contains a digression on the rise
and decline of all bodies politic; see ibid., 108–9.
[38] Ibid., 111.
[39] Ibid., 112.

form in general and the best general form of a monarchy.[40] The remaining seven-eighths goes to concrete institutional analysis of Roman
democracy, Venetian aristocracy, and French monarchy,[41] and of that
remainder Seyssel devotes almost three-quarters to a consideration of
the structural strong points of France in his day.[42]

This trait of La Monarchie—its focus on the particular as against
the general, the concrete as against the abstract—is even more distinctly visible in the sections that in form are a treatise de regimine
principum. It starts conventionally enough with a chapter entitled
"Of the Education and Instruction of Princes and Monarchs in General."[43] The title is the only conventional thing about the chapter. In
the chapter itself Seyssel notes that if kings were always good and
wise, there would be no abuses to correct, but adds that since they
are not, more particular instruction seems necessary. Then instead of
going on to offer the sort of instruction that fills the ordinary prince
book, he produces rather surprisingly a short bibliographical essay
on treatises de regimine principum and pays his small respects to the
whole genre by pointing out that the advice so lavishly dispensed in
such exercises "is hard to retain because of the fragility and imperfec-
tion of human nature." He ends his observations with the wry remark
that "if they are wise and virtuous, . . . men of high degree are ordinarily occupied with great affairs so that they scarcely have idle time
to spend on reading lengthy writing, and if young and willful, they
are given over to lewdness and other vain and voluptuous doings."[44]

With an almost palpable sigh of relief Seyssel then turns from monarchs in general to "Particular Instruction . . . for the King . . . of
France," in which he says he will concern himself with "what seems
most necessary for the present maintenance and increase of this monarchy" dealing with "several points which call for special attention
because it has been observed during the lives of those still living
that on them hinges the good or the ill, the prosperity or the misery
of the realm."[45] And he is as good as his word. It is precisely with
such matters—policy and administration, social and economic and
military, internal and external—that he thereafter deals for the rest
of La Monarchie.[46] Again it is the relative allocation of space that is
startling—three pages to a rather cool evasion of the standard banali-
ties of treatises de regimine principum followed by eighty pages of
reasoned and reasonably detached suggestions about royal policy based

[40] Ibid., 103–4, 110–11.
[41] Ibid., 104–10, 112–28.
[42] Ibid., 112–28.
[43] Ibid., 130.
[44] Ibid., 132.
[45] Ibid., 133.
[46] Ibid., 133–221.

on a consideration of recent French history, things "observed during the lives of those still living." Overall then in *La Monarchie* one-twentieth of the work concerns itself rather casually with the standard topics of the standard works in its putative genres, nineteen-twentieths with the *modus operandi* of three actual political societies, one of the past and two of Seyssel's own day. And nine-tenths deals with France, the political society which he knew best from that long experience in a variety of posts by which Machiavelli set such great store.

The consequence of Seyssel's intense focus on France was that *La Monarchie* dealt, although less vividly yet a bit more sensibly than *Il Principe* and *Utopia*, with a number of matters which preoccupied men concerned with politics in that day—the use of mercenary soldiers,[47] for example, and the problems of counsel for rulers.[48] But most significant is Seyssel's handling of the crucial dilemma of politics in the age of Machiavelli. Lack of governance, weakness at the center, had prevailed in the era that preceded, and having tasted its bitter fruits, men in the politically advanced lands of Europe wanted an end to it. They wanted to be ruled, and if they were to have what they wanted, they must allow their rulers the power needed to govern. If the prince were truly to rule, his will must be effective, and to be effective, it had to be law or something very like law. But in the common opinion law ought never to be the mere expression of any mortal's mere will; it ought to be inextricably bound into the complex pattern of perdurable relations in which justice, reason, experience, custom, nature, and virtue were indispensable terms. The pressing problem was how to keep law bound into that pattern of relations and at the same time allow rulers the power to rule, which meant in effect the power to make rules with the force of law.

In France, Seyssel argued, this problem was as near to being solved as—given the weakness and wickedness of men—it could be, because there the hazards of abuse of power on the part of the king were limited by three bridles. The term itself is significant. A bridle is not to stop action but to regulate it, to subject it to rule. The verb Seyssel uses in describing the function of the bridles is never *dominer*; it is always *regler*. The king cannot be *dominé*; he is *absolu*; no man or body of men can exercise dominion over him. The bridles are not to command his action, but to conform it to order, to prevent it from becoming *desordiné*, inordinate; *volontaire*, merely willful; *dereglé*, unruly.[49]

The bridles that perform this work are religion, justice, and police. Medieval and more recent writers on the duties of rulers had long

---

[47] *La Monarchie*, 169–73; *Utopia*, 149–51; *Il Principe*, 12–14.

[48] *La Monarchie*, 133–41; *Utopia*, 55–59, 85–103; *Il Principe*, 22–23.

[49] For this set of rhetorical ploys, see especially *La Monarchie*, 113–15, 120.

harangued monarchs on their obligation to maintain religion and execute justice; indeed in their coronation oaths most kings solemnly undertook to do both. The trouble was that while good rulers hardly needed written exhortations about their duties, bad ones were not likely to pay much heed to them, or, for that matter, to coronation oaths. In speaking of the bridles, Seyssel had something more in mind than mere exhortation; according to him religion, justice, and police actually functioned in day-to-day politics to prevent or limit the merely willful exercise of royal authority.

Because the French people are religious Christians, he points out, the king must make it clear to them *"by example and by present and overt demonstration"* that he too is a zealous Christian. But to do this, he will have to live like a Christian, which in effect means that he cannot act tyrannically. If he is so willful as to do so, he can be reprehended to his face by any mere preacher. Even should the king desire to take action against such a preacher, he would not dare to brave the popular disapproval that such a deed would generate. The effective sanction throughout is the wrath of a religious people against a manifestly sacrilegious ruler—the king's "fear of provoking the ill will and indignation of the people," his awareness that, if through his acts he appeared indifferent to his religion, "the people would hate him and perhaps obey him but ill, . . . imputing all the realm's troubles" to the king's religious defect. In the monarchy of France the bridle of religion is neither an abstraction nor a mere pious hope; it is the ruler's understanding and fear that, if in his management of public affairs he does not at least outwardly conform to the minimal demand of Christian conduct, he will suffer rejection at the hands of the French people.[50]

As with religion, so with justice. The justice that bridles the king is not a remote inoperative ideal; it is embodied in the ancient and rooted practices of the king's own courts of law, and especially of the parlements. The eminence and authority of the judges of these courts are such that in civil matters a petitioner can get a judgment against the king as well as against another person; that in cases at private law the king cannot intervene in favor of one party to the detriment of the other, since his writs are subject to judgment not merely with respect to their fraudulent procurement but with respect to their legality as well; and that in criminal matters, the parlement so thoroughly debates the king's acts of grace and pardon and puts those who have wrongfully procured them through such an interrogation, that few indeed are foolish enough to rely on such acts. Moreover, since judges can be dismissed only on charges over which

[50] Ibid., 115–17. On Religion, the first bridle of kings.

the sovereign courts themselves have jurisdiction, they are able to act independently on their view of the law of the realm without fear of removal by a willful king.[51]

The third bridle, police, works in a similar way. Police is "the many ordinances made by the kings of France themselves and afterwards confirmed and approved from time to time, which tend to the conservation of the realm. . . ." Such, for example, is the rule against alienation of the royal domain except in case of necessity. The parlements, whose approval of such exceptional alienations alone legalizes them, stall so long while considering them that they simply ruin the market for them. At the same time the accounting court (*chambre des comptes*) reviews the king's outlays. Between the two they dampen the appetites of those who seek to fatten off special favor, diminish the need for the king to rely on extraordinary exactions in emergencies, and keep the monarchy strong by restraining the overgreat liberality of individual monarchs. In general, police serves as a bridle on the monarchy because, should French kings willfully derogate from the time-sanctioned ordinances of their predecessors, "their commands would not be obeyed at all."[52]

Such were the bridles on the kings of France to prevent their *puissance absolu* from becoming *volontaire* and *desordiné*. Let us make two further points about them. First, as a clear-eyed man who knew a good bit both about human orneriness, especially in high places, and about the history of the French monarchy, Seyssel did not delude himself that the bridles were perfectly and instantaneously efficacious. He did believe that they were tough, resilient, and durable, capable of surviving the heavy strains put on them by wicked rulers and by kings who were children or idiots, and of doing their work when these plagues of God had passed. They had their imperfections, and by the whim of an arbitrary ruler they "might be bent, but they have been maintained so long that they can scarcely be broken."[53]

Second, the so-called bridles were also the great reservoirs of royal power. The power the king needed to rule effectively in large part derived from his authority as protector of religion, as source of justice, and as initiator of ordinances. Thus Seyssel is not whistling in the dark or indulging in the usual make-believe when he states his judgment that without the bridles the absolute power of the King of France would be "worse and more imperfect," just as "the power of God is not less but rather more perfect because he cannot sin or do ill," and that the bridles rendered the king's power "more perfect and

---

[51] Ibid., 117–18. On Justice, the second bridle.
[52] Ibid., 119. On Police, the third bridle. There is not space here to consider what Seyssel meant when he used the term—ubiquitous in *La Monarchie*—*la police*.
[53] Ibid., 118.

complete and also more firm and lasting."[54] Finally it is precisely in the area of religion, justice, and police, taken quite concretely as we have seen, and in the ruler's role as guarantor of a historically specific social order that the relation between law as the emanation of the king's will on the one hand and law and custom as a part of a value pattern that includes reason, nature, experience, virtue, and justice on the other is firmly fixed, fixed by links that connect both of them with the actual needs and operative institutions of the government and society of sixteenth-century France. It is precisely at this point that Seyssel does in *La Monarchie* what neither More nor Machiavelli tries to do or cares to do in their extraordinary and extravagant little books. He finds a way to bring the empirical observation of political actuality into effective relation with the conventional wisdom about the ends of political association and therefore with the perennial aspirations of man, the political animal. However involutely, however fortuitously, the policy of the absolute King of France is therefore bound to reason and nature and virtue and justice and bound to make at least a pretense of conformity to them.

Between 1513 and 1516, then, in three small books three modern modes of thinking about politics attained maturity so abruptly that two of them at least give the impression of being born like Athene, full grown from the head of Zeus. The first mode, the predatory, found its first clear expression in *Il Principe*; the second the utopian, in *Utopia*; the third, the constitutional, in *La Monarchie*.[55] None of the books could

---

[54] Ibid., 120.

[55] The author has misgivings not so much about his taxonomic scheme here as about the labels he has applied to it. He has least concern about the label *predatory*, mainly because it is not at the moment widely current among the words of art for describing political posture, but also because it so neatly fits the posture prescribed for would-be rulers in *Il Principe*. The word *utopian* creates far more difficulty, so much so indeed that in 1965 a more than ordinarily intelligent group of twenty-odd scholars spent two days chasing it around in hopes of pinning it down. The author hopes that he made it clear that in using *utopian* he does not refer to the form of political fantasy which constitutes the bulk of the "literature of Utopias," but rather to the political posture of those whose contemplation of the fabric of imperatives, professed by their own society or deemed possible by them, has profoundly alienated them from the actual life lived in that society. (For a more elaborate discussion, see above, chapter IV.) *Constitutional* has even worse drawbacks. It has been used to describe some forms of political theory in the Middle Ages and the political theorizing of part of Machiavelli's *Discorsi*. As here used it does not fit either of these—not the first because medieval writers did not exhibit publicly (although they may have possessed) the necessary grasp of the relations between theory and practice; not the second because therein Machiavelli seems mainly concerned with the stability and expansive force of political structures and scarcely at all with their legitimacy or capacity to achieve justice. The term *political*, with its reference to Aristotle's conception of the *politeia*, would have done better justice on sixteenth-century usage than *constitutional*, a word coined more than two hundred years later. Unfortunately, however, the present-day connotations of *political* are too all-embracing, so *faute de mieux*. . . .

have been written a century earlier, because one characteristic common to thinking in all three modes had not yet developed adequately. All three demanded a close scrutiny of the general principles men professed as the norms of political conduct in intimate conjunction with the networks of actual practice manifested in established institutions and recurrent patterns of political behavior. Since in the time before the age of Machiavelli the second element was either hopelessly fragmented or wholly absent, one of the necessary conditions for the emergence of all these modes of thinking was not fulfilled.

But it is not an accident that of the three early exemplars of the predatory, the utopian, and the constitutional modes of thinking, two are classics of politics, still current today, while the third is remembered by few and read by fewer. For if there is an unbridgeable chasm between the norms of political conduct and actual political practice, only two active options are open to a writer who would concern himself seriously with politics. One is to prescind entirely from the avowed normative principles and treat politics as an exercise in predation, in which those who seek domination treat the body politic as prey. Then the only relevant question is how to acquire the prey, how to keep one's hold on it, how to avoid losing it or having it taken away by a rival predator. In this game reason, virtue, justice, and law, along with force and fraud, are merely instrumental to the wills of the predators; they are the weapons used in the struggle; and the name of the game is power. Or as it was once put with perhaps a trace of poetic license:

> Force should be right, or rather right and wrong . . .
> Should lose their names, and so should justice too.
> Then everything concludes itself in power,
> Power into will, will into appetite,
> And appetite a universal wolf . . .
> Must make a universal prey,
> And last eat up himself.[56]

Though by no means inevitable, it is still intelligible that the first man who was bright and bold enough to envisage this extravagant option at all should be also bright and bold enough to grasp it fully. And this was what Machiavelli did in *Il Principe*.

So, conversely, with the alternative option. If on analysis actual institutions appear to be means not of approximating the professed norms of a society but rather means of thwarting them in the interest of the rich and the powerful, then one may inquire what institutions and patterns of behavior must replace them in order to realize those

---

[56] William Shakespeare, *Troilus and Cressida*, I, iii.

norms. And again the first man bright and bold enough to grasp this option might be bright and bold enough to grasp it fully. And that was what More did in *Utopia*.

The position of the constitutional mode is different. In the first place the transition from earlier modes of thinking about politics is less abrupt and dramatic. Constitutional thought is not faced with a simple either/or option, but with the more prosaic task of shoving and hauling medieval normative theory on the one side and medieval legal thinking and administrative practice on the other into bridge-able distance of each other. Moreover, this task requires the patient and tentative modulation of both of these earlier forms in the process. Perhaps this is why, although the quest for medieval and Renaissance precursors in any serious sense for *Il Principe* and *Utopia* has failed, we may discern precursors of *La Monarchie* in such diverse places as Fortescue's *Governance of England*, Commines' *Mémoires*, Mas-selin's *Journal* and the debates of the Pratiche. Second, whatever the overt avowals of its practitioners, the constitutional mode of political thinking requires that they treat nature and justice and order and virtue and reason as not forever fixed with complete precision in the human understanding and that they treat the actual institutions of society and its particular current patterns of activity as subject to gradual modification and amelioration. And this means that the con-stitutional mode of thinking about politics will always lack the clarity, the incisiveness, and the finality of predatory and utopian thinking and that works written in a mode dominantly constitutional will suffer from a tonal greyness, a tendency to obsolescence, an element of the ephemeral.[57]

I say "dominantly constitutional" because these three modern modes of thinking about politics are not wholly discrete. In one direction constitutional thinking lies closer to utopian, in the other to predatory thinking. Yet it would be a mistake to conceive of the relation to each other of these modes of thought, whose origins we have just explored, as a straight-line continuum with predatory thinking at one extreme, utopian at the other, and constitutional in the middle. A triangle provides a better model. Constitutional and predatory thought con-verge in their common concern with the range of maneuver possible within the bounds of an existing political structure and situation. But as we have seen in the case of *Utopia* and *Il Principe*, utopian and predatory thought also converge in their common despair of the con-stitutional enterprise of maintaining contact between virtue and reason

---

[57] Something of the sort has happened to many sections of *The Federalist Papers*, for example, and to those parts of *Le Contrat Social* in which Rousseau tries to relate his utopian conception of politics to the actualities of Europe in the later eighteenth century.

and nature and justice on the one hand and the going political and social order on the other. Thus we may conceive that the constitutional mode is most secure when broadly based, when it retains for itself a comfortable range of maneuver amid the hard and resistant political actualities without surrendering its purpose of providing the means whereby men who aspire to a good life may attain as good a life as circumstances and the human condition permit. In this way it can encompass and possess within itself the means of adjustment to change. It also thus maintains a wide angle opposite to it between the utopian and the predatory modes of thinking. And it needs to do so, for the narrowing of that angle, the closing together of those modes of thinking, are symptomatic of a revolutionary situation.

This way of considering these three modern modes of political thinking, whose beginnings we have just explored, may require us to change our very conception of the nature of understanding and truth as it applies to the constitutional mode. We are habituated to the Platonic dogma that political truth and understanding involve the discovery of a fixed set of rules or formulas establishing the right order among a changeless set of facts. Perhaps we should resign ourselves to the actuality that neither the current rules embodying the perdurable human aspiration to a world based on order and reason and justice and nature nor the facts embodied in time-bound, place-bound institutions and patterns of actions are, or can, or should be, fixed or changeless. In the constitutional mode we can retain our concern for nature and reason and justice and order in our social cosmos without binding ourselves to an impossible quest for final and definitive solutions. Truth about political life then ceases to be a goal that the human mind can attain once and for all. It becomes that measure of prudence and judgment and wisdom that men deploy in the ever-changing process of seeking to maintain living and effective contact between the realm of justice and reason and nature and order on the one hand and the sphere of men's daily doing in an actual political society on the other, a continual rethinking of our belief about the one and a continual reforming of our doings in the other. Whether such a notion of the meaning of truth and understanding in the constitutional mode of political thought would survive the rigor of philosophical analysis, I do not know. Nor do I much care, since I suspect that our very notions of truth and understanding may be on the verge of a period of ecumenical redefinition.

BIBLIOGRAPHY

Adams, Robert P. *The Better Part of Valor* (Seattle, 1962).
Allen, J. W. *A History of Political Thought in the Sixteenth Century* (London, 1960).
Ames, Russell. *Citizen Thomas More and His Utopia* (Princeton, 1949).
Ba., Ro. *The Life of Syr Thomas More*, ed. E. V. Hitchcock and P. E. Hallett, Early English Text Society, Original Series, *222* (London, 1950).
Baillie, John. *Our Knowledge of God* (New York, 1959).
Baldwin, Frances E. *Sumptuary Legislation and Personal Regulation in England*, Johns Hopkins University Studies in Historical and Political Science, *44*:1 (Baltimore, 1926).
Baron, Hans. *The Crisis of the Early Italian Renaissance*, 1 vol. in 2 (Princeton, 1955).
————. "Machiavelli: The Republican Citizen and the Author of 'The Prince'," *English Historical Review*, *76* (1961), 217–53.
Bataillon, Marcel. *Erasme et l'Espagne* (Paris, 1937).
Berelson, Bernard. *Content Analysis in Communication Research* (Glencoe, Ill., 1952).
Berlin, Isaiah. *Karl Marx* (London, 1939).
Campbell, W. E. *More's Utopia and His Social Teaching* (London, 1930).
Carlyle, R. W. and A. J. *A History of Medieval Political Theory in the West*, *1* (Edinburgh, 1903); *2* (1904); *5* (1928).
Caspari, Fritz. *Humanism and the Social Order in Tudor England* (Chicago, 1954).
Cassirer, Ernst. "Giovanni Pico Della Mirandola," *Journal of the History of Ideas*, *3* (1942), 123–44.
Caviglia, Alberto. *Claudio di Seyssel (1450–1520): La vita mella storia di suoi tempi* ("Miscellanea di Storia Italiana," Vol. LIV, Turin, 1928).
Chambers, R. W. *Thomas More* (London, 1935).
Chartier, Alain. *Le Quadrilogue invectif*, ed. E. Droz (Paris, 1950).
Chiappelli, Fredi. *Studi sul linguagio del Machiavelli* (Florence, 1952).
Choisy, Eugène. *La Théocratie à Genève au temps de Calvin* (Geneva, n.d.).
Church, W. F. *Constitutional Thought in Sixteenth-Century France* (Cambridge, Mass., 1941).

Colet, John. *An Exposition of St. Paul's First Epistle to the Corinthians*, tr. J. H. Lupton (London, 1874).

Condorelli, Grazio. "Per la storia del Nome 'Stato' (il nome 'stato' in Machiavelli)," *Archivio Guerdico LXXXIX* (1923), 223–35; *XL* (1923), 77–112.

Curtis, Mark. *Oxford and Cambridge in Transition, 1558–1642* (Oxford, 1959).

De Roover, Raymond. *The Medici Bank* (New York, 1948), pp. 5–13.

———. "The Concept of the Just Price: Theory and Economic Policy," *Journal of Economic History, 18* (1958), 418–34.

Dictionnaire de theologie catholique, "Guerre."

Donner, H. W. *Introduction to Utopia* (London, 1945).

Doumergue, Émile. *Jean Calvin, les hommes et les choses de son temps* (7 vols. Lausanne and Neuilly-sur-Seine, 1899–1927), 6.

Duhamel, P. Albert. "Medievalism of More's *Utopia*," *Studies in Philology, 52* (1955), 99–126.

———. "The Oxford Lectures of John Colet," *The Journal of the History of Ideas, 14* (1953), 493–510.

Dunham, W. H., Jr. "Lord Hastings' Indentured Retainers," *Transactions of the Connecticut Academy of Arts and Sciences, 39* (New Haven, 1955).

Ehrenberg, R. *Das Zeitalterder Fugger*, 2 vols. (Jena, 1912), *1*.

Elyot, Sir Thomas. *The Boke named the Governour*, ed. H. H. S. Crofts, 2 vols. (London, 1880), II.

Erasmus, Desiderius. *Education of a Christian Prince*, trans. L. K. Born (New York, 1936).

———. *Opera Omnia*, ed. Jean Leclerc, 10 vols. in 11 (Louvain, 1703–1706) 6*3–*4v.

———. *Opus Epistolarum Des. Erasmi Roterdami*, ed. P. S. Allen, et al., 12 vols. (Oxford, 1906–58).

Ercole, Francesco. *La politica di Machiavelli* (Rome, 1926).

d'Entrèves, Allesandro Passerin. *Medieval Contributions to Political Thought* (Oxford, Eng., 1939).

Ferguson, Arthur B. *The Articulate Citizen and the English Renaissance* (Durham, N.C., 1965).

Garin, Eugenio. *L' educazione in Europa* (1400–1600) (Bari, 1957).

Gibson, W. R., and J. Max Patrick. *St. Thomas More: A Preliminary Bibliography* (New Haven, 1961).

Gilbert, A. H. *Machiavelli's Prince and its Forerunners* (Durham, N.C., 1938).

Gilbert, Felix. *Machiavelli and Guicciardini: Politics and History in Sixteenth Century Florence* (Princeton, 1965).

———. "Machiavelli's Idea of Virtù," *Renaissance News*, IV (1951), 53–55 and V (1952), 21–23.

Gregory the Great, "Regulae Pastoralis Liber," pt. 3, chap. 21; *Patrologia Latina*, ed. J.-P. Migne, 77 (1896), 87.

Guicciardini, Francesco. *Opere*, ed. Vittorio de Caprariis (*La Letteratura Italiana, Storia e Testi*, XXX [Milan, n.d.]).

Hale, John. *Machiavelli and Renaissance Italy* (London, 1961).

———. "War and Public Opinion in the Fifteenth and Sixteenth Centuries," *Past and Present*, 22 (1962), 18–20.

Harpsfield, Nicholas. *The Life and Death of Sr Thomas Moore, Knight*, ed. E. V. Hitchcock, Early English Text Society, Original Series, *186*. (London, 1932).

Hexter, J. H. "The Education of the Aristocracy in the Renaissance," *Reappraisals in History* (London, 1961), pp. 45–70.

———. *More's "Utopia": The Biography of an Idea*, History of Ideas Series, 5 (Princeton, 1952), Torchbook Edition (New York, 1965).

———. "Thomas More: On the Margins of Modernity," *Journal of British Studies*, 1 (1961), 20–37.

Hill, Christopher. *Puritanism and Revolution* (London, 1958).

Hillerbrand, Hans J. *The Reformation in Its Own Words* (London, 1964).

Hoyoux, Jean. "Les Moyens d'existence d'Erasme," *Bibliothèque d'Humanisme et Renaissance*, 5 (Paris, 1944), 7–59.

Hyma, Albert. *The Christian Renaissance* (New York, 1925).

Jacob, E. F. *The Fifteenth Century* (Oxford, 1961).

Jordan, W. K. *The Development of Religious Toleration in England from the Beginning of the English Reformation to the Death of Queen Elizabeth* (Cambridge, 1932).

Kidd, B. J. *Documents Illustrative of the Continental Reformation* (Oxford, 1911).

Kristeller, P. O. *Il Pensiero Filosofico di Marsiglio Ficino* (Florence, 1953).

———. *Renaissance Thought* (New York, 1961).

———. *Studies in Renaissance Thought and Letters* (Rome, 1956).

Laertes, Diogenes. *Lives of Eminent Philosophers*, trans. R. D. Hicks, 2 vols. (London, 1950), *1*.

Lane, Frederick. *Venetian Ships and Shipbuilders of the Renaissance* (Baltimore, 1934).

Lavisse, E. ed. *Histoire de France*, 9 vols., V. 1, H. Lemonnier, *Les Guerres d'Italie.—La France sous Charles VIII, Louis XII et François I* (Paris, 1911).

Letters and Papers, Foreign and Domestic, of the Reign of Henry VIII, ed. J. S. Brewer, James Gairdner, and R. H. Brodie (London, 1862–1932), *1515–1516*.

Limmer, Rudolf. *Bildungszustände und Bildungsideen des 13 Jahrhunderts* (Munich, 1928).

Lovejoy, Arthur. *The Great Chain of Being* (Cambridge, Mass., 1936).

Lupton, J. H. *A Life of John Colet* (London, 1887).

Luther, Martin. *Lectures on Romans*, tr. and ed. Wilhelm Pauck, Library of Christian Classics, vol. 15 (Philadelphia, 1961).

MacKinney, Loren C. "Gilbert's 'On Machiavelli's Idea of Virtù'," *Renaissance News*, V (1952), 21–23.

McNeill, John T. *The History and Character of Calvinism* (New York, 1957).

Machiavelli, Niccolò. *The Discourses of Niccolò Machiavelli*, ed. and trans. Leslie J. Walker (London, 1950).

———. *Il Principe*, ed. A. L. Burd (Oxford, 1891).

———. *Opere*, 1, *Il Principe e Discorsi; 2, Arte della Guerra e Scritti Politici Minori*, ed. S. Bertelli (Milan, 1960).

———. *Opere*, 6, *Lettere*, ed. F. Gaeta, (Milan, 1961).

———. *Tutte le opere . . . di Niccolò Machiavelli* (Florence, 1929).

Madan, F. ed. "Day Book of John Dorne," *Collecteana*, ed. C. R. L. Fletcher, *1, 71–177, Oxford Historical Society, 5* (1885).

Mallet, C. E. *History of the University of Oxford*, 3 vols. (London, 1924–27).

Masselin, Jehan. *Journal des Etats Généraux . . . en 1484 . . .* , ed. and trans. A. Bernier (Paris, 1835).

Mattingly, Garrett. *The Armada* (Boston, 1959).

———. *Renaissance Diplomacy* (London, 1955).

Mayer, E. W. *Machiavellis Geschichtsauffassung und sein begriff Virtù* (Munich, 1912).

Meinecke, Friedrich. *Die Idee der Staatsräson in der Neuen Geschichte* (3rd ed.; Munich, 1929).

———. *Machiavellism*, tr. Douglas Scott (New Haven, Conn., 1957).

Merriman, Roger B. *The Rise of the Spanish Empire*, 4 vols., 2 (New York, 1918–34).

Merton, Robert K. "Role of the Intellectual in a Public Bureaucracy," *Social Forces, 23* (1945).

Mohl, Ruth. *The Three Estates in Medieval and Renaissance Literature* (New York, 1933).

More, Thomas. *The Apologye of Syr Thomas More, Knyght*, ed. A. I. Taft, Early English Text Society, Original Series, *180* (London, 1930).

———. *The Correspondence of Sir Thomas More*, ed. E. F. Rogers (Princeton, 1947).

———. *The History of King Richard III*, ed. R. S. Sylvester, The Yale Edition of the Complete Works of St. Thomas More, Vol. 2 (New Haven, 1963).

———. *The Latin Epigrams of Thomas More*, ed. and trans. Leicester Bradner and Charles Arthur Lynch (Chicago, 1953).

———. *St. Thomas More: Selected Letters*, E. F. Rogers ed. (New Haven, 1961).

———. *Utopia*, ed. J. H. Lupton (Oxford, 1895).

———. *Utopia*, tr. into German by Gerhard Ritter, intro. by Hermann Oncken (Berlin, 1922).

———. *Utopia*, ed. Edward Surtz, S.J., and J. H. Hexter, The Yale Edition of the Complete Works of St. Thomas More, Vol. 4 (New Haven and London, 1965).

———. *The Workes of Sir Thomas More, Knyght . . . in the Englysh Tongue* (London, 1557).

Mullinger, James B. *The University of Cambridge*, 2 vols., (Cambridge, 1873–1911).

Nelson, Benjamin. "Usurer and Merchant Prince," *Journal of Economic History*, 7 (1947), Supplement, pp. 104–22.

Owst, G. R. *Literature and Pulpit in Medieval England* (Cambridge, 1933).

———. *Preaching in Medieval England* (Cambridge, 1926).

Plato, *Laws* (trans. R. G. Bury).

Pineas, Rainer. "Erasmus and More: Some Contrasting Theological Opinions," *Renaissance News*, 13 (1960).

Pollard, A. F. *Factors in Modern History* (New York, 1907).

———. *Wolsey* (London, 1929).

Prezzolini, Giuseppe. *Machiavelli Anticristo* (Rome, 1954).

Reed, A. W. *Early Tudor Drama* (London, 1926).

Remy, Y., and Dunil-Marquebreucq, R. *Collection Latomus*, 8 (Brussels, 1953).

Rice, Eugene F., Jr. "John Colet and the Annihilation of the Natural," *Harvard Theological Review*, 45 (1952), 141–63.

Renaudet, Augustin. *Humanisme et Renaissance*, Travaux d'Humanisme et Renaissance, 30 (Geneva, 1958).

———. *Preréforme et Humanisme* (Paris, 1953).

Ridolfi, Roberto. *The Life of Girolamo Savonarola* (New York, 1959).

———. *Vita di Niccolò Machiavelli* (Rome, 1954).

Roper, William. *The Lyfe of Sir Thomas Moore, Knighte*, ed. E. V. Hitchcock, Early English Text Society, Original Series, 197.

di Sciullo, John. *Il vocabolario politico di Niccolò Machiavelli* (MA Thesis, Columbia University, 1950).

Schottenloher, Otto. *Erasmus im Ringen um die humanistische Bildungsforem*, Reformationgeschichtliche Studien und Text, 61, 1933.

de Seyssel, Claude. *La Monarchie de France*, ed. J. Poujol (Paris, 1961).

Smith, Preserved. *Erasmus* (New York, 1923).

Smith, Sir Thomas. *De Republica Anglorum*, ed. L. Alston (Cambridge, Eng., 1906).

Stone, Lawrence. "Marriage among the English Nobility in the Sixteenth and Seventeenth Centuries," *Comparative Studies in History and Society*, 3 (1961), 182–83.

Sullivan, Frank and Majie Padberg. *Moreana* (Kansas City, 1946).

Surtz, Edward. *The Praise of Pleasure* (Cambridge, Mass., 1957).

———. *The Praise of Wisdom* (Chicago, 1957).

———. "Sir Thomas More and His Utopian Embassy of 1515," *The Catholic Historical Review*, 39 (1953), 272–98.

Tawney, R. H. *Agrarian Problems in the Sixteenth Century* (London, 1912).

——. *Equality* (New York, 1931).

——. *Religion and the Rise of Capitalism* (New York, 1947).

——. "Rise of the Gentry: A Postscript," *Economic History Review*, Series 2, 7 (1954–56), 91–97.

Tillyard, E. M. W. *The Elizabethan World Picture* (London, 1952).

Troeltsch, Ernst. *The Social Teaching of the Christian Churches*, 1 vol. in 2, trans. O. Wyon (New York, 1931).

Tucker, Robert. *Philosophy and Myth in Karl Marx* (Cambridge, Eng., 1961).

Vespucci, Amerigo. *The First Four Voyages of Amerigo Vespucci* (see Waldseemüller).

Waldseemüller, Martin. *The Cosmographiae Introductio*, ed. C. G. Herbermann, United States Catholic Historical Society Monograph 4 (1907).

Weber, Max. *The Protestant Ethic and the Spirit of Capitalism*, trans. T. Parsons (London, 1930).

Whitfield, J. H. *Machiavelli* (Oxford, 1947).

——. "On Machiavelli's use of *ordini*," *Italian Studies*, X (1955), 19–39.

Woodward, W. H. *Studies in Education During the Age of the Renaissance, 1400–1600* (Cambridge, 1906).

——. *Vittorino de Feltre and Other Humanist Educators* (Cambridge, 1897).

INDEX